FOR NEARLY 5000 YEARS THE

I CHING ORACLE

HAS ACCURATELY PROPHESIED MANKIND'S QUESTIONS OF:

Luck and Wishes
Love and Marriage
Children and Pregnancies
Sickness
Missing People and Things
Moving or Traveling
Loans
Business Ventures
Jobs
The Market

Every aspect of Human Endeavor,
including wars and invasions.

KGI PUBLICATIONS, A Subsidiary of Kheper Group Inc., now presents a decidedly Occidental approach
to this ancient Oriental philosophical concept in the published form as:

I CHING, The Illustrated Primer

And in culturally enhancing computer software form as:

I CHING IN 4 EASY STEPS

I CHING
The Illustrated Primer

** AUTHORS **

Barry R. Trosper
Gin-Hua Leu

** ARTIST / ILLUSTRATOR **

Ken C. Yang

** EDITOR **

Robin M. Thompson

KGI Publications   1986   San Jose, California

I CHING
The Illustrated Primer

Library of Congress Cataloging in Publication Data

Library of Congress Catalog Card Number: 86-81905

Trosper, Barry R., 1941–
I ching: the illustrated primer = [I ching]

1. I ching.   I. Leu, Gin-Hua, 1957–

II. Yang, Ken C., 1940–   .   III. Title.

PL2464.Z7T73   1986   299'.51282   86-81905

ISBN 0-939231-02-6

Manufactured in the United States of America

12 11 10 9 8 7 6 5 4 3 2

Design by Ken C. Yang and Barbara Day

The Authors and Illustrator dedicate this book to the members of their families, who have also had to endure the labors of its composition, and to persons of free and independent will who—from time to time—may find satisfaction or entertainment in its contents.

Barry R. Trosper

Gin-Hua Leu

Ken C. Yang

For nearly 5000 years the advice and wisdom of the I CHING has provided improvement in lifestyles—as well as accurately predicting events and situations—to many millions of people.

No person, however, is compelled to follow the advice of the I CHING Oracle, and the advice of the Oracle needs to be weighed carefully with the circumstances within one's own life to be truly effective. The sincerity with which responses are sought— and the sincerity with which they are applied—will have significant import on the validity of the responses and, as such, are beyond the domain and control of the authors or the illustrator.

FORWARD

ABOUT THIS BOOK

This book is the product of the authors' desire to provide a meaningful and simplified method of consulting the I CHING oracle for prophesy, education, and entertainment.

The reader, or "Player," is encouraged to become familiar with the introductory material. We have not attempted to present the detailed reasons for the organization of the I CHING, but rather a base of fundamentals allowing each Player to intelligently explore this fascinating subject further.

This publication approaches the I CHING from an Occidental, or Western, viewpoint with emphasis on 20th century interpretations. We have not included the literal translations due to the confusion they generally invoke. However, the original translations which follow in this publication have been interpreted, in the authors' opinions, in strict accordance with the intent of the ancient text.

Many of the key words contained in the ancient text have been literally translated when they enhance or clarify interpretations. The Player will find frequent use of "Good Fortune," "Success," "Progress," "Error," as well as other words or phrases which have been strictly translated to relate the intent of the ancient text.

Even today significant differences remain between Occidental and Oriental behavioral concepts which have evolved from the respective cultures. This book addresses these differences from the Occidental viewpoint, while also presenting the Oriental cultural basis.

This publication presents the primary techniques of the I CHING organized into 4 fundamental steps.

STEP 1: CONSULTING THE I CHING ORACLE.

This Step explains the simplified methods of Consulting the Oracle, or "asking the question." The alternatives of both "Coin Toss" and "Yarrow Stick Manipulation" are presented in this Step.

STEP 2: THE CONSTRUCTION OF THE HEXAGRAM.

This Step provides the regularly occurring attributes of each Hexagram in a composite form. The explanations of the Orderly, Polarity, and Calendary sequences are also contained within this Step.

STEP 3: THE I CHING PROPHESIZES.

This Step contains the illustrated theme, the prophetic theme, and the description of the construction of the Hexagram in condensed formats. The translated prophesies of this Step also include the Changing Line representations for evaluation of future circumstances.

STEP 4: ELEMENTARY ANALYSIS OF TRIGRAMS.

This Step allows the Player to apply the attributes of the individual Trigrams to the prophesies of the I CHING. This publication separates the study of I CHING at this point as the novice Player may not necessarily benefit from the advanced concepts, while advanced Players will want to delve into the Plum Blossom I, Geomancy, and Astrological aspects of the I CHING. The publisher also provides **I CHING, THE ADVANCED TECHNIQUES** for the more serious Players, and **THE YEARLY I CHING,** which is a daily planning, appointment, and memorandum package for all Players.

ABOUT THE ASSOCIATED PROGRAM

The Program is organized in precisely the same manner as the published book. Variations occur in the format, but the Player will find that the Data Base used by the Program is exactly the same as printed in this text.

In Step 1, however, the Program does allow for Random Number Generation methods of Consulting the Oracle, as well as allowing for specific construction of the Hexagrams to facilitate Advanced and Astrological I CHING consultations.

The Program provides Display Panels which contain the instructions for advancing the Player through the Steps in a seemingly automatic fashion without reference to separate publications. The Program does not, however, provide graphic display of Mr. Yang's work.

Conventional attached printer compatibility is provided with the Program. A separate booklet, supplied with the diskette, provides loading and start-up instructions for operation of the Program. Methods for saving prophesies are also contained within this booklet supplied with the Program.

The especially struck I CHING coins are regularly supplied with the Program. These coins may also be available from the dealer where this publication was purchased, and are also available as a mail order item as explained on Page 3.

ACKNOWLEDGMENTS

Many persons have assisted in the production of this material and we would like to specifically acknowledge the efforts of the following individuals:

Tsung-Hwa Jou, for cultural introductions into the philosophical aspects of this material.

Robin M. Thompson, for the valuable contribution of editing this material prior to printing.

Lily F. Chin, for the extension of resources relating to ancient Chinese attire and artifacts.

Barbara Day, for the graphics design and composition of the finished text.

Dennis C. Hansen, for retail and distributor exposure of New-Age material.

Ivy Lau, for graphics design, artwork, and advice relating to this material.

MAIL ORDER, UPDATE, AND CORRESPONDENCE

Appendix D of this publication provides a listing of I CHING material which is available from the publisher on a mail order basis. As noted in Appendix D, all orders require the name of the dealer where the original material was purchased or encountered.

Update servicing of the Program is provided when the Warranty and Registration Card is completed and returned to the publisher.

Correspondence with the authors or the publisher is welcome, especially with comments for future improvement. Address such correspondence as follows:

KGI Publications, I CHING
(Name of Author)
7280 Blue Hill Drive, #4
San Jose, CA 95129

All correspondence requesting a reply will be answered, but results from telephone inquiries cannot be insured.

TABLE OF CONTENTS

INTRODUCTION

 The I CHING, or Book of Changes as it is most commonly translated, is a book of wisdom most properly used as a philosophical approach to intuitive introspection for improvement of one's lifestyle. It has survived centuries of change in the Orient and is as contemporary today as it was nearly 5000 years ago.

The I CHING applies one's travels through the Universal Order, or "Tao," to the natural workings of Heaven and Earth. For this reason, the I CHING Oracle, when sincerely consulted, has provided accurate prophesies regarding all phases of human endeavor throughout the centuries.

A modern-day translation, from the Chinese, for a person engaging in an endeavor in any varying degree, is "Player." Although this term is included in the Vocabulary of Appendix B, it is included in this introduction as it will be used throughout the remainder of this text.

Various aspects of the I CHING are also introduced in the Steps which follow when particular subject matter is addressed, but the topics of History, Primal Forces, Culture, and Coins are introduced separately within this Introduction as they represent topics leading to the understanding of either the I CHING itself or this particular material.

THE HISTORICAL INTRODUCTION TO THE "I CHING".

The origin of the I CHING is credited to a legendary Emperor of China, Fu Hsi, circa 3000 B.C. Fu Hsi is also credited with forming the first civilized society within China. The I CHING is believed to be the set of principles for behavior presented by Fu Hsi in forming this early civilized society. Fu Hsi is shown as conventionally depicted in the illustration on page 28.

The eminent value in Fu Hsi's set of principles was its recognition that all things undergo change. Consequently the title of this work, I CHING, is translated as the "Book of Changes." Of course the original work was not in book form as we know it today and tortoise shells, bones, and other paraphernalia were originally used for record keeping, counting, and reading. These earliest of primitive methods were replaced by bamboo slats—joined by leather thongs—and the I CHING was inked onto these slats.

Fu Hsi originated the I CHING with a set of eight "Trigrams," or a stack of three lines, each of which have specific attributes relative to the Earth, Mankind, and Heaven. These lines are always read and referred to from the bottom to the top and are either Yang (Solid) indicating a strong nature or Yin (Broken) indicating a yielding nature. For example:

THE TRIGRAM LI; FIRE, SUN; THE MIDDLE DAUGHTER.

3rd Line	▬▬▬	(Yang, Solid)—Heavenly Influences
2nd Line	▬▬ ▬▬	(Yin, Broken)—Human Influences
1st Line	▬▬▬	(Yang, Solid)—Earthly Influences

Changes in Earthly and Heavenly affairs follow a predictable natural order, with permutations caused by fate. The Earthly and Heavenly behavior is regarded as beyond the ability of mankind to control and represents the Universal or Cosmic Order. The single word "Tao," which translates as "Way," represents this Universal or Cosmic Way and is used in this sense throughout this text.

Mankind, on the other hand, exercises free will and possesses the ability to change behavior by choice. I CHING captures Mankind's travel through the Universal Order (Tao) and provides advice with which one can make meaningful change for improvement in one's own life. As the I CHING identifies Mankind's position within the Tao, it is also able to portray and predict circumstances as easily as one can predict snow falling in the winter or hot days in the summer.

This leads to one of the important precepts of the I CHING;

"To Superior Persons the I CHING gives advice,
Regarding Inferior Persons it makes predictions."

The "Superior Person" is considered to be one who is striving for improvement in lifestyle, behavior, and the accumulation of wisdom. The "Inferior Person" is regarded as being cast about by the whims of fate.

The I CHING is based upon the Two Principles of "Yang" and "Yin", which, when relating to their extreme polarities, represent Heaven and Earth, high and low, or positive and negative. As with a magnet, these two polarities exist in varying degrees between the respective extremes—the two opposite poles—and neither principle is complete without the complementary portion of the other. Try to imagine Heaven without Earth, or Earth without Heaven.

The "T'ai Chi" is a pictorial representation of the changing of the Two Principles, Yang and Yin. The growing seed of the opposite Principle is always contained within the other. Thus Yang changes and Yin grows within Yang; Yin changes and Yang grows within Yin.

Two misconceptions are associated with the representation of duality. The first is in associating "Yin" with the destructive negative. In reality Yin is only the opposing principle of Yang, positive. This also applies to the second misconception, where Yang is related to "Man" and Yin to "Woman." In expressing the natural order of Mankind, man and woman—certainly different—are both required in equal measure to continue and perpetuate human life as we know it.

Men and Women form relationships, have conflicts, produce children, engage in careers, and share happiness together. The Yang and Yin principles emulate these natural relationships without true regard to sex.

In step 2, page 23, a chart is provided, showing the organization of the duality, Yang and Yin, from the T'ai Chi, through the Two Principles of Yang and Yin, the Four Symbols of Greater and Lesser Influences, the Eight Trigrams, to the 64 individual Hexagrams.

The Hexagrams are stacks of 6 Lines (Yang—Solid or Yin-Broken) which are composites of a Lower Trigram (BELOW) and an Upper Trigram (ABOVE). The appropriateness of a Yang (Strong) or Yin (Yielding) influence in any one of the six positions is the primary factor in determining the degree of favorableness of any prophesy. Strength where yielding is required, and vice-versa, are examples of inappropriate positioning.

Returning to the historical aspect of the I CHING, it is significant to note that it, and it alone, has survived centuries of changes and purges, due primarily to the fact that it is not a political work. Nor is it a religious work, although many religions have embraced its lessons either totally or in large measure.

The true aspect of I CHING is philosophical, and its cultural value is truly exhilarating.

In approximately 2200 B.C. another Emperor, the Great Yu, is believed to have further promoted the I CHING as a book of wisdom for society. The Great Yu is credited with flood and water control projects, and when engaged in one of these projects a magic tortoise is said to have come from the waters with Fu Hsi's original markings on its back.

Regardless of the authenticity of the magic tortoise, it is noteworthy that the I CHING had not only survived for 800 years, but was in active use when writing and record keeping implements were in their most primitive form.

As noted above, the 64 Hexagrams of the I CHING are made up from combinations of the 8 Trigrams of Fu Hsi (8 X 8 = 64). The upper Trigram is the Heavenly influence and the lower Trigram is the Earthly influence. 64 sets of circumstances are represented by the 64 Hexagrams, and all lines have the ability to change, forming the future—also represented by any one of the 64 Hexagrams. In this manner 4,096 (64 X 64) situations are defined. Some scholars have expanded this even further, but, in a general sense, they have not added further to meaningful definition, and the I CHING is still most commonly represented by the original 64 Hexagrams. The current arrangement and appended commentaries to the Hexagrams are attributed to King Wen, circa 1200 B.C., at a time when he was cast into prison by a conquering tyrant, King Chou (Hsin). Because of King Wen's position, the hexagrams convey warnings as well as descriptions of circumstances and prophesies. Or the prophesy itself is associated with the warning.

This brings up another important precept of the I CHING;
"One who is conscious of danger creates their own peace.
One who treats things lightly brings their own downfall.
In the Middle and Without Blame is the Tao (Way) of I CHING from Beginning to End."

King Wen was a ruler of great virtue, but ruled only a small province. When attempting to overthrow the despot, King Chou (Hsin), his efforts were discovered and he was condemned into prison. King Wen had five sons, and one, King Wu, was able to overthrow the tyrant, forcing him to death. A second son, the Duke of Chou, became an able administator within the new reign, as well as the reign of King Wu's son, King Chen. The Duke of Chou's substantial contribution to the I CHING was his continuance of his father's work by providing the definitions of the individual lines.

The tyrant King Chou (Hsin) and King Wen are both depicted on the illustration of MING I, Hexagram #36, on page 152.
King Chou (Hsin) is shown wearing the imperial headdress, containing 288 jewels, which could be brought down over the face to obscure view in either direction.
King Wen is shown shackled in chains.
The Duke of Chou, the administrator and scholar, is shown in the illustration below.

THE DUKE OF CHOU

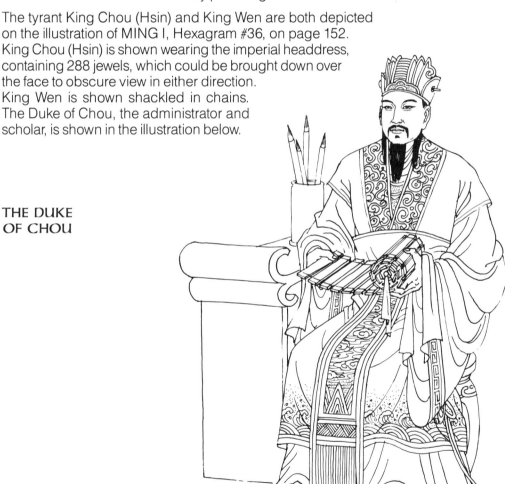

It should be noted that I CHING is not a submissive philosophical concept, but one which expects the "Player" to recognize times when yielding to circumstances is required to prevent disaster from being visited upon oneself.

In approximately 500 B.C., Confucius added the "Symbols" and limited commentaries to the I CHING, but probably never completed his work, or a substantial portion was lost. Late in his life he was quoted as saying; "If I had fifty more years to live I would devote them all to the I CHING." Confucius is shown in a separate illustration on page 222.

Five persons—Fu Hsi, King Wen, the Duke of Chou, Confucius, and the Great Yu (all mentioned above)—are reputed to have organized and passed down the I CHING as it exists and is used today.

In the Occidental world interest in the I CHING began with the "Legge" translation into English in the late 19th century. Interest spread throughout Europe and this work, as well as the "Wilhelm" German translation of 1923, are common to all European languages. These translations eventually appeared in America.

In the United States the popularity of I CHING began in the 1930s as more literal and interpretive translations began to appear. But its original popularity was chiefly as a "parlor game." In the 1940s the I CHING began to take on significant prominence as a book of wisdom when the eminent Swiss pyschologist, C. G. Jung, embraced its philosophical concepts.

Today interest in the I CHING is experiencing rapid growth and rediscovery as society becomes more attuned to and conscious of orders and powers available to them although largely ignored up to now. Even the entertainment or "parlor game" aspect of the I CHING is experiencing expanding popularity.

The accuracy associated with correct use and application of the I CHING stands far in advance of Tarot Cards, Palmistry, etc., and the I CHING, since it is based upon natural order, requires no special pyschic power. The I CHING also employs horoscopes and numerology in prophesies, and the results are fascinating and realistic.

In closing this historical brief another precept of the I CHING should be related:

"The words of persons of Good Fortune are few."

This statement in itself explains the difficulty of arriving at correct and meaningful interpretations of the I CHING. The ancient text exists in an abbreviated form of very few characters, often cryptic, and written as parables or examples. Even our translations, at times, had to be laboriously picked apart character by character, and sometimes stroke by stroke of each character.

USAGE OF THE CHINESE LANGUAGE.

Our text uses a modification of the Wade-Giles system of Romanization of the Chinese characters. Not only is it the most widely used in texts relating to the I CHING material, but also best conforms to "Western" printing equipment. In modifying the Wade-Giles system we have dropped the representation of inflected vowels. The Occidental user has available many other texts to enhance the understanding of the Oriental languages which this publication does not address. The Chinese character depictions are carried into this publication as a matter of cultural appreciation.

The extreme differences between Mandarin and Cantonese pronunciations cannot be simply expressed, and over 800 dialects of the Chinese language actually exist. It is indeed remarkable that the characters share the same meaning in most all dialects, and even translate nearly the same in Japanese—in spite of the differences in pronunciation.

REPRESENTATION OF THE PRIMAL FORCES.

The dualism concept of the two primal forces, Creative Power and Natural Strength, can be best related as co-existence in the same manner that opposite ends of a magnet co-exist. The total positive resides at one end, while the total negative resides at the other, and varying intensities exist in between. Neither force can be represented as better or worse than the other, as they are both equally required for the balance required by nature.

CH'IEN, The Creative Power, Yang, is symbolized by a Solid bar and represents the male of a species. It has been assigned the attributes of Heaven, Light, and Positive. Like one end of the magnet, it combines with the opposite Primal Force, K'UN.

K'UN, Natural Strength, Yin, is symbolized by a Broken bar and represents the female of a species. It has been assigned the attributes of Earth, Dark, and Negative. Again, like one end of the magnet, it combines with the opposite Primal Force, CH'IEN.

CH'IEN and **K'UN** (Yang and Yin) join and originate the I CHING as complements to each other, and their profound examples serve as lessons illustrating how one may achieve the superior life of the Superior Person. When the two Primal Forces are represented as being combined together, CH'IEN-K'UN, the meaning is interpreted as "Universe," and represents all the extremes: Heaven-Earth, Light-Dark, Positive-Negative, Male-Female, and all intensities which can be found existing between them.

REPRESENTATION OF CULTURAL ASPECTS.

This material has been prepared as a representation of the intellectual and philosophical aspects associated with the I CHING. Since the I CHING is based upon philosophies which have been studied and followed in the Orient for nearly 5000 years, we ask the reader to note that it may often be difficult to understand the cultural aspects without also appreciating other cultural issues, either from ancient or modern times.

During the course of translation and interpretation of this material the authors experienced many significantly different cultural aspects relating to conduct. These are related in the Occidental wording of this text and often literal and even interpretive translations do not fully convey the original Oriental thought.

As a simple example, the DRAGON, from the Occidental viewpoint, is thought of as a fierce and destructive creature requiring severe methods to subdue. But in the Orient the DRAGON is viewed as a highly charged energy source associated with wisdom, justice, proper conduct, and success.

Not so simply related, however, is the Oriental concept of MODESTY. Although mention is made of this clash in Step 3 regarding Hexagram Number 15, CH'IEN, MODESTY, its significance justifies duplication here. From the Oriental viewpoint it represents a positive and unpretentious attitude of self-effacement, as a virtue of the highest order associated with Good Fortune. But from the Occidental viewpoint it frequently represents shy retirement and possibly meager positions.

To derive the full value from the I CHING it will often be necessary to abandon preconceived notions about words and the thoughts they may represent. For this reason we have included a Vocabulary in this publication as Appendix B. In addition to DRAGON and MODESTY, we have included such words and phrases as SUCCESS, GOOD FORTUNE, and BLAME, as well as some of their modifications, since these words and phrases are frequently literally translated in this material when they enhance the circumstances to which they relate.

When so understood, the I CHING is a fascinating text—available to persons of free and intelligent will for individual improvement and enhancement, as well as a powerful aid in meditation.

We have also avoided the detailed derivations of TRIGRAM and HEXAGRAM construction, which are generally cultural in nature, and have presented only the most salient points. Many fine authors have preceded this work with such explanations, and for deeper understanding of these concepts the Player is referred to the many works which explain such construction in detail and which are available in bookstores and libraries throughout the world.

The illustrations, designs, and page borders of this publication have also been prepared to be culturally correct, either as the direct effort of Artist/Illustrator Ken C. Yang, or under his specific direction.

THE COINS SUPPLIED BY KGI PUBLICATIONS.

The replicated coins supplied either with the Program Package or as separately ordered items, are also the product of the research and talent of Artist and Illustrator, Ken C. Yang, without whose effort the significant cultural presentation contained herein would not have been possible.

YANG
TAIL = 3

YIN
HEAD = 2

The replicated coin is 5/24ths of a Teal of the T'ang Dynasty, 621-975 AD. This coin is generally considered to be "Good Luck." The Teal is no longer of any equitable monetary value, although they are certainly collector pieces. Coins relating to 5 units of a monetary value are considered to bring the Good Fortune associated with the 5th Line of the Hexagram. We invite you to use such coins representing 5 units within your own national monetary system. In the United States a 5-cent coin or "Nickel" will serve to invite this same Good Fortune upon yourself.

Prior to the period represented by the depicted coins, Chinese coins were generally blank on one side and inscribed on the other with the monetary value. The inscribed side became the representation of the Earthly value and was assigned the number Two. The blank side became the representation of the Heavenly value and was assigned the number Three. "Heads" became Yin and designated as 2. "Tails" became Yang and designated as 3.

We have indicated our preference regarding the use of "Heads" and "Tails" of the coins and ask you to note that it makes no absolute difference, as long as you are consistent, as to which side you use to represent Heads or Tails, since these coins are merely the instrument you are using to seek intuitive answers to your questions.

Because Mr. Yang has done such a fine job in replicating the coin, we have included the wording **"NOT LEGAL TENDER"** on the coin to preclude confusion between it and any token of monetary or collector value.

STEP 1: CONSULTING THE I CHING ORACLE

When consulting the I CHING with a question it is sincerity which makes the difference between receiving a meaningful prophesy and a "parlor game" response from the I CHING Oracle. It is said of the I CHING:

"To Superior Persons the I CHING gives advice, Regarding Inferior Persons it makes predictions."

This work is prepared on the basis that the Player using this material is a Superior Person attempting to combine virtue and sincere effort in the improvement of his or her lifestyle.

Many methods are used to invoke sincerity when consulting the I CHING, including physical positioning, selection of the time of day, lighting candles, burning incense, dropping of bamboo cups, prayers, as well as a variety of other approaches.

Players already familiar with the I CHING may have their own method of invoking sincerity, but we recommend:

— Firmly establishing your question of the I CHING Oracle in your mind, using as emotional description as possible.

— If you know the answer, don't ask. It would be pointless to ask the I CHING, "Am I reading this book?"

— Choose a time when you will not be interrupted.

— Remember that you are consulting your intuitive senses and the first answer you receive is the response of the I CHING Oracle.

— Write your question on a copy of the Worksheet, the Program Display, or some other writing media of your choice.

— As you write your question, attempt to include the time reference you have in mind—a day, a year, soon, etc.—Think of nothing else but your question until the Oracle has prophesized.

Once the Oracle has prophesized it will be necessary for you to evaluate the response objectively. Wishful thinking will only cause a misinterpretation. All of our lives are made up of both favorable and unfavorable circumstances.

We also recommend that once you are finished with your consultations, the I CHING material be wrapped and placed in a high place. This is also an expression of sincerity.

YES-NO QUESTIONS.

When consulting the I CHING it must be kept in mind that you are consulting the Cosmic Order or Way ("Tao") to determine your own position within the Order.

Great thought needs to be given to the YES-NO question since the tense of the question will alter the meaning of an answer. The expected response from a favorably assembled prophesy should be "YES," and "NO" for the unfavorable.

Consider the possible responses from the following similarly organized questions:
   1) Will I be successful this year?
   2) Will I be unsuccessful this year?
   3) Will success come to me this year?
   4) Will my efforts in violin study be theatrically successful this year?

The preferred approach is shown in question number 4. Success can be of many different types, and depends on the individual Player's association with the meaning of success. Even theatrical success could mean either financial gain, or recognition of talent, or both, to any different Player.

When the Program Display constructs the Hexagram, a simplified evaluation of the Present/Recent Past, Controlling Line, and the Future Hexagram is displayed. There are 4,096 derivations and, due both to the length and complexity of indexing, they have not been printed in this book.

Step 4 also provides another method of deriving YES-NO answers which the Player may choose to employ.

GAMBLING.

Although many regard life as a gamble, the I CHING recognizes life as methodically proceeding in accordance with the Universal Order, again the "Tao." Consequently the I CHING regards pure gambling as an insincere endeavor, not intended for Superior Persons. Many have found favorable results from gambling based upon the prophesies of the I CHING, but the authors of this book offer a warning against any reliance upon the prophesies when engaging in any gambling endeavors.

THE WORKSHEET.

Printed on the inside of the back cover of this publication the Player will find a copy of the authors' preferred Worksheet. This Worksheet provides for the elements of Hexagram construction and evaluation. The Player may choose to photocopy the Worksheet. This paragraph also serves as written permission for the Player to make such a photocopy. The Program will also produce a replication of this Worksheet on either the Display Screen or an attached Printer.

The Worksheet is shown in progressive stages of construction throughout this text with the explanations contained for its completion as each segment of the consultation is addressed.

METHODS OF CONSULTING THE ORACLE.

Two primary methods of consulting the I CHING Oracle have evolved through the centuries. The Program allows a third, in the form of a Random Number Generator, as well as specifying the construction of a Hexagram for Advanced or Astrological consultations.

The Player may select either the Coin Toss method or the Yarrow Stick method. The Program, as mentioned above, also provides for a Random Number generation method which replicates the Coin Toss method exactly.

The methods using Yarrow Sticks are the most ancient described in this text, although even more remotely in time, the cracks obtained from heating tortoise shells were used for this purpose. The method of Coin Toss is presented first as it is the most common and easily used method.

COIN TOSS METHOD OF CONSULTING THE ORACLE.

This method evolved approximately 2000 years ago when coinage came into use. Original Chinese coins were blank on one side with the value inscribed on the other. The Program Package is supplied with three of the Publisher's especially struck I CHING coins of the T'ang Dynasty—described in the Introduction, page 13. These coins are also available as mail order items.

When selecting your own coins we suggest three coins of equal size and denomination. The fifth line of a Hexagram is generally favorable, and coins representing 5 units of a monetary value are seen as inviting good fortune upon one's consultation. In the United States a "Nickel," or 5-cent coin, is favored for this reason.

After your question has been carefully formulated or written onto a Worksheet (see page 18), continue by:

— Removing the Coins from their container and holding them in your hand until you are comfortable with their temperature and feel.

— While forming each of the Six Lines, continue to carefully consider your question. – Beginning at the First, or Bottom, Line repeat the following procedure for all Six Lines.

— Drop the coins onto a hard flat surface, allowing them to bounce and fall to one side or the other. Mark the Worksheet with the respective sides of the three coins using "H" for Heads and "T" for Tails (see page 18).

— If Three Heads are shown mark "H,H,H". The Head is the Symbol of Earth and assigned the value of Two. Add 2 for each Head displayed, $2+2+2 = 6$. Mark the Six on the Worksheet following the fall of the Coins: "H,H,H 6". This is the representation of Old Yin changing to Yang in the Future and a Yin, Broken Line, is drawn on the Worksheet with an "X" between the two segments. Our example shows this contruction on Line 4.

— If Three Tails are shown mark "T,T,T". The Tail is the Symbol of Heaven and assigned the value of Three. Add 3 for each Tail displayed, $3+3+3 = 9$. Mark the Nine on the Worksheet following the fall of the Coins: "T,T,T 9". This is the representation of Old Yang changing to Yin in the Future, and a Yang, Solid, Line is drawn on the Worksheet with an "O" in the center. Our example shows this construction on Line 2.

— If Two Heads and One Tail are shown mark "H,H,T". The order is not important. Add 2 for each Head and 3 for each Tail, $2+2+3 = 7$. Mark the Seven on the Worksheet following the fall of the Coins: "H,H,T 7". This is the representation of New Yang growing and continuing into the Future. A Yang, Solid, Line is drawn on the Worksheet without any other markings. Our example shows this construction on Lines 1 and 3.

— If Two Tails and One Head are shown mark "T,T,H". The order is not important. Add 3 for each Tail and 2 for each Head displayed, $3+3+2 = 8$. Mark Eight on the Worksheet following the fall of the Coins: "T,T,H 8". This is the representation of New Yin growing and continuing into the Future. A Yin, Broken, Line is drawn on the Worksheet without any other markings. Our example shows this construction on Lines 5 and 6.

— When all six lines are completed, replace the coins into their container and continue with Step 2—defining the construction of the Hexagram.

Other methods of tossing coins also exist, some requiring as many as twelve coins, which involve more complexity. The method described herein is considered wholly adequate for the Player to address intuitive positions within the Tao, or Universal Order.

I CHING WORKSHEET

QUESTION	WILL I RECEIVE GREAT VALUE FROM	DATE 4 SEPT '86
	CONSULTING THE I CHING ?	

RECENT. PAST. PRESENT

FUTURE

NO	NAME		NO	NAME
TITLE			TITLE	

YANG
TAIL = 3

YIN
HEAD = 2

6th *H, T, T 8* —— ——   ABOVE

5th *T, H, T 8* —— ——

4th *H, H, H 6* —X—

3rd *T, H, H 7* ————   BELOW

2nd *T, T, T 9* —O—

1st *H, T, H 7* ————

—X— 3 HEADS = 6 CHANGING

———— 2 HEADS. 1 TAIL = 7

—— —— 1 HEAD 2 TAILS = 8

—O— 3 TAILS = 9 CHANGING

INTERNAL. MOTIVATING

PROPHESY REMARKS

KGI PUBLICATIONS

YARROW STICK METHOD OF CONSULTING THE ORACLE.

The more ancient method of consulting the I CHING is with the use of 50 "Yarrow Sticks." A Yarrow Stick is a particular reed, cut 15 to 18 inches long for this purpose. The original method is approximately six times more complex than the method presented in this publication or the Program, but the method presented in this text is considered wholly adequate for the Player to address intuitive positions within the Tao, or Universal Order. Inexpensive and commercially available "barbeque" skewers can also be used in place of the actual reeds.

The method of Yarrow Stick manipulation we have presented actually produces two Trigrams designated " ABOVE" and "BELOW", which form the Hexagram, and always one Changing Line, which becomes the Controlling Line referred to in Step 3.

After your question has been carefully formulated and written onto a Worksheet continue by:

— Removing the 50 Yarrow Sticks from their container and wrappings and holding them in your hand until you are comfortable in continuing. Some Players, as an indication of sincerity, will choose to pass the Yarrow Sticks over burning incense.

— Select one of the Yarrow Sticks and remove it from the 50. Place this Stick into a jar, or by itself, in front of you. This Stick represents the "T'ai Chi," or the Absolute, and it relates to the origin of all things. It must not be moved during the consultation.

— While forming both of the Trigrams and the Changing Line, continue to carefully consider your question.

    — Without counting, divide the remaining 49 Sticks into two bundles, keeping one bundle in the left hand and one bundle in the right hand. This operation represents the separation of the two principles, Yang and Yin.

    — Remove one Stick from the right-hand bundle. This Stick is held in the left hand between the little and ring fingers.

    — Continue by removing two Sticks at a time from the bundle in the left hand and make smaller groups of Eight.

    — When no more groups of eight can be formed, count the number of sticks remaining. Add the one held in the hand to this count. For example:

        0 Remain, Add One from the Hand, Total = 1
        5 Remain, Add One from the Hand, Total = 6
        7 Remain, Add One from the Hand, Total = 8

    This will always produce a number between One and Eight.

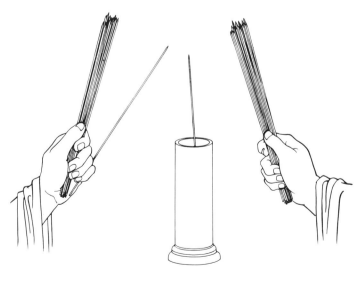

— The following table, explained more fully in Step 4, relates these numbers to the individual Trigrams.

1	CH'IEN		2	TUI	
3	LI		4	CHEN	
5	SUN		6	K'AN	
7	KEN		8	K'UN	

When defining the Lower Trigram begin at Line 1; when defining the Upper Trigram begin at Line 4. Copy the Trigram associated with the appropriate number onto the Worksheet from the bottom upwards (see page 21).

— Reassemble the Yarrow Sticks into a bundle of 49 Sticks. Remember that the Stick in the middle and is not to be gathered into the bundle or even moved.

— When the Lower Trigram is completed, repeat the above procedure to produce the Upper Trigram. When the Upper Trigram is complete, proceed to the following paragraph to define the Changing Line.

— Without counting divide the 49 Sticks into two bundles, keeping one in the right hand and one in the left hand.

— Remove one Stick from the right-hand bundle. This Stick is held in the hand between the little and ring fingers of the left hand as before.

— Continue by removing two Sticks at a time from the left-hand bundle, making groups of Six.

— When no more groups of six can be formed, count the number of sticks remaining. Add the one held in the hand to this count. For example:

    0 Remain, Add One from the Hand, Total = 1
    3 Remain, Add One from the Hand, Total = 4
    5 Remain, Add One from the Hand, Total = 6
This will always produce a number between One and Six.

— This is the number of the Changing Line. If the designated bar on this line is Solid, draw an "O" in the center of the Line. If the designated bar on this line is Broken, place an "X" between the two segments.

— When both Trigrams and the Changing Line are completed, replace all 50 of the sticks into their container and continue with Step 2, defining the construction of the Hexagram.

The Program can replicate the Yarrow Stick manipulation by allowing the Player to manually position Cursors, or by Random Number generation. The Display Panels provide the instructions for each manipulation.

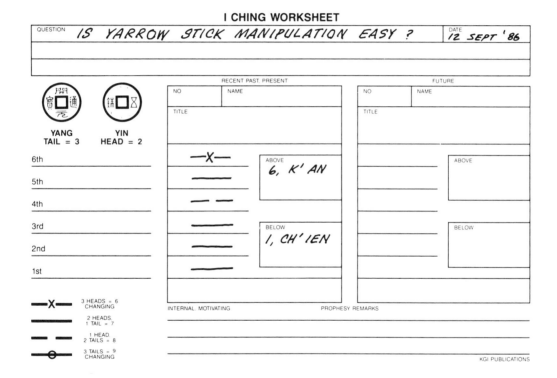

RANDOM NUMBER METHOD OF CONSULTING THE ORACLE.

This method is only associated with the Program, and the instructions for its use are contained on the appropriate Display Panels. This method exactly replicates the Coin Toss method, providing additional convenience and efficiency to the Player. It is also considered wholly adequate for consultation of the Oracle, when the Oracle is sincerely questioned.

The Program will automatically advance the Player into Step 2 and define the construction of the Hexagram on either the Display Screen or an attached Printer.

STEP 2: THE CONSTRUCTION OF THE HEXAGRAMS

The Hexagram completed in Step 1 is known as the "Pen Kua" and reflects the Present, or Recent Past—it is the beginning of the prophesy.

The I CHING represents changes we are experiencing in our own life cycles, and it must be remembered that if we receive a prophesy we do not like, the situation can be corrected with new and positive attitudes while resolving the difficulties. In this way a poor prophesy may bring a better future than good prophesies that are wasted with a careless or intemperate attitude.

The chart at the right relates all 64 Hexagrams as two sets of Trigrams in a regular scheme that is based first on the relationship of the lower Trigram, then the upper.

To easily locate the number of a Hexagram, find its lower Trigram, the lower three lines, in the "BELOW" row. Our example uses a lower Trigram of CH'IEN (three Solid lines at the bottom), indicating the Hexagram will be found in the left-most column of Hexagrams. Next locate the upper Trigram, the upper three lines, in the left-hand "ABOVE" column of Trigrams. Our example uses K'UN (three Broken lines at the top). The point where the BELOW row and the ABOVE column intersect provides the Hexagram number. Our example, K'UN-ABOVE and CH'IEN-BELOW intersects at Hexagram number 11. Compare the Hexagram printed in the box with the actual Hexagram formed. They will be the same when correctly located.

Step 1 also produced "Changing Lines" which represent the transition from the Present/Recent Past to the Future. A line can only change from Solid (Yang) to Broken (Yin) or vice versa. Thus the Future Hexagram is formed by changing these lines to their exact opposites.

Any number of lines from zero to six can be changing. Our example uses two lines changing, the 2nd and 4th. Reading up from the bottom (as is always done with Hexagrams), or the 1st Line, the Present/Recent Past Hexagram, #11, was constructed as Solid, Solid, Solid, Broken, Broken, Broken. Changing the 2nd and 4th lines, the Future Hexagram becomes Solid, Broken, Solid, Solid, Broken, Broken. The Program performs this function automatically, and the Worksheet example on page 24 depicts this completion.

RELATIONSHIPS OF THE 64 HEXAGRAMS

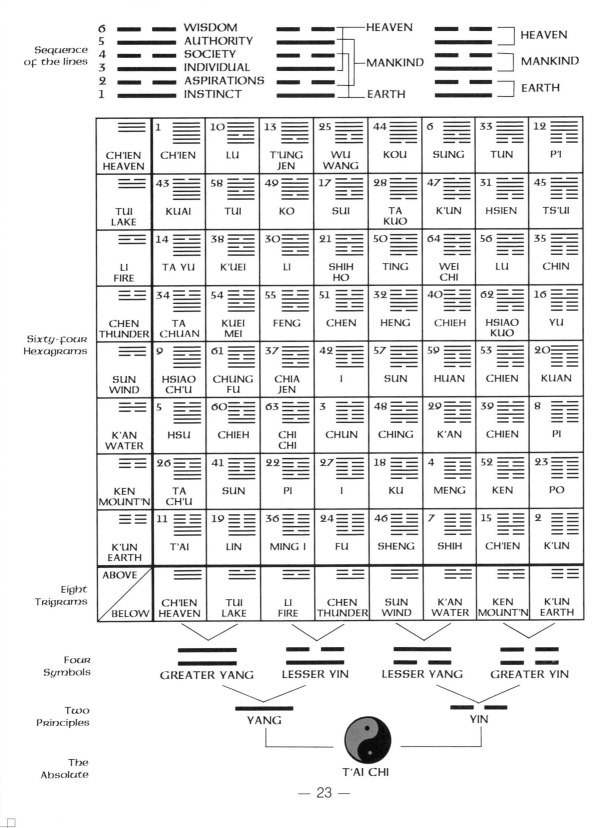

Sequence of the lines

6 — WISDOM
5 — AUTHORITY
4 — SOCIETY
3 — INDIVIDUAL
2 — ASPIRATIONS
1 — INSTINCT

HEAVEN
MANKIND
EARTH

HEAVEN
MANKIND
EARTH

Sixty-four Hexagrams

ABOVE / BELOW	CH'IEN HEAVEN	TUI LAKE	LI FIRE	CHEN THUNDER	SUN WIND	K'AN WATER	KEN MOUNT'N	K'UN EARTH
CH'IEN HEAVEN	1 CH'IEN	10 LU	13 T'UNG JEN	25 WU WANG	44 KOU	6 SUNG	33 TUN	12 P'I
TUI LAKE	43 KUAI	58 TUI	49 KO	17 SUI	28 TA KUO	47 K'UN	31 HSIEN	45 TS'UI
LI FIRE	14 TA YU	38 K'UEI	30 LI	21 SHIH HO	50 TING	64 WEI CHI	56 LU	35 CHIN
CHEN THUNDER	34 TA CHUAN	54 KUEI MEI	55 FENG	51 CHEN	32 HENG	40 CHIEH	62 HSIAO KUO	16 YU
SUN WIND	9 HSIAO CH'U	61 CHUNG FU	37 CHIA JEN	42 I	57 SUN	59 HUAN	53 CHIEN	20 KUAN
K'AN WATER	5 HSU	60 CHIEH	63 CHI CHI	3 CHUN	48 CHING	29 K'AN	39 CHIEN	8 PI
KEN MOUNT'N	26 TA CH'U	41 SUN	22 PI	27 I	18 KU	4 MENG	52 KEN	23 PO
K'UN EARTH	11 T'AI	19 LIN	36 MING I	24 FU	46 SHENG	7 SHIH	15 CH'IEN	2 K'UN

Eight Trigrams

| ABOVE / BELOW | CH'IEN HEAVEN | TUI LAKE | LI FIRE | CHEN THUNDER | SUN WIND | K'AN WATER | KEN MOUNT'N | K'UN EARTH |

Four Symbols

GREATER YANG   LESSER YIN   LESSER YANG   GREATER YIN

Two Principles

YANG   YIN

The Absolute

T'AI CHI

— 23 —

Our sample of the Future Hexagram reads as LI-BELOW (Solid, Broken, Solid) and is found in the 3rd column from the left in the row of Trigrams. Our upper Trigram of CHEN-ABOVE (Solid, Broken, Broken) is located in the left-hand column of Trigrams. The two intersect at Hexagram number 55. The printed Hexagram is lastly compared to the Hexagram actually formed to insure it was correctly located.

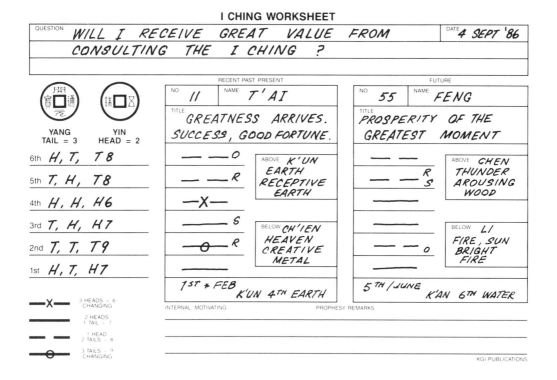

I CHING WORKSHEET

| QUESTION | *WILL I RECEIVE GREAT VALUE FROM CONSULTING THE I CHING ?* | DATE *4 SEPT '86* |

RECENT PAST PRESENT — FUTURE

NO *11* NAME *T'AI*

TITLE *GREATNESS ARRIVES. SUCCESS, GOOD FORTUNE.*

NO *55* NAME *FENG*

TITLE *PROSPERITY OF THE GREATEST MOMENT*

YANG TAIL = 3   YIN HEAD = 2

6th *H, T, T8*
5th *T, H, T8*
4th *H, H, H6*
3rd *T, H, H7*
2nd *T, T, T9*
1st *H, T, H7*

ABOVE *K'UN EARTH RECEPTIVE EARTH*

BELOW *CH'IEN HEAVEN CREATIVE METAL*

ABOVE *CHEN THUNDER AROUSING WOOD*

BELOW *LI FIRE, SUN BRIGHT FIRE*

*1ST * FEB K'UN 4TH EARTH*

5TH / JUNE K'AN 6TH WATER

INTERNAL MOTIVATING — PROPHESY REMARKS

—X— 3 HEADS = 6 CHANGING
—— 2 HEADS 1 TAIL = 7
— — 1 HEAD 2 TAILS = 8
—o— 3 TAILS = 9 CHANGING

KGI PUBLICATIONS

The following pages in this Step explain the organization of the chart on the preceeding page, and then the composite Hexagrams which are contained in this Step. Users of the Program will note that the Display Screen produces these Hexagrams automatically. Players using the book may want to include the various attributes indicated in this Step on the worksheet. Experience, especially with particular types of questions, will enable Players to discover their own short cuts.

Players can proceed to Step 3 at this point when satisfied that they have extracted the pertinent information from the composites within this Step. Beginners may choose not to include any information from this Step and proceed directly to Step 3.

The chart on page 23, "THE RELATIONSHIPS OF THE 64 HEXAGRAMS," is the regular organization of the Hexagrams by their associative Trigrams. The three Hexagrams at the top of the page define the sequential relationships of the lines within the Hexagram, with each line in its "Natural" state (Solid, Broken, Solid, Broken, Solid, and Broken).

When Hexagrams are fully analyzed, the Strong (Solid, Yang) and the Yielding (Broken, Yin) have specific and important meanings.

The Hexagram at the upper left of page 23 associates the attributes of the line position with the Hexagram and the Prophesy. The natural states are:

— The beginning (bottom) line is Strong and represents Instinct and Intuition. Coin toss, Yarrow Stick movement, or Random Number Generation likewise represent instinctive or intuitive responses from the I CHING. This line is considered Natural when Strong and Unyielding.

— The 2nd Line is Yielding, as should be our Motives, Desires, Aspirations, and Goals in meeting the changing circumstances of life.

— The 3rd Line is Strong and represents Individual Interest. This is seen as a feature of human nature which most frequently works against oneself. In the I CHING, Line 3 is generally unfavorable and serves as a warning against selfishness and self-centered considerations.

— The 4th Line is Yielding and represents the interaction with Society. Social and community relationships require a yielding and adaptability to render them successful. This line also represents an administrator of a higher authority (The Minister of a King) who operates on behalf of both the higher authority and the Society, or the mass of people.

— The 5th Line is Strong and represents Authority. The Authority is Strong, but emphasis is also placed on fairness and justice to render it successful. In antiquity this Authority was represented by the King.

— The Top, or 6th Line, is Yielding and represents Wisdom. The wisdom of yielding to the circumstances and, more particularly, the wisdom of developing high virtues, is represented by this line. A sage, or holy person, is associated with this line, emphasizing the aspect of wisdom. This line also functions as the passing from the theme of one Hexagram to another as they relate to the "Orderly Sequence," which is explained later in this step.

The Hexagram at the upper center of page 23 correlates the lines of the Lower and Upper Trigrams together.

— The 1st and the 4th lines are considered to have corresponding positions to each other and both represent Earthly and Material influences.

— The 2nd and the 5th lines are considered to have corresponding positions to each other and both represent the influences of Mankind.

— The 3rd and the 6th Line are considered to have corresponding positions to each other and both represent Heavenly and Spiritual influences.

Note that correspondence requires both a Strong and a Yielding line. When corresponding, these lines are also referred to as being "Matched." Matched lines are either Natural, when as shown, or Unnatural when reversed. Both matches tend to be favorable, even though the positions may be unfavorable. This occurs as both attributes are present.

The Hexagram at the upper right of page 23 relates the Earthly, Human, and Heavenly influences to the Hexagram as a whole, without emphasis on correspondence between the lines of the different Trigrams. This relationship is particularly useful in defining a third Hexagram, called the "Hu Kua," and is explained later in this Step as the "Motivational Influence."

— The 1st and 2nd lines, when the Hexagram is considered as a whole, represent the Earthly and Material influences.

— The 3rd and 4th lines, when the Hexagram is considered as a whole, represent the influences of Mankind.

— The 5th and 6th lines, when the Hexagram is considered as a whole, represent Heavenly and Spiritual influences.

As the I CHING Oracle prophesizes all of these factors are considered. Thousands of years have been applied to defining and analyzing the structure of both the Hexagrams and the prophesies—seemingly contradictory presentations will perfectly meld together with careful study.

The Chart, page 23, is organized from the bottom up, as are all Hexagrams. The T'AI CHI, at the bottom, is representative of the Absolute, where Yang changes to Yin with the seed of Yin growing within it, and Yin changes to Yang with the seed of Yang growing within it. The T'AI CHI is born of the WU CHI, which is a simple circle encompassing all things—yet representing nothing. Red is the color associated with Yang, and Black with Yin. These two colors were prominent among the inks or dyes in nearly all ancient civilizations as they were the most readily produced.

The T'AI CHI divides into Two Principles, the Yang and the Yin, which exist and are counterbalanced equally in nature. In the scientific sense, Sir Isaac Newton stated "that for every action there is an equal and opposite reaction." The Two Principles of the I CHING, the Yang and Yin, are likewise expressions of the two opposite extremes of polarity, but more importantly are extremes which do not exist without the influence or reaction of the other.

A common Chinese word for Line is "Yao." Yao Bars—(Line Bars)—were made of wood and had a Solid red inset which identified it as "Yang," and a Broken black inset which identified it as "Yin." For this reason we have shown the Two Principles as red and black, respective to Yang and Yin. Normally the printing of these Two Principles is only in black to be more easily read.

The Two Principles divide into the Four Symbols by again working up from the bottom, placing the new principle above the pre-existing principle. When both principles appear together they are considered the Greater influence; when associated with the opposite they are considered the Lesser influence. The Four Symbols are formed as follows:

Note that the Principle (Yang or Yin) continues to be specified by the LOWER line. This will remain consistent with the Trigrams and Hexagrams as well.

The division of the Four Symbols into Trigrams, nearly 5000 years ago, was made on the same basis, and the characteristic names and family associations were assigned. (This is attributed to the legendary Fu Hsi and his markings on tortoise shells.)

FU HSI, INVENTOR OF THE EIGHT TRIGRAMS

The Trigrams were formed in the same manner and associated with attributes as:

CH'IEN
(Father)   ☰   **Greater Yang**
                                          YANG

This Trigram is composed of all strong lines and represents the Firmness of the Father in family relationships.

TUI
(Youngest Daughter)   ☱   **Greater Yang**
                                          YANG

This Trigram has two strong lines below with the female influence at the top, or most recent. The most recent female is interpreted as the Joyous and Cheerful Youngest Daughter.

LI
(Middle Daughter)   ☲   **Lesser Yin**
                                          YANG

This Trigram has one strong line at the bottom and one at the top, with the female influence in the middle. This is interpreted as the Brilliant and Radiant Middle Daughter.

CHEN
(Oldest Son)   ☳   **Lesser Yin**
                                          YANG

This Trigram has one strong line at the bottom and it is the only male influence. Being at the beginning, bottom, it is interpreted as the Moving and Arousing Oldest Son.

SUN (Oldest Daughter)		**Lesser Yang** YIN

This Trigram has one yielding line at the bottom and it is the only female influence. Being at the beginning, bottom, it is interpreted as the Gentle and Penetrating Oldest Daughter.

K'AN (Middle Son)		**Lesser Yang** YIN

This Trigram has one yielding line at the bottom and one at the top, with the male influence in the middle. This is interpreted as the Dangerous and Abysmal Middle Son.

KEN (Youngest Son)		**Greater Yin** YIN

This Trigram has two yielding lines below, with the male influence at the top, or most recent. The most recent male is interpreted as the Still and Silent Youngest Son.

K'UN (Mother)		**Greater Yin** YIN

This Trigram is composed of all yielding lines and represents the Receptivity of the Mother in family relationships.

Again, note that the bottom line continues to specify the Principle and the bottom two lines continue to specify the Symbol. This continues into the construction of the Hexagrams, explained below.

Each of the Eight Lower Trigrams corresponds with each of the Eight Upper Trigrams to form the Hexagrams which relate to Yang (Greater Yang and Lesser Yin) and Yin (Lesser Yang and Greater Yin) in the sequence shown.

The full sequence of the Hexagrams, by the intensity of their polarities from Total Yang to Total Yin, can be followed by starting at the upper left hand corner (Hexagram #1, CH'IEN), then reading down to the bottom (#11, T'AI). Restart at the top of the next column (#10 LU) and continue through all eight columns until the lower right hand corner is reached (#2, K'UN). This is known as the "Polarity Sequence."

The system in which the Hexagrams are numbered is discussed in this Step under the heading, "The Orderly Sequence of the Hexagrams," and obviously differs from the above polarity sequence. The composites of the Hexagrams following the narrative in this Step, page 38, and in the Illustrated Step 3, are arranged according to this "Orderly Sequence of the Hexagrams," from 1 to 64.

The Orderly Sequence of the Hexagrams divides the Hexagrams into Two Sections. The First (Hexagrams 1 through 30) contains the Basic Theory of the I CHING, and these Hexagrams are the dramatizations of the workings of Heaven and Earth upon Mankind. The Second Section (Hexagrams 31 through 64) contains the precepts for Human Behavior.

The Player will find this numbering system universally used in the text of any language. Between the text of the composite Hexagrams, on the following pages, the reader will find a short paragraph describing the Orderly Sequence as it relates to the Hexagrams on that particular page. (This description is not resident within the Program.)

The Name of the Hexagram.

This Name is taken from our modification of the Wade-Giles System of Romanization and is the most common representation of the names. Some names appear to be the same, and in fact are spelled the same, but are actually different as they relate to the Oriental character. Pronunciations are dependent upon vowel inflections and usage within sentence structures. The introduction contains a more detailed explanation of our selection of the Wade-Giles System.

The Title of the Hexagram.

Our Title makes use of the translation of the character within the circumstances implied by the Hexagram. Strict translations of the characters often create confusion as to the signficance of the Hexagram. For example,#18, KU, translates as "Decay," and the Occidental word carries a certain negative connotation. However, the intended interpretation is the "Repair of Decay," with certain positive connotations. Because this Title is also used in conjunction with the Program Data Base, we have allowed two lines of 38 characters each, and have included all these implications within our title. Thus #18 is titled "Prepare in Advance. Eliminate the Decay and Rebuild, Completing Swiftly." This will resemble the "Symbol" referred to in other texts, but there is no attempt here to portray it as the"Symbol" of the Hexagram, which is reputed to have been originated by Confucius.

ABOVE: The essential attributes of the Upper Trigram, (see step 4).

BELOW: The essential attributes of the Lower Trigram, (see step 4).

The Hexagram Line Numbers.

The Line Numbers are arranged vertically from 6 down to 1 on the left hand side. The Hexagrams begin at the bottom, line number 1, and continue upward to the top, line number 6. To avoid confusion this can be seen as the height of a person in 1-foot increments, and some interpretations actually use this analogy to describe physical relationships of the body. The Hexagram KEN, #52, specifically relates to parts of the body in this specific order. Each line contains the following composite information:

— **The Yang (Solid) or Yin (Broken) Yao Bar.** This bar represents the line, Yang or Yin. Your actual Worksheet, and the Program Display, will additionally contain an "O" through a Yang line and an "X" in a Yin line when the referenced line is indicating a Change.

— **The Ruling Line Indication.** "R" to right side of the Bar indicates a Ruling Line. The selection of this line is made by the application of certain guidelines relating to the center line of each Trigram, the 5th (Authoritative) line, and the structure of the Hexagram itself. Initially these guidelines are confusing, but once understood are surprisingly meaningful. Step 3 gives a more detailed explanation of the Ruling Lines within each Hexagram.

— **The Subject (Self) or Object (Other) Indication.** Either "S" or "O" appears to indicate that the line is the Subject or the Object of the Hexagram. Step 3 gives further amplification of these lines, which are always separated from each other by three lines and always relate to the particular Trigram in which they are contained.

— **The Natural Line Indication.** An "N" indicates that the line is in a "Natural" position. As explained on Page 25, the Odd numbered lines are naturally Solid or Yang, and the Even numbered lines are naturally Broken or Yin.

— **The Matched Line Indication.** A connecting line indicates a correspondence with the associative line. Line 1 can correspond with line 4, line 2 to 5, and line 3 to 6. This "Correspondence" occurs when the two lines contain the opposite principles. Correspondence is either natural or unnatural.

— **The Twelve Hourly Branches.** These branches are indicated by 12 two-hour periods through the day and night. The first represents 11PM to 1AM, they progressively continue until the 12th, 9PM to 11PM. This cycle is also represented in Step 4 as part of the "Hu Tien." (These hourly branches are also referred to in the Horary Branches, particularly in Advanced or Astrological texts,) and also relate to positions in astrological or horoscope charts.

— The Element Name. Each Hourly Branch symbol is associated with one of the five elements as follows:

11 PM to 1 AM	T'zu	WATER	Shui
1 AM to 3 AM	Ch'ou	EARTH	T'u
3 AM to 5 AM	Yin	WOOD	Mu
5 AM to 7 AM	Mao	WOOD	Mu
7 AM to 9 AM	Ch'en	EARTH	T'u
9 AM to 11 AM	Ssu	FIRE	Ho
11 AM to 1 PM	Wu	FIRE	Ho
1 PM to 3 PM	Wei	EARTH	T'u
3 PM to 5 PM	Shen	METAL	Chin
5 PM to 7 PM	Yu	METAL	Chin
7 PM to 9 PM	Hsu	EARTH	T'u
9 PM to 11 PM	Hai	WATER	Shui

The elements are applied with the element of the "House," described below, under the Principles of Mutual Creation and Destruction to form the Personifications described below. The Principles of Mutual Creation and Destruction are explained fully in Step 4. We have also included the Chinese name for each of the branches and elements above for cultural reference.

— The Personification. The Personification is arrived at by applying the Principles of Mutual Creation and Destruction of the Element of the House to the Element of the Line. Although more fully described in Step 4, the Principles and the derivation of the Personifications are as follows:

WATER Creates WOOD	WATER Destroys FIRE
EARTH Creates METAL	EARTH Destroys WATER
WOOD Creates FIRE	WOOD Destroys EARTH
FIRE Creates EARTH	FIRE Destroys METAL
METAL Creates WATER	METAL Destroys WOOD

When the HOUSE and LINE are the same, the Personification is
Brothers, Sisters, and Peers.

When the HOUSE Creates the LINE, the Personification is
Sons, Daughters, Descendants.

When the HOUSE Destroys the LINE, the Personification is
Wife, Husband, Money, Business.

When the LINE Creates the HOUSE, the Personification is
Fathers, Mothers, Ancestors.

When the LINE Destroys the HOUSE, the Personification is
Officials, Boss, Troublemakers.

A degree of familiarity and expertise in using the I CHING will be required before the Personifications can be used effectively by the Player, but the examples in Appendix A will provide some insight into this advanced topic.

The House, Position, and Element.

The House and Position of a Hexagram are taken from ancient tables described in Step 4. These tables also provide the Subject (Self) and Object (Other) Line indication referred to above. The Element is the same as normally associated with the Trigram representing the House. The First Position always refers to a "Pure" Hexagram, where both the upper and lower Trigrams are the same. The Seventh Position is indicative of "Souls Departing" and represents a particular graveness when the I CHING is consulted regarding Sickness. The Eighth Position is indicative of "Souls Returning" and represents a return of Health when consulting regarding Sickness. The other positions have Advanced applications and are presented in this publication for reference.

The Motivational Influence Hexagram Number.

This is an internal Hexagram made by using Lines 2, 3, and 4 for the lower Trigram and Lines 3, 4, and 5 for the upper Trigram—forming a new Hexagram referred to as "Hu Kua." This new Hexagram emphasizes the human influence upon circumstances regarding a consultation. More advanced users will derive more from this Hexagram, and we have not provided for it on either the Worksheet or in the Program, other than to indicate its number. There are sixteen of these influences as follows:

HEXAGRAM	INFLUENCE
1 — CH'IEN	Great Strength and Creative Power.
2 — K'UN	Natural Strength and Receptivity.
23 — PO	Collapse and Splitting Apart.
24 — FU	Natural Return and Correction of Faults.
27 — I	Invigoration and Cultivation of Virtue.
28 — TA KUO	Great Behavior with Unusual Changes.
37 — CHIA JEN	Harmony and Order within a Family.
38 — K'UEI	Opposing Elements Effecting Achievement.
39 — CHIEN	Difficulty from a Personal Restraint.
40 — CHIEH	Liberation from Restraints and Resolution.
43 — KUAI	Great Strength in Eliminating Corruption.
44 — KOU	Inferior Elements Appear as Temptation.
53 — CHIEN	Gradual Progress and Development.
54 — KUEI MEI	Subordination and Agreement.
63 — CHI CHI	Complete, Finished. Disorder follows Order.
64 — WEI CHI	Incomplete, Undone. Order follows Disorder.

The numbers of these Hexagrams are enclosed in brackets in the lower right-hand corner of each of the composites beginning on page 38.

Hexagrams associated with the Time of Year.

The cyclic changes through the calendar year portray particular relevances to the Hexagrams of the I CHING. We have included two phrases, "The Primary Hexagram of the . . . Month," and "A Hexagram of the . . . Month" to indicate particular relevancy. The Chinese calendar year is represented with the Western equivalents. The Chinese New Year begins on approximately February 5th on Western calendars, but the date actually varies as the Chinese calendar is based upon the cycles of the moon, or "lunar" cycles.

The lunar cycle is based upon slightly less than 30 days, and the total year loses 5 days which are periodically made up by incorporating an inter-calendary month. Thus the actual New Year's Day varies from late January to the middle of February. The First Month, however, corresponds most closely with February. The following table and explanation summarizes the correspondence with the months, but we have purposely begun with the 11th Month as it relates to the passing of the Winter Solstice in December.

In the "Calendar Sequence," which follows, notice the upward movement of the Solid Lines in the beginning as the days lengthen to the Summer Solstice, followed by the upward movement of the Broken lines as the days shorten to the Winter Solstice.

24, FU, Natural Return and Correction of Faults, is the Primary Hexagram of the Eleventh Month, December. The days first become longer after the passing of the Winter Solstice, represented by the Solid bottom line. The return of the living giving forces.
The other Hexagrams are:

3 - CHUN	Difficulties of New Beginnings and Life.
15 - CH'IEN	Modest Behavior Greatens Good Fortune.
38 - K'UEI	Opposing Elements Affecting Achievement.
46 - SHENG	Opportunity to Advance and Accumulate.
* 29 - K'AN	Overcoming Difficulties by Perseverance.

19, LIN, Approaching Greatness, is the Primary Hexagram of the Twelfth Month, January. The days continue to lengthen and the greatness of Spring is approaching. The two Solid lines at the bottom are rising and there is evidence of new life.
The other Hexagrams are:

62 - HSIAO KUO	Advantage in Tending to Small Affairs.
4 - MENG	Youthful Folly and Innocence in Development.
42 - I	Individual Advantage from Common Benefit.
53 - CHIEN	Gradual Progress and Development.
* 29 - K'AN	Overcoming Difficulties by Perseverance.

11, T'AI, Arrival of Greatness, Peace, and Harmony is the Primary Hexagram of the First Month, February. Days continue to lengthen and Spring arrives. The bottom three Solid lines indicate the arrival of greatness. Blossoms appear while peace and harmony prevail.
The other Hexagrams are:

5 - HSU	Resting, Nourishing for Better Times Ahead.
17 - SUI	Following Nature's Way as Autumn Does Spring.
35 - CHIN	Progress and Esteem from Virtuous Efforts.
40 - CHIEH	Freed of Restraints, Difficulties Resolved.
* 52 - KEN	Devout Meditation to Improve Virtue.

34, TA CHUAN, Great Strength and Power Increase is the Primary Hexagram of the Second Month, March. The days continue to lengthen, the Vernal (Spring) Equinox passes, and weather improves. The four Solid lines are increasing in power over the Yielding lines.
The other Hexagrams are:

16 - YU	Enthusiasm and Devotion in New Undertakings.
6 - SUNG	Contention, Lawsuits, Conflicts are Resolved.
18 - KU	Elimination and Swift Repair of Decay.
45 - TS'UI	Gather Together in Pursuit of Common Goals.
* 52 - KEN	Devout Meditation to Improve Virtue.

43, KUAI, Great Strength in Eliminating Corruption is the Primary Hexagram of the Third Month, April. The days continue to lengthen while plantlife greens and grows and temperatures increase. The five Solid lines are overtaking the remaining Yielding line.
The other Hexagrams are:

56 - LU	Correct Traveling into Strange Circumstances.
7 - SHIH	Army, Strength Stored in the Mass of People.
8 - PI	Union with Loyal and Sincere Relationships.
9 - HSIAO CH'U	Small and Weak Forces Restrain the Great.
* 52 - KEN	Devout Meditation to Improve Virtue.

1, CH'IEN, Great Strength and Creative Power is the Primary Hexagram of the Fourth Month, May. The days have fully lengthened while the warmth and clearness of early Summer prevails. All six lines are Solid and there are no Yielding lines.
The other Hexagrams are:

14 - TA YU	Possession of Great Strength and Virtue.
37 - CHIA JEN	Harmony and Order within a Family.
48 - CHING	The Well Nourishes Those Who Come and Go.
31 - HSIEN	Natural Influence without Designs or Schemes.
* 30 - LI	Ascent by Clinging to Honesty and Sincerity.

44, KOU, The Inferior has Appeared as Temptation, is the Primary Hexagram of the Fifth Month, June. The Summer Solstice has passed, the days begin to shorten, and darkness begins to ascend. Temptation appears in the pleasant and balmy time of Summer.
The other Hexagrams are:

50 - TING	The Cauldron Nourishes for Great Progress.
55 - FENG	Prosperity, Abundance, the Greatest Moment.
59 - HUAN	Dissolution of or Casting out the Inferior.
10 - LU	Considerate Conduct toward Others.
* 30 - LI	Ascent by Clinging to Honesty and Sincerity.

33, TUN, Strength Yielding to the Circumstances is the Primary Hexagram of the Six Month, July. The Summer's heat is beginning to wane and crops are maturing for harvest. The four Solid lines above are now Yielding to the lower Broken lines as they continue ascent.
The other Hexagrams are:

32 - HENG	Sincerity in Preserving Relationships.
60 - CHIEH	Regulations for Orderly Attainment.
13 - T'UNG JEN	Fellowship, Peaceful Union among Colleagues.
41 - SUN	Individual Sacrifice for the Benefit of All.
* 30 - LI	Ascent by Clinging to Honesty and Sincerity.

12, P'I, Stagnation and Lesser Influences Arrive is the Primary Hexagram of the Seventh Month, August. The days continue to shorten, temperatures begin to drop, and the leaves begin the change to Autumn Colors. The Broken lines occupy the bottom three places.
The other Hexagrams are:

57 - SUN	Gentle Penetration to Influence Movement.
49 - KO	Revolution and Corrections for Advantage.
26 - TA CH'U	Great Restraint Providing Great Accumulation.
22 - PI	Grace as Simplistic Virtue, Beauty of Form.
* 58 - TUI	Cheerful Encouragement for Attainment.

20, KUAN, Observation for Future Improvement is the Primary Hexagram of the Eighth Month, September. The days continue to shorten, harvests are completed, and the Autumnal Equinox passes. The remaining Solid lines are seen preparing for the future.
The other Hexagrams are:

54 - KUEI MEI	Subordination and Agreement, as in Marriage.
25 - WU WANG	The Unexpected Even with Sincere Efforts.
36 - MING I	Darkening of the Light, Virtue is Obscured.
47 - K'UN	Adapting to Difficulties with Bravery.
* 58 - TUI	Cheerful Encouragement for Attainment.

23, PO, Collapse and Splitting Apart is the Primary Hexagram of the Ninth Month, October. The days continue to shorten, leaves begin falling along with temperatures. The Broken lines offer no support or strength, and Autumn begins a collapse to Winter.
The other Hexagrams are:

51 - CHEN	Shocking and Arousing Power in Development.
63 - CHI CHI	Complete, Finished. Disorder follows Order.
21 - SHIH HO	Biting Through to Correct Serious Problems.
28 - TA KUO	Great Behavior with Unusual Changes.
* 58 - TUI	Cheerful Encouragement for Attainment.

2, K'UN, Natural Strength and Receptivity is the Primary Hexagram of the Tenth Month, November. The days shorten into cold Winter. All items are received by the earth for rebirth and regrowth. All lines are Broken.
The Other Hexagrams are:

64 - WEI CHI	Incomplete, Undone. Order follows Disorder.
39 - CHIEN	Difficulty from a Personal Restraint.
27 - I	Invigoration and Cultivation of Virtue.
61 - CHUNG FU	Inner Sincerity Advances Undertakings.
* 29 - K'AN	Overcoming Difficulties by Perseverance.

* These Hexagrams are regarded as seasonal influences or as having inter-calendary signficance.

Each Month is assigned five Hexagrams, excluding the seasonal, or inter-calendary, influences. When the Oriental Month of 30 days is divided by 5, the resulting 6 provides 1 line for each day of the 5 periods.

* * * * * *

This Step has introduced the three primary sequences of Hexagrams.
    First—The Polarity Sequence, from total Yang to total Yin.
    Second—The Orderly Sequence, which explains the regular numbering progression of the Hexagrams according to King Wen.
    Third—The Calendar Sequence, beginning on page 34, explains the sequence of the Hexagrams according to the natural order, with their relationship to the time of year.

All three give particular insight when evaluating a prophesy. Very proficient Players, or "Masters," will evaluate all three, and possibly more—as more exist—when revealing the prophesy of the Oracle.

1   CH'IEN

THE HEAVENLY PRIMAL FORCE OF CREATIVE POWER AND FIRMNESS, MAKING STRONG.

ABOVE: CH'IEN   Heaven, Sky   Creative, Firmness   Father
BELOW: CH'IEN   Heaven, Sky   Creative, Firmness   Father

Line				Time	Element
6	▬▬▬▬▬	S		7pm - 9pm	EARTH
				Fathers, Mothers, Ancestors	
5	▬▬▬▬▬	R N		3pm - 5pm	METAL
				Brothers, Sisters, Peers	
4	▬▬▬▬▬			11am - 1pm	FIRE
				Officials, Bosses, Troublemakers	
3	▬▬▬▬▬	O N		7am - 9am	EARTH
				Fathers, Mothers, Ancestors	
2	▬▬▬▬▬			3am - 5am	WOOD
				Wife, Husband, Money, Business	
1	▬▬▬▬▬	N		11pm - 1am	WATER
				Sons, Daughters, Descendants	

House: CH'IEN, 1st Position; METAL   PURE   [1]
The Primary Hexagram of the 4th Month, (MAY).

2   K'UN

THE EARTHLY PRIMAL FORCE OF NATURAL STRENGTH, RECEPTIVENESS AND SERVICE.

ABOVE: K'UN   Earth, Land   Natural, Receptive   Mother
BELOW: K'UN   Earth, Land   Natural, Receptive   Mother

Line				Time	Element
6	▬▬ ▬▬	S N		5pm - 7pm	METAL
				Sons, Daughters, Descendants	
5	▬▬ ▬▬			9pm- 11pm	WATER
				Wife, Husband, Money, Business	
4	▬▬ ▬▬	N		1am - 3am	EARTH
				Brothers, Sisters, Peers	
3	▬▬ ▬▬	O		5am - 7am	WOOD
				Officials, Bosses, Troublemakers	
2	▬▬ ▬▬	R N		9am - 11am	FIRE
				Fathers, Mothers, Ancestors	
1	▬▬ ▬▬			1pm - 3pm	EARTH
				Brothers, Sisters, Peers	

House: K'UN, 1st Position; EARTH   PURE   [2]
The Primary Hexagram of the 10th Month, (NOVEMBER).

CH'IEN, Heaven, #1, and K'UN, Earth, #2, brought all other things into being. The Heaven and Earth combine to represent the Universe, and everything in between. The space between Heaven and Earth came to be filled with all other things as new life. These beginnings came to know their first difficulties, and CHUN, #3, follows.

3   CHUN

THE DIFFICULTIES ASSOCIATED WITH NEW
BEGINNINGS AND THE BIRTH OF LIFE.

ABOVE: K'AN   Water, Rain   Danger, Abysmal   Middle Son
BELOW: CHEN   Thunder   Movement, Arousing   Oldest Son

6	▬▬ ▬▬	N	11pm - 1am	WATER
			Brothers, Sisters, Peers	
5	▬▬▬▬	R O N	7pm - 9pm	EARTH
			Officials, Bosses, Troublemakers	
4	▬▬ ▬▬	N	3pm - 5pm	METAL
			Fathers, Mothers, Ancestors	
3	▬▬ ▬▬		7am - 9am	EARTH
			Officials, Bosses, Troublemakers	
2	▬▬ ▬▬	S N	3am - 5am	WOOD
			Sons, Daughters, Descendants	
1	▬▬▬▬	R N	11pm - 1am	WATER
			Brothers, Sisters, Peers	

House: K'AN, 3rd Position; WATER   [23]
A Hexagram of the 11th Month, (DECEMBER).

4   MENG

YOUTHFUL FOLLY AND INNOCENCE ARE
EXCUSED WHEN LEARNING AND DEVELOPING.

ABOVE: KEN   Mountain   Stillness, Silence   Youngest Son
BELOW: K'AN   Water, Rain   Danger, Abysmal   Middle Son

6	▬▬▬▬		3am - 5am	WOOD
			Fathers, Mothers, Ancestors	
5	▬▬ ▬▬	R	11pm - 1am	WATER
			Officials, Bosses, Troublemakers	
4	▬▬ ▬▬	S N	7pm - 9pm	EARTH
			Sons, Daughters, Descendants	
3	▬▬ ▬▬		11am - 1pm	FIRE
			Brothers, Sisters, Peers	
2	▬▬▬▬	R	7am - 9am	EARTH
			Sons, Daughters, Descendants	
1	▬▬ ▬▬	O	3am - 5am	WOOD
			Fathers, Mothers, Ancestors	

House: LI, 5th Position; FIRE   [24]
A Hexagram of the 12th Month, (JANUARY).

CH'IEN, #1, and K'UN, #2, created new life and beginnings, and there followed the difficulties associated with CHUN, #3. New life grows from CHUN through an innocent and underdeveloped time of folly known as MENG, #4. New life rests to gather strength and is nourished in preparation for the better times ahead, so HSU, #5, follows.

5   HSU

PATIENTLY WAITING AND WORKING TOWARD
A BETTER TIME. RESTING AND NOURISHING.

ABOVE: K'AN   Water, Rain   Danger, Abysmal   Middle Son
BELOW: CH'IEN   Heaven, Sky   Creative, Firmness   Father

6	▬▬ ▬▬	N	11pm - 1am	WATER
			Wife, Husband, Money, Business	
5	▬▬▬▬	R N	7pm - 9pm	EARTH
			Brothers, Sisters, Peers	
4	▬▬ ▬▬	S N	3pm - 5pm	METAL
			Sons, Daughters, Descendants	
3	▬▬▬▬	N	7am - 9am	EARTH
			Brothers, Sisters, Peers	
2	▬▬▬▬		3am - 5am	WOOD
			Officials, Bosses, Troublemakers	
1	▬▬▬▬	O N	11pm - 1am	WATER
			Wife, Husband, Money, Business	

House: K'UN, 7th Position; EARTH   SPIRITS DEPART   [38]
A Hexagram of the 1st Month, (FEBRUARY).

6   SUNG

DISAGREEMENTS AND LAWSUITS. CONFLICTS
AND OPPOSITION ARE MET AND RESOLVED.

ABOVE: CH'IEN   Heaven, Sky   Creative, Firmness   Father
BELOW: K'AN   Water, Rain   Danger, Abysmal   Middle Son

6	▬▬▬▬		7pm - 9pm	EARTH
			Sons, Daughters, Descendants	
5	▬▬▬▬	R N	3pm - 5pm	METAL
			Wife, Husband, Money, Business	
4	▬▬▬▬	S	11am - 1pm	FIRE
			Brothers, Sisters, Peers	
3	▬▬ ▬▬		11am - 1pm	FIRE
			Brothers, Sisters, Peers	
2	▬▬▬▬		7am - 9am	EARTH
			Sons, Daughters, Descendants	
1	▬▬ ▬▬	O	3am - 5am	WOOD
			Fathers, Mothers, Ancestors	

House: LI, 7th Position; FIRE   SPIRITS DEPART   [37]
A Hexagram of the 2nd Month, (March).

The growth from MENG, #4, leads to the patient waiting, resting, and nourishment of HSU, #5, which describes the way meat and drink are provided. There are certain to be conflicts and contention over the supply of meat and drink, hence SUNG, #6, follows. The masses arise when in contention, so SHIH, #7, follows.

7   SHIH

ARMY, STRENGTH STORED IN A MASS OF
PEOPLE. ORGANIZATION AND LEADERSHIP.

ABOVE: K'UN	Earth, Land	Natural, Receptive	Mother
BELOW: K'AN	Water, Rain	Danger, Abysmal	Middle Son

6	▬▬ ▬▬	O N	5pm - 7pm	METAL
			Fathers, Mothers, Ancestors	
5	▬▬ ▬▬	R	9pm - 11pm	WATER
			Brothers, Sisters, Peers	
4	▬▬ ▬▬	N	1am - 3am	EARTH
			Officials, Bosses, Troublemakers	
3	▬▬ ▬▬	S	11am - 1pm	FIRE
			Wife, Husband, Money, Business	
2	▬▬▬▬▬	R	7am - 9am	EARTH
			Officials, Bosses, Troublemakers	
1	▬▬ ▬▬		3am - 5am	WOOD
			Sons, Daughters, Descendants	

House: K'AN, 8th Position; WATER   SPIRITS RETURN   [24]
A Hexagram of the 3rd Month, (APRIL).

8   PI

THE GROUP IS UNITED AND HELD TOGETHER
WITH SINCERE AND LOYAL RELATIONSHIPS.

ABOVE: K'AN	Water, Rain	Danger, Abysmal	Middle Son
BELOW: K'UN	Earth, Land	Natural, Receptive	Mother

6	▬▬ ▬▬	O N	11pm - 1am	WATER
			Wife, Husband, Money, Business	
5	▬▬▬▬▬	R N	7pm - 9pm	EARTH
			Brothers, Sisters, Peers	
4	▬▬ ▬▬	N	3pm - 5pm	METAL
			Sons, Daughters, Descendants	
3	▬▬ ▬▬	S	5am - 7am	WOOD
			Officials, Bosses, Troublemakers	
2	▬▬ ▬▬	N	9am - 11am	FIRE
			Fathers, Mothers, Ancestors	
1	▬▬ ▬▬		1pm - 3pm	EARTH
			Brothers, Sisters, Peers	

House: K'UN, 8th Position; EARTH   SPIRITS RETURN   [23]
A Hexagram of the 3rd Month, (APRIL).

The conflicts and contention of SUNG, #6, have caused the masses to arise as seen in SHIH, #7. The masses are signified as being at arms—as in an Army—and they need binding together as in a union, and thus PI, #8, follows. Such unions require restraint, which is provided by the small forces of HSIAO CH'U, #9.

9 HSIAO CH'U

A SMALL, WEAK FORCE RESTRAINING
A POWERFUL AND VITAL FORCE.

ABOVE: SUN   Wind, Wood   Gentle, Penetrating   Oldest Daughter
BELOW: CH'IEN   Heaven, Sky   Creative, Firmness   Father

Line		Marks		Time	Element
6	▬▬▬▬▬			5am - 7am	WOOD
				Brothers, Sisters, Peers	
5	▬▬▬▬▬	R N		9am - 11am	FIRE
				Sons, Daughters, Descendants	
4	▬▬ ▬▬	O N		1pm - 3pm	EARTH
				Wife, Husband, Money, Business	
3	▬▬▬▬▬	N		7am - 9am	EARTH
				Wife, Husband, Money, Business	
2	▬▬▬▬▬			3am - 5am	WOOD
				Brothers, Sisters, Peers	
1	▬▬▬▬▬	S N		11pm - 1am	WATER
				Fathers, Mothers, Ancestors	

House: SUN, 2nd Position; WOOD   [38]
A Hexagram of the 3rd Month, (APRIL).

10 LU

CONSIDERATE CONDUCT WITH RESPECT
TOWARDS OTHERS. TREADING PROPERLY.

ABOVE: CH'IEN   Heaven, Sky   Creative, Firmness   Father
BELOW: TUI;   Lake, Marsh   Joyous, Cheerful   Youngest Daughter

Line		Marks		Time	Element
6	▬▬▬▬▬			7pm - 9pm	EARTH
				Brothers, Sisters, Peers	
5	▬▬▬▬▬	R S N		3pm - 5pm	METAL
				Sons, Daughters, Descendants	
4	▬▬▬▬▬			11am - 1pm	FIRE
				Fathers, Mothers, Ancestors	
3	▬▬ ▬▬			1am - 3am	EARTH
				Brothers, Sisters, Peers	
2	▬▬▬▬▬	O		5am - 7am	WOOD
				Official, Bosses, Troublemakers	
1	▬▬▬▬▬	N		9am - 11am	FIRE
				Fathers, Mothers, Ancestors	

House: KEN, 6th Position; EARTH   [37]
A Hexagram of the 5th Month, (JUNE).

The union of PI, #8, requires restraint to maintain order and HSIAO CH'U, #9, follows. The weak and fragile restraining force requires the careful conduct and consideration of LU, #10, which follows. Treading carefully gives rise to the peace and harmony of T'AI, #11.

11   T'AI

PEACE, HARMONY. THE BAD DEPARTS, THE GREAT ARRIVES. SUCCESS, GOOD FORTUNE.

ABOVE: K'UN   Earth, Land   Natural, Receptive   Mother
BELOW: CH'IEN   Heaven, Sky   Creative, Firmness   Father

6	▬▬ ▬▬	O N	5pm - 7pm	METAL
			Sons, Daughters, Descendants	
5	▬▬ ▬▬	R	9pm - 11pm	WATER
			Wife, Husband, Money, Business	
4	▬▬ ▬▬	N	1am - 3am	EARTH
			Brothers, Sisters, Peers	
3	▬▬▬▬	S N	7am - 9am	EARTH
			Brothers, Sisters, Peers	
2	▬▬▬▬	R	3am - 5am	WOOD
			Officials, Bosses, Troublemakers	
1	▬▬▬▬	N	11pm - 1am	WATER
			Wife, Husband, Money, Business	

House: KU'N, 4th Position; EARTH   [54]
The Primary Hexagram of the 1st Month, (FEBRUARY).

12   P'I

ENDURING DISORDER, STAGNATION. LESSER INFLUENCES ARRIVE. THE GREAT DEPARTS.

ABOVE: CH'IEN   Heaven, Sky   Creative, Firmness   Father
BELOW: K'UN   Earth, Land   Natural, Receptive   Mother

6	▬▬▬▬	O	7pm - 9pm	EARTH
			Fathers, Mothers, Ancestors	
5	▬▬▬▬	R N	3pm - 5pm	METAL
			Brothers, Sisters, Peers	
4	▬▬▬▬		11am - 1pm	FIRE
			Officials, Bosses, Troublemakers	
3	▬▬ ▬▬	S	5am - 7am	WOOD
			Wife, Husband, Money, Business	
2	▬▬ ▬▬	N	9am - 11am	FIRE
			Officials, Bosses, Troublemakers	
1	▬▬ ▬▬		1pm - 3pm	EARTH
			Fathers, Mothers, Ancestors	

House: CH'IEN, 4th Position; METAL   [53]
The Primary Hexagram of the 7th Month, (AUGUST).

The careful conduct of LU, #10, produces the peace and harmony of T'AI, #11. Peace and harmony provides freedom, without discipline, which leads to the stagnation of P'I, #12. Progress cannot be held back by stagnation forever, and colleagues join in fellowship as T'UNG JEN, #13.

13   T'UNG JEN

FELLOWSHIP AND PEACEFUL UNION AMONG COLLEAGUES. PROGRESS, SUCCESS.

ABOVE: CH'IEN	Heaven, Sky	Creative, Firmness	Father
BELOW: LI;	Fire, Sun	Brilliance, Clarity	Middle Daughter

6	▬▬▬▬	O		7pm - 9pm	EARTH
				Sons, Daughters, Descendants	
5	▬▬▬▬	R N		3pm - 5pm	METAL
				Wife, Husband, Money, Business	
4	▬▬▬▬			11am - 1pm	FIRE
				Brothers, Sisters, Peers	
3	▬▬▬▬	S N		9pm - 11pm	WATER
				Officials, Bosses, Troublemakers	
2	▬▬ ▬▬	R N		1am - 3am	EARTH
				Sons, Daughters, Descendants	
1	▬▬▬▬	N		5am - 7am	WOOD
				Fathers, Mothers, Ancestors	

House: LI, 8th Position; FIRE   SPIRITS RETURN   [44]
A Hexagram of the 6th Month, (JULY).

14   TA YU

POSSESSION OF VIRTUE AND STRENGTH PRODUCES PROGRESS AND SUCCESS.

ABOVE: LI	Fire, Sun	Brilliance, Clarity	Middle Daughter
BELOW: CH'IEN	Heaven, Sky	Creative, Firmness	Father

6	▬▬▬▬	O		9am - 11am	FIRE
				Officials, Bosses, Troublemakers	
5	▬▬ ▬▬	R		1pm - 3pm	EARTH
				Fathers, Mothers, Ancestors	
4	▬▬▬▬			5pm - 7pm	METAL
				Brothers, Sisters, Peers	
3	▬▬▬▬	S N		7am - 9am	EARTH
				Fathers, Mothers, Ancestors	
2	▬▬▬▬			3am - 5am	WOOD
				Wife, Husband, Money, Business	
1	▬▬▬▬	N		11pm - 1am	WATER
				Sons, Daughters, Descendants	

House: CH'IEN, 8th Position; METAL   SPIRITS RETURN   [43]
A Hexagram of the 4th Month, (MAY).

The restraints and containment of P'I, #12, motivate colleagues to join together in T'UNG JEN, #13. When persons so unite, then comes the ability to acquire possession in great measure as TA YU, #14. Such great possession and fullness require the humility and modesty in CH'IEN, #15, to bring satisfaction.

15   CH'IEN
MODEST BEHAVIOR GREATENS GOOD FORTUNE.
SUCCESS MUST NOT BRING ARROGANCE.

ABOVE: K'UN	Earth, Land	Natural, Receptive	Mother
BELOW: KEN	Mountain	Stillness, Silence	Youngest Son

#				Time	Element
6	▬▬ ▬▬	N		5pm - 7pm	METAL
				Brothers, Sisters, Peers	
5	▬▬ ▬▬	S		9pm- 11pm	WATER
				Sons, Daughters, Descendants	
4	▬▬ ▬▬	N		1am - 3am	EARTH
				Fathers, Mothers, Ancestors	
3	▬▬▬▬	R N		3pm - 5pm	METAL
				Brothers, Sisters, Peers	
2	▬▬ ▬▬	O N		11am - 1pm	FIRE
				Officials, Bosses, Troublemakers	
1	▬▬ ▬▬			7am - 9am	EARTH
				Fathers, Mothers, Ancestors	

House: TUI, 6th Position; METAL   [40]
A Hexagram of the 11th Month, (DECEMBER).

16   YU
ENTHUSIASM AS THE JOINING OF ENERGY
AND DEVOTION IN NEW UNDERTAKINGS.

ABOVE: CHEN	Thunder	Movement, Arousing	Oldest Son
BELOW: K'UN	Earth, Land	Natural, Receptive	Mother

#				Time	Element
6	▬▬ ▬▬	N		7pm - 9pm	EARTH
				Wife, Husband, Money, Business	
5	▬▬ ▬▬			3pm - 5pm	METAL
				Officials, Bosses, Troublemakers	
4	▬▬▬▬	R O		11am - 1pm	FIRE
				Sons, Daughters, Descendants	
3	▬▬ ▬▬			5am - 7am	WOOD
				Brothers, Sisters, Peers	
2	▬▬ ▬▬	N		9am - 11am	FIRE
				Sons, Daughters, Descendants	
1	▬▬ ▬▬	S		1pm - 3pm	EARTH
				Wife, Husband, Money, Business	

House: CHEN, 2nd Position; EARTH   [39]
A Hexagram of the 2nd Month, (MARCH).

The great possession of TA YU, #14, requires the humility of CH'IEN, #15, for satisfaction. When such satisfaction and contentment are attained, the enthusiastic joy and energy of YU, #16, follows with energetic new undertakings. Such enthusiastic undertakings naturally attract the sincere followers represented by SUI, #17.

17   SUI

FOLLOWING NATURE'S WAY, AS AUTUMN
DOES SPRING, LEADS TO GREAT SUCCESS.

ABOVE: TUI   Lake, Marsh   Joyous, Cheerful   Youngest Daughter
BELOW: CHEN   Thunder   Movement, Arousing   Oldest Son

6	▬▬ ▬▬	O N	1pm - 3pm	EARTH
			Wife, Husband, Money, Business	
5	▬▬▬▬	R N	5pm - 7pm	METAL
			Officials, Bosses, Troublemakers	
4	▬▬▬▬		9pm - 11pm	WATER
			Fathers, Mothers, Ancestors	
3	▬▬ ▬▬	S	7am - 9am	EARTH
			Wife, Husband, Money, Business	
2	▬▬ ▬▬	N	3am - 5am	WOOD
			Brothers, Sisters, Peers	
1	▬▬▬▬	R N	11pm - 1am	WATER
			Fathers, Mothers, Ancestors	

House: CHEN, 8th Position; WOOD   SPIRITS RETURN   [53]
A Hexagram of the 1st Month, (FEBRUARY).

18   KU

PREPARE IN ADVANCE. ELIMINATE THE
DECAY AND REBUILD, COMPLETING SWIFTLY.

ABOVE: KEN   Mountain   Stillness, Silence   Youngest Son
BELOW: SUN   Wind, Wood   Gentle, Penetrating   Oldest Daughter

6	▬▬▬▬	O	3am - 5am	WOOD
			Brothers, Sisters, Peers	
5	▬▬ ▬▬	R	11pm - 1am	WATER
			Fathers, Mothers, Ancestors	
4	▬▬ ▬▬	N	7pm - 9pm	EARTH
			Wife, Husband, Money, Business	
3	▬▬▬▬	S N	5pm - 7pm	METAL
			Officials, Bosses, Troublemakers	
2	▬▬▬▬		9pm - 11pm	WATER
			Fathers, Mothers, Ancestors	
1	▬▬ ▬▬		1am - 3am	EARTH
			Wife, Husband, Money, Business	

House: SUN, 8th Position; WOOD   SPIRITS RETURN   [54]
A Hexagram of the 2nd Month, (MARCH).

The enthusiasm of YU, #16, has naturally attracted followers as in SUI, #17. The followers are certain to have duties to perform in correcting decay and rebuilding, so follows KU, #18. Those who perform valuable services are certain to become great, and the greatness approaches, with proper leadership, in LIN, #19.

19   LIN

GREATNESS APPROACHES WITH WELL-DEVELOPED LEADERSHIP.

ABOVE: K'UN	Earth, Land	Natural, Receptive	Mother
BELOW: TUI	Lake, Marsh	Joyous, Cheerful	Youngest Daughter

6	▬▬ ▬▬	N	5pm - 7pm	METAL
			Sons, Daughters, Descendants	
5	▬▬ ▬▬	O	9pm - 11pm	WATER
			Wife, Husband, Money, Business	
4	▬▬ ▬▬	N	1am - 3am	EARTH
			Brothers, Sisters, Peers	
3	▬▬ ▬▬		1am - 3am	EARTH
			Brothers, Sisters, Peers	
2	▬▬▬▬	R S	5am - 7am	WOOD
			Officials, Bosses, Troublemakers	
1	▬▬▬▬	R N	9am - 11am	FIRE
			Fathers, Mothers, Ancestors	

House: K'UN, 3rd Position; EARTH   [24]

The Primary Hexagram of the 12th Month (JANUARY).

20   KUAN

OBSERVATION OF THE CONDITIONS AND CONTEMPLATION FOR IMPROVEMENT.

ABOVE: SUN	Wind, Wood	Gentle, Penetrating	Oldest Daughter
BELOW: K'UN	Earth, Land	Natural, Receptive	Mother

6	▬▬▬▬	R	5am - 7am	WOOD
			Wife, Husband, Money, Business	
5	▬▬▬▬	R N	9am - 11am	FIRE
			Officials, Bosses, Troublemakers	
4	▬▬ ▬▬	S N	1pm - 3pm	EARTH
			Fathers, Mothers, Ancestors	
3	▬▬ ▬▬		5am - 7am	WOOD
			Wife, Husband, Money, Business	
2	▬▬ ▬▬	N	9am - 11am	FIRE
			Officials, Bosses, Troublemakers	
1	▬▬ ▬▬	O	1pm - 3pm	EARTH
			Fathers, Mothers, Ancestors	

House: CH'IEN, 5th Position; METAL   [23]

The Primary Hexagram of the 8th Month (SEPTEMBER).

The performance of valuable services in KU, #18, brings the approach of greatness in LIN, #19. Greatness leads to contemplation for improvement of situations in the future, as in KUAN, #20. Such contemplation brings a resolve to correct serious problems, as one would ''bite through''—represented by SHIH HO, #21.

21   SHIH HO

BITING THROUGH, TENACIOUSLY WORKING TO CORRECT SERIOUS PROBLEMS SUCCEEDS.

ABOVE: LI   Fire, Sun   Brilliance, Clarity   Middle Daughter
BELOW: CHEN   Thunder   Movement, Arousing   Oldest Son

Line			Time	Element
6	▬▬▬▬		9am - 11am	FIRE
			Sons, Daughters, Descendants	
5	▬▬ ▬▬	R S	1pm - 3pm	EARTH
			Wife, Husband, Money, Business	
4	▬▬▬▬		5pm - 7pm	METAL
			Officials, Bosses, Troublemakers	
3	▬▬▬▬		7am - 9am	EARTH
			Wife, Husband, Money, Business	
2	▬▬ ▬▬	O N	3am - 5am	WOOD
			Brothers, Sisters, Peers	
1	▬▬▬▬	N	11pm - 1am	WATER
			Fathers, Mothers, Ancestors	

House: SUN, 6th Position; WOOD   [39]
A Hexagram of the 9th Month, (OCTOBER).

22   PI

OUTWARD BEAUTY PROVIDES NO GUARANTEE OF INNER CONTENTS.

ABOVE: KEN   Mountain   Stillness, Silence   Youngest Son
BELOW: LI   Fire, Sun   Brilliance, Clarity   Middle Daughter

Line			Time	Element
6	▬▬▬▬	R	3am - 5am	WOOD
			Officials, Bosses, Troublemakers	
5	▬▬ ▬▬		11pm - 1am	WATER
			Wife, Husband, Money, Business	
4	▬▬ ▬▬	O N	7pm - 9pm	EARTH
			Brothers, Sisters, Peers	
3	▬▬▬▬	N	9pm - 11pm	WATER
			Wife, Husband, Money, Business	
2	▬▬ ▬▬	R N	1am - 3am	EARTH
			Brothers, Sisters, Peers	
1	▬▬▬▬	S N	5am - 7am	WOOD
			Officials, Bosses, Troublemakers	

House: KEN, 2nd Position; EARTH   [40]
A Hexagram of the 7th Month, (AUGUST).

The contemplation for improvement, KUAN, #20, has brought the union and resolve to correct serious problems, as is SHIH HO, #21. Such union cannot be organized in a reckless or irresponsible way, so follows grace, which warns of vanity, in the form of PI, #22. When adornment and vanity prevails, the collapse represented by PO, #23, follows.

23   PO

DETERIORATION AND BREAKING APART
AS THE INFERIOR BECOMES DOMINANT.

ABOVE: KEN   Mountain   Stillness, Silence   Youngest Son
BELOW: K'UN   Earth, Land   Natural, Receptive   Mother

6	▬▬▬▬	R	3am - 5am	WOOD
			Wife, Husband, Money, Business	
5	▬▬ ▬▬	S	11pm - 1am	WATER
			Sons, Daughters, Descendants	
4	▬▬ ▬▬	N	7pm - 9pm	EARTH
			Fathers, Mothers, Ancestors	
3	▬▬ ▬▬		5am - 7am	WOOD
			Wife, Husband, Money, Business	
2	▬▬ ▬▬	O N	9am - 11am	FIRE
			Officials, Bosses, Troublemakers	
1	▬▬ ▬▬		1pm - 3pm	EARTH
			Fathers, Mothers, Ancestors	

House: CH'IEN, 6th Position; METAL   [2]
The Primary Hexagram of the 9th Month, (OCTOBER).

24   FU

NATURAL RETURN FROM ERROR AND
CORRECTION OF FAULTS BRINGS ADVANTAGE.

ABOVE; K'UN   Earth, Land   Natural, Receptive   Mother
BELOW: CHEN   Thunder   Movement, Arousing   Oldest Son

6	▬▬ ▬▬	N	5pm - 7pm	METAL
			Sons, Daughters, Descendants	
5	▬▬ ▬▬		9pm - 11pm	WATER
			Wife, Husband, Money, Business	
4	▬▬ ▬▬	O N	1am - 3am	EARTH
			Brothers, Sisters, Peers	
3	▬▬ ▬▬		7am - 9am	EARTH
			Brothers, Sisters, Peers	
2	▬▬ ▬▬	N	3am - 5am	WOOD
			Officials, Bosses, Troublemakers	
1	▬▬▬▬	R S N	11pm - 1am	WATER
			Wife, Husband, Money, Business	

House: K'UN, 2nd Position; EARTH   [2]
The Primary Hexagram of the 11th Month, (DECEMBER).

The outward appointment of PI, #22, fail to provide substance, and so follows the deterioration and collapse of PO, #23. Collapse is overcome by the correction of faults, and such a natural return to order is indicated by FU, #24. Return to order is associated with the honest and sincere efforts of WU WANG, #25, which also brings unexpected adversity.

25

WU WANG

THE UNEXPECTED APPEARS EVEN WITH HONEST AND SINCERE EFFORTS.

ABOVE: CH'IEN   Heaven, Sky   Creative, Firmness   Father
BELOW: CHEN   Thunder   Movement, Arousing   Oldest Son

6	▬▬▬▬			7pm - 9pm	EARTH
				Wife, Husband, Money, Business	
5	▬▬▬▬	R N		3pm - 5pm	METAL
				Officials, Bosses, Troublemakers	
4	▬▬ ▬▬	S		11am - 1pm	FIRE
				Sons, Daughters, Descendants	
3	▬▬ ▬▬			7am - 9am	EARTH
				Wife, Husband, Money, Business	
2	▬▬ ▬▬	N		3am - 5am	WOOD
				Brothers, Sisters, Peers	
1	▬▬▬▬	R O N		11pm - 1am	WATER
				Fathers, Mothers, Ancestors	

House: SUN, 5th Position; WOOD   [53]
A Hexagram of the 8th Month, (SEPTEMBER).

TA CH'U

GREAT RESTRAINT PROVIDES GREAT SAVING, ACCUMULATING STRENGTH AND WEALTH.

ABOVE: KEN   Mountain   Stillness, Silence   Youngest Son
BELOW: CH'IEN   Heaven, Sky   Creative, Firmness   Father

6	▬▬ ▬▬	R		3am - 5am	WOOD
				Officials, Bosses, Troublemakers	
5	▬▬ ▬▬	R O		11pm - 1am	WATER
				Wife, Husband, Money, Business	
4	▬▬ ▬▬	N		7pm - 9pm	EARTH
				Brothers, Sisters, Peers	
3	▬▬▬▬	N		7am - 9am	EARTH
				Brothers, Sisters, Peers	
2	▬▬▬▬	S		3am - 5am	WOOD
				Officials, Bosses, Troublemakers	
1	▬▬▬▬	N		11pm - 1am	WATER
				Wife, Husband, Money, Business	

House: KEN, 3rd Position; EARTH   [54]
A Hexagram of the 7th Month, (AUGUST).

The return of order in FU, #24, brings forth the honest and sincere efforts of WU WANG, #25, but unexpected adversity still appears. The Unexpected dictates the need for great restraint and saving to accumulate the strength and wealth sought in TA CH'U, #26. This is followed by a need for the invigoration and nourishment of such greatness as I, #27.

27   I

INVIGORATE AND CULTIVATE THE GROWING
AS DOES THE MOUTH PROVIDE NOURISHMENT.

ABOVE: KEN   Mountain   Stillness, Silence   Youngest Son
BELOW: CHEN;   Thunder   Movement, Arousing   Oldest Son

Line		Marker	Time	Element	Relationship
6	▬▬▬▬	R	3am - 5am	WOOD	Brothers, Sisters, Peers
5	▬▬ ▬▬	R	11pm - 1am	WATER	Fathers, Mothers, Ancestors
4	▬▬ ▬▬	S N	7pm - 9pm	EARTH	Wife, Husband, Money, Business
3	▬▬ ▬▬	N	7am - 9am	EARTH	Wife, Husband, Money, Business
2	▬▬ ▬▬	N	3am - 5am	WOOD	Brothers, Sisters, Peers
1	▬▬▬▬	O N	11pm - 1am	WATER	Fathers, Mothers, Ancestors

House: SUN, 7th Position; WOOD   SPIRITS DEPART   [2]
A Hexagram of the 10th Month, (NOVEMBER).

28   TA KUO

GREAT BEHAVIOR OR MATERIAL EXCESSES
PREDOMINATE, EXPECT UNUSUAL CHANGE.

ABOVE: TUI   Lake, Marsh   Joyous, Cheerful   Youngest Daughter
BELOW: SUN   Wind, Wood   Gentle, Penetrating   Oldest Daughter

Line		Marker	Time	Element	Relationship
6	▬▬ ▬▬	N	1pm - 3pm	EARTH	Wife, Husband, Money, Business
5	▬▬▬▬	N	5pm - 7pm	METAL	Officials, Bosses, Troublemakers
4	▬▬▬▬	R S	9pm - 11pm	WATER	Fathers, Mothers, Ancestors
3	▬▬▬▬	N	5pm - 7pm	METAL	Officials, Bosses, Troublemakers
2	▬▬▬▬	R	9pm - 11pm	WATER	Fathers, Mothers, Ancestors
1	▬▬ ▬▬	O	1am - 3am	EARTH	Wife, Husband, Money, Business

House: CHEN, 7th Position; WOOD   SPIRITS DEPART   [1]
A Hexagram of the 9th Month, (OCTOBER).

The great accumulation of TA CH'U, #26, has brought forth the need for invigoration and nourishment of such accumulation in I, #27. Such invigorated nourishment provides for the great behavior and material excesses signified by TA KUO, #28. Great excess and extraordinary progress bring forth the state of peril represented by K'AN, #29.

29 K'AN

PERSISTENCE SUCCESSFULLY OVERCOMES DIFFICULTIES AND HARDSHIPS.

| ABOVE: K'AN | Water, Rain | Danger, Abysmal | Middle Son |
| BELOW: K'AN | Water, Rain | Danger, Abysmal | Middle Son |

6	▬▬ ▬▬	S N	11pm - 1am	WATER
			Brothers, Sisters, Peers	
5	▬▬▬▬▬	R N	7pm - 9pm	EARTH
			Officials, Bosses, Troublemakers	
4	▬▬ ▬▬	N	3pm - 5pm	METAL
			Fathers, Mothers, Ancestors	
3	▬▬ ▬▬	O	11am - 1pm	FIRE
			Wife, Husband, Money, Business	
2	▬▬▬▬▬	R	7am - 9am	EARTH
			Officials, Bosses, Troublemakers	
1	▬▬ ▬▬		3am - 5am	WOOD
			Sons, Daughters, Descendants	

House: K'AN, 1st Position; WATER   PURE   [27]
A Hexagram of months 10—12. (NOVEMBER—JANUARY).

30 LI

CLINGING TO SINCERITY AND HONESTY BRINGS ASCENT AND ENLIGHTENMENT.

| ABOVE: LI | Fire, Sun | Brilliance, Clarity | Middle Daughter |
| BELOW: LI | Fire, Sun | Brilliance, Clarity | Middle Daughter |

6	▬▬▬▬▬	S	9am - 11am	FIRE
			Brothers, Sisters, Peers	
5	▬▬ ▬▬	R	1pm - 3pm	EARTH
			Sons, Daughters, Descendants	
4	▬▬▬▬▬		5pm - 7pm	METAL
			Wife, Husband, Money, Business	
3	▬▬▬▬▬	O N	9pm - 11pm	WATER
			Officials, Bosses, Troublemakers	
2	▬▬ ▬▬	R N	1am - 3am	EARTH
			Sons, Daughters, Descendants	
1	▬▬▬▬▬	N	5am - 7am	WOOD
			Fathers, Mothers, Ancestors	

House: LI, 1st Position; FIRE   PURE   [28]
A Hexagram of months 4—6. (MAY—JULY).

The extraordinary progress of TA KUO, #28, is beset by peril from the movement and changing times of K'AN, #29. When in peril, one clings and attaches oneself to another as related in LI, #30. From such joining follows the unscheming and natural influence of HSIEN, #31. The lessons and order of heaven and earth are hereby passed to mankind.

31   HSIEN

NATURAL INFLUENCE WITHOUT DESIGNS OR
SCHEMES FORMS SINCERE RELATIONSHIPS.

ABOVE: TUI   Lake, Marsh   Joyous, Cheerful   Youngest Daughter
BELOW: KEN   Mountain   Stillness, Silence   Youngest Son

6	▬▬ ▬▬	O N	1pm - 3pm EARTH Fathers, Mothers, Ancestors
5	▬▬▬▬	R N	5pm - 7pm METAL Brothers, Sisters, Peers
4	▬▬▬▬	R	9pm - 11pm WATER Sons, Daughters, Descendants
3	▬▬▬▬	S N	3pm - 5pm METAL Brothers, Sisters, Peers
2	▬▬ ▬▬	N	11am - 1pm FIRE Officials, Bosses, Troublemakers
1	▬▬ ▬▬		7am - 9am EARTH Fathers, Mothers, Ancestors

House: TUI, 4th Position; METAL   [44]
A Hexagram of the 4th Month, (MAY).

32   HENG

CONTINUED CONSIDERATION AND SINCERITY
PRESERVES NATURAL RELATIONSHIPS.

ABOVE: CHEN   Thunder   Movement, Arousing   Oldest Son
BELOW: SUN   Wind, Wood   Gentle, Penetrating   Oldest Daughter

6	▬▬ ▬▬	O N	7pm - 9pm EARTH Wife, Husband, Money, Business
5	▬▬ ▬▬		3pm - 5pm METAL Officials, Bosses, Troublemakers
4	▬▬▬▬		11am - 1pm FIRE Sons, Daughters, Descendants
3	▬▬▬▬	S N	5pm - 7pm METAL Officials, Bosses, Troublemakers
2	▬▬▬▬	R	9pm - 11pm WATER Fathers, Mothers, Ancestors
1	▬▬ ▬▬		1am - 3am EARTH Wife, Husband, Money, Business

House: CHEN, 4th Position; WOOD   [43]
A Hexagram of the 6th Month, (JUNE).

The radiant attachment of LI, #30, has passed the order of heaven and earth to mankind as the unscheming and natural influence in HSIEN, #31. Such influence should be long-enduring and sincere, as husband and wife, and so follows HENG, #32. Preservation of such influences is achieved by the yielding and withdrawing nature of TUN, #33.

33   TUN

STRENGTH YIELDS AND WITHDRAWS
AS APPROPRIATE TO THE CIRCUMSTANCES.

ABOVE: CH'IEN   Heaven, Sky   Creative, Firmness   Father
BELOW: KEN   Mountain   Stillness, Silence   Youngest Son

6	▬▬▬▬		7pm - 9pm	EARTH
			Fathers, Mothers, Ancestors	
5	▬▬▬▬	R O N	3pm - 5pm	METAL
			Brothers, Sisters, Peers	
4	▬▬▬▬		11am - 1pm	FIRE
			Officials, Bosses, Troublemakers	
3	▬▬▬▬	N	3pm - 5pm	METAL
			Brothers, Sisters, Peers	
2	▬▬ ▬▬	S N	11am - 1pm	FIRE
			Officials, Bosses, Troublemakers	
1	▬▬ ▬▬		7am - 9am	EARTH
			Fathers, Mothers, Ancestors	

House: CH'IEN, 3rd Position; METAL   [44]
The Primary Hexagram of the 6th Month, (JULY).

34   TA CHUAN

GREAT STRENGTH AND POWER INCREASE
BUT CANNOT BE ABUSED OR USED AS FORCE.

ABOVE: CHEN   Thunder   Movement, Arousing   Oldest Son
BELOW: CH'IEN   Heaven, Sky   Creative, Firmness   Father

6	▬▬ ▬▬	N	7pm - 9pm	EARTH
			Brothers, Sisters, Peers	
5	▬▬ ▬▬		3pm - 5pm	METAL
			Sons, Daughters, Descendants	
4	▬▬▬▬	R S	11am - 1pm	FIRE
			Fathers, Mothers, Ancestors	
3	▬▬▬▬	N	7am - 9am	EARTH
			Brothers, Sisters, Peers	
2	▬▬▬▬		3am - 5am	WOOD
			Officials, Bosses, Troublemakers	
1	▬▬▬▬	O N	11pm - 1am	WATER
			Wife, Husband, Money, Business	

House: K'UN, 5th Position; EARTH   [43]
The Primary Hexagram of the 2nd Month, (MARCH).

The Continuing consideration and sincerity, as in HENG, #32, is prolonged by withdrawing strength as appropriate, so TUN, #33, follows. But great strength cannot be continually held in check and TA CHUAN, #34, issues forward. Then follows the advance, progress, and enlightenment of CHIN, #35.

35 CHIN
PROGRESS AND RECOGNITION FROM
ENLIGHTENED AND VIRTUOUS EFFORTS.

ABOVE: LI   Fire, Sun   Brilliance, Clarity   Middle Daughter
BELOW: K'UN   Earth, Land   Natural, Receptive   Mother

6	▬▬▬		9am - 11am	FIRE
			Officials Bosses, Troublemakers	
5	▬ ▬	R	1pm - 3pm	EARTH
			Fathers, Mothers, Ancestors	
4	▬▬▬	S	5pm - 7pm	METAL
			Brothers, Sisters, Peers	
3	▬ ▬		5am - 7am	WOOD
			Wife, Husband, Money, Business	
2	▬ ▬	N	9am - 11am	FIRE
			Officials, Bosses, Troublemakers	
1	▬ ▬	O	1pm - 3pm	EARTH
			Fathers, Mothers, Ancestors	

House: CH'IEN, 7th Position; METAL   SPIRITS DEPART   [39]
A Hexagram of the 1st Month, (FEBRUARY).

36 MING I
THE DARKENING OF THE LIGHT AS VIRTUE
AND INTELLECT ARE OBSCURED.

ABOVE: K'UN   Earth, Land   Natural, Receptive   Mother
BELOW: LI   Fire, Sun   Brilliance, Clarity   Middle Daughter

6	▬ ▬	N	5pm - 7pm	METAL
			Fathers, Mothers, Ancestors	
5	▬ ▬	R	9pm - 11pm	WATER
			Brothers, Sisters, Peers	
4	▬ ▬	S N	1am - 3am	EARTH
			Officials, Bosses, Troublemakers	
3	▬▬▬	N	9pm - 11pm	WATER
			Brothers, Sisters, Peers	
2	▬ ▬	R N	1am - 3am	EARTH
			Officials, Bosses, Troublemakers	
1	▬▬▬	O N	5am - 7am	WOOD
			Sons, Daughters, Descendants	

House: K'AN, 7th Position; WATER   SPIRITS DEPART   [40]
A Hexagram of the 8th Month, (SEPTEMBER).

The increasing strength of TA CHUAN, #34, produces the advance, progress, and enlightenment of CHIN, #35. Such advance and progress invite the envy and suppression represented by MING I, #36. The obscuration of virtue and intellect is overcome by returning to the harmonious affairs of the family and CHIA JEN, #37, follows.

37   CHIA JEN

HARMONY AND ORDER WITHIN THE FAMILY PROMOTES SUCCESS IN ALL AFFAIRS.

ABOVE: SUN   Wind, Wood   Gentle, Penetrating   Oldest Daughter
BELOW: LI   Fire, Sun   Brilliance, Clarity   Middle Daughter

6	▬▬▬		5am - 7am	WOOD
			Brothers, Sisters, Peers	
5	▬▬▬	R O N	9am - 11am	FIRE
			Sons, Daughters, Descendants	
4	▬ ▬	N	1pm - 3pm	EARTH
			Wife, Husband, Money, Business	
3	▬▬▬	N	9pm - 11pm	WATER
			Fathers, Mothers, Ancestors	
2	▬ ▬	R S N	1am - 3am	EARTH
			Wife, Husband, Money, Business	
1	▬▬▬	N	5am - 7am	WOOD
			Brothers, Sisters, Peers	

House: SUN, 3rd Position; WOOD   [64]
A Hexagram of the 4th Month, (MAY).

38   K'UEI

SEPARATE AND OPPOSED ELEMENTS CAN SUCCESSFULLY ACHIEVE A COMMON GOAL.

ABOVE: LI   Fire, Sun   Brilliance, Clarity   Middle Daughter
BELOW: TUI   Lake, Marsh   Joyous, Cheerful   Youngest Daughter

6	▬▬▬		9am - 11am	FIRE
			Fathers, Mothers, Ancestors	
5	▬ ▬	R	1pm - 3pm	EARTH
			Brothers, Sisters, Peers	
4	▬▬▬	S	5pm - 7pm	METAL
			Sons, Daughters, Descendants	
3	▬ ▬		1am - 3am	EARTH
			Brothers, Sisters, Peers	
2	▬▬▬	R	5am - 7am	WOOD
			Officials, Bosses, Troublemakers	
1	▬▬▬	O N	9am - 11am	FIRE
			Fathers, Mothers, Ancestors	

House: KEN, 5th Position; EARTH   [63]
A Hexagram of the 11th Month, (DECEMBER).

The obscuration of virtue and intellect in MING I, #36, is overcome by the return to the harmonious affairs of the family, and CHIA JEN, #37, follows. Even within the family, divisions and misunderstandings occur—as represented by K'UEI, #38—though common goals can be attained. Misunderstandings lead to the difficulties of CHIEN, #39.

39 CHIEN

THE DIFFICULTIES ASSOCIATED WITH A
PERSONAL RESTRAINT OR INJURY, LIMPING.

ABOVE: K'AN   Water, Rain   Danger, Abysmal   Middle Son
BELOW: KEN   Mountain   Stillness, Silence   Youngest Son

6	▬ ▬		N	11pm - 1am	WATER
				Sons, Daughters, Descendants	
5	▬▬▬	R	N	7pm - 9pm	EARTH
				Fathers, Mothers, Ancestors	
4	▬ ▬	S	N	3pm - 5pm	METAL
				Brothers, Sisters, Peers	
3	▬ ▬		N	3pm - 5pm	METAL
				Brothers, Sisters, Peers	
2	▬ ▬		N	11am - 1pm	FIRE
				Officials, Bosses, Troublemakers	
1	▬ ▬		O	7am - 9am	EARTH
				Fathers, Mothers, Ancestors	

House: TUI, 5th Position; METAL   [64]
A Hexagram of the 10th Month, (NOVEMBER).

40 CHIEH

LIBERATION AND LOOSENING OF RESTRAINTS
BY TIMELY RESOLUTION OF DIFFICULTIES.

ABOVE: CHEN   Thunder   Movement, Arousing   Oldest Son
BELOW: K'AN   Water, Rain   Danger, Abysmal   Middle Son

6	▬ ▬		N	7pm - 9pm	EARTH
				Wife, Husband, Money, Business	
5	▬ ▬	R	O	3pm - 5pm	METAL
				Officials, Bosses, Troublemakers	
4	▬▬▬			11am - 1pm	FIRE
				Sons, Daughters, Descendants	
3	▬▬▬			11am - 1pm	FIRE
				Sons, Daughters, Descendants	
2	▬▬▬	R	S	7am - 9am	EARTH
				Wife, Husband, Money, Business	
1	▬ ▬			3am - 5am	WOOD
				Brothers, Sisters, Peers	

House: CHEN, 3rd Position; WOOD   [63]
A Hexagram of the 1st Month, (FEBRUARY).

The division and misunderstandings represented by K'UEI, #38, have led to the difficulties associated with personal restraint or injury indicated by CHIEN, #39. The complications are eased with relaxation and the resolving of difficulties—bringing the liberation of CHIEH, #40. Liberation and relaxation bring the losses represented by SUN, #41.

41 SUN

THE VIRTUE OF INDIVIDUAL DECREASE OR SACRIFICE FOR THE BENEFIT OF ALL.

ABOVE: KEN — Mountain — Stillness, Silence — Youngest Son
BELOW: TUI — Lake, Marsh — Joyous, Cheerful — Youngest Daughter

6	▬▬▬	O		3am - 5am	WOOD
				Officials, Bosses, Troublemakers	
5	▬ ▬	R		11pm - 1am	WATER
				Wife, Husband, Money, Business	
4	▬ ▬	N		7pm - 9pm	EARTH
				Brothers, Sisters, Peers	
3	▬ ▬	S		1am - 3am	EARTH
				Brothers, Sisters, Peers	
2	▬▬▬			5am - 7am	WOOD
				Officials, Bosses, Troublemakers	
1	▬▬▬	N		9am - 11am	FIRE
				Fathers, Mothers, Ancestors	

House: KEN, 4th Position; EARTH [24]
A Hexagram of the 6th Month, (JULY).

42 I

INDIVIDUAL ADVANTAGE IS DERIVED FROM THE COMMON BENEFIT IN ITS TIME.

ABOVE: SUN — Wind, Wood — Gentle, Penetrating — Oldest Daughter
BELOW: CHEN — Thunder — Movement, Arousing — Oldest Son

6	▬▬▬	O		5am - 7am	WOOD
				Brothers, Sisters, Peers	
5	▬▬▬	R N		9am - 11am	FIRE
				Sons, Daughters, Descendants	
4	▬ ▬	N		1pm - 3pm	EARTH
				Wife, Husband, Money, Business	
3	▬ ▬	S		7am - 9am	EARTH
				Wife, Husband, Money, Business	
2	▬ ▬	R N		3am - 5am	WOOD
				Brothers, Sisters, Peers	
1	▬▬▬	N		11pm - 1am	WATER
				Fathers, Mothers, Ancestors	

House: SUN, 4th Position; WOOD [23]
A Hexagram of the 12th Month, (JANUARY).

The liberation derived from CHIEH, #40, has brought decrease from lessening of efforts represented by SUN, #41. But such losses are viewed as sacrifices for the common good, and the common good provides for individual increase and advantage in the proper time as I, #42. Such advantage brings the resolute decision and breakthrough of KUAI, #43.

43   KUAI

RESOLUTE DECISION TO EXPOSE
AND REMOVE CORRUPTION.

ABOVE: TUI   Lake, Marsh   Joyous, Cheerful   Youngest Daughter
BELOW: CH'IEN   Heaven, Sky   Creative, Firmness   Father

Line	Marks	Time	Element	
6	N	1pm - 3pm	EARTH	Brothers, Sisters, Peers
5	R S N	5pm - 7pm	METAL	Sons, Daughters, Descendants
4		9pm - 11pm	WATER	Wife, Husband, Money, Business
3	N	7am - 9am	EARTH	Brothers, Sisters, Peers
2	O	3am - 5am	WOOD	Officials, Bosses, Troublemakers
1	N	11pm - 1am	WATER	Wife, Husband, Money, Business

House: K'UN, 6th Position; EARTH   [1]
The Primary Hexagram of the 3rd Month, (APRIL).

44   KOU

ADVANTAGE IS FOUND BY AVOIDING
STRONG AND INFERIOR TEMPTATION.

ABOVE: CH'IEN   Heaven, Sky   Creative, Firmness   Father
BELOW: SUN   Wind, Wood   Gentle, Penetrating   Oldest Daughter

Line	Marks	Time	Element	
6		7pm - 9pm	EARTH	Fathers, Mothers, Ancestors
5	R N	3pm - 5pm	METAL	Brothers, Sisters, Peers
4	O	11am - 1pm	FIRE	Officials, Bosses, Troublemakers
3	N	5pm - 7pm	METAL	Brothers, Sisters, Peers
2	R	9pm - 11pm	WATER	Sons, Daughters, Descendants
1	S	1am - 3am	EARTH	Fathers, Mothers, Ancestors

House: CH'IEN, 2nd Position; METAL   [1]
The Primary Hexagram of the 5th Month, (JUNE).

The individual advantage and increase of I, #42, brings resolute decision in the removal of corruption—as "breakthrough"—and KUAI, #43, follows. Dispersion of corruption is followed by the temptation of the impure as KOU, #44. Avoiding the inferior temptation produces the gathering together, or collection, of TS'UI, #45.

45   TS'UI

GATHERING TOGETHER AS ONE PROMOTES
SUCCESS IN PURSUIT OF COMMON GOALS.

ABOVE: TUI   Lake, Marsh   Joyous, Cheerful   Youngest Daughter
BELOW: K'UN   Earth, Land   Natural, Receptive   Mother

Line		Relation		Time	Element
6	▬▬ ▬▬	N		1pm - 3pm	EARTH
				Fathers, Mothers, Ancestors	
5	▬▬▬▬▬	R O N		5pm - 7pm	METAL
				Brothers, Sisters, Peers	
4	▬▬▬▬▬	R		9pm - 1pm	FIRE
				Sons, Daughters, Descendants	
3	▬▬ ▬▬			5am - 7am	METAL
				Wife, Husband, Money, Business	
2	▬▬ ▬▬	S N		9am - 11am	WATER
				Officials, Bosses, Troublemakers	
1	▬▬ ▬▬			1pm - 3pm	EARTH
				Fathers, Mothers, Ancestors	

House: TUI, 3rd Position; METAL   [53]
A Hexagram of the 2nd Month, (MARCH).

46   SHENG

OPPORTUNITY TO RISE AND ADVANCE BY
ACCUMULATING VIRTUE UNTIL GREAT.

ABOVE: K'UN   Earth, Land   Natural, Receptive   Mother
BELOW: SUN   Wind, Wood   Gentle, Penetrating   Oldest Daughter

Line		Relation		Time	Element
6	▬▬ ▬▬	N		5pm - 7pm	METAL
				Officials, Bosses, Troublemakers	
5	▬▬ ▬▬	R		9pm - 11pm	WATER
				Fathers, Mothers, Ancestors	
4	▬▬ ▬▬	S N		1am - 3am	EARTH
				Wife, Husband, Money, Business	
3	▬▬▬▬▬	N		5pm - 7pm	METAL
				Officials, Bosses, Troublemakers	
2	▬▬▬▬▬			9pm - 11pm	WATER
				Fathers, Mothers, Ancestors	
1	▬▬ ▬▬	O		1am - 3am	EARTH
				Wife, Husband, Money, Business	

House: CHEN, 5th Position; WOOD   [54]
A Hexagram of the 11th Month, (DECEMBER).

Meeting and avoiding the inferior temptation of KOU, #44, has allowed the gathering together of virtuous elements to pursue common goals, represented by TS'UI, #45. Such pursuit provides the opportunity to greatly rise and advance, so follows SHENG, #46. Such great ascent brings forth the difficulties and isolation of K'UN, #47.

47 K'UN

HONESTY AND BRAVERY WHILE ADAPTING TO
DIFFICULTIES. COMPLAINTS GO UNHEARD.

ABOVE: TUI   Lake, Marsh   Joyous, Cheerful   Youngest Daughter
BELOW: K'AN   Water, Rain   Danger, Abysmal   Middle Son

6	▬▬ ▬▬	N	1pm 3pm	EARTH
			Fathers, Mothers, Ancestors	
5	▬▬▬▬	R N	5pm - 7pm	METAL
			Brothers, Sisters, Peers	
4	▬▬▬▬	O	9pm - 11pm	WATER
			Sons, Daughters, Descendants	
3	▬▬ ▬▬		11am - 1pm	FIRE
			Officials, Bosses, Troublemakers	
2	▬▬ ▬▬	R	7am - 9am	EARTH
			Fathers, Mothers, Ancestors	
1	▬▬ ▬▬	S	3am - 5am	WOOD
			Wife, Husband, Money, Business	

House: TUI, 2nd Position; METAL   [37]
A Hexagram of the 8th Month, (SEPTEMBER).

48 CHING

THE NOURISHING WELL IS THE ABUNDANT
SOURCE OF WISDOM TO BENEFIT ALL.

ABOVE: K'AN   Water, Rain   Danger, Abysmal   Middle Son
BELOW: SUN   Wind, Wood   Gentle, Penetrating   Oldest Daughter

6	▬▬ ▬▬	N	11pm - 1am	WATER
			Fathers, Mothers, Ancestors	
5	▬▬▬▬	R S N	7pm - 9pm	EARTH
			Wife, Husband, Money, Business	
4	▬▬▬▬	N	3pm - 5pm	METAL
			Officials, Bosses, Troublemakers	
3	▬▬▬▬	N	5pm - 7pm	METAL
			Officials, Bosses, Troublemakers	
2	▬▬▬▬	O	9pm - 11pm	WATER
			Fathers, Mothers, Ancestors	
1	▬▬ ▬▬		1am - 3am	EARTH
			Wife, Husband, Money, Business	

House: CHEN, 6th Position; WOOD   [38]
A Hexagram of the 4th Month, (MAY).

The great rise and advance of SHENG, #46, is followed by the difficulties, isolation, and exhaustion of K'UN, #47. Such exhaustion requires the nourishment of CHING, #48, for the betterment of all. As nourishment provides energy, there follows change and revolution to remove corruption, and KO, #49, follows.

49

KO

REVOLUTION AND CHANGE FROM THE BELIEF
THAT CORRUPTION REQUIRES REMOVAL.

ABOVE: TUI	Lake, Marsh	Joyous, Cheerful	Youngest Daughter
BELOW: LI	Fire, Sun	Brilliance, Clarity	Middle Daughter

6	▬▬ ▬	N		1pm - 3pm	EARTH
				Officials, Bosses, Troublemakers	
5	▬▬▬▬	R N		5pm - 7pm	METAL
				Fathers, Mothers, Ancestors	
4	▬▬▬▬	S		9pm - 11pm	WATER
				Brothers, Sisters, Peers	
3	▬▬▬▬	N		9pm - 11pm	WATER
				Brothers, Sisters, Peers	
2	▬▬ ▬	N		1am - 3am	EARTH
				Officials, Bosses, Troublemakers	
1	▬▬▬▬	O N		5am - 7am	WOOD
				Sons, Daughters, Descendants	

House: K'AN, 5th Position; WATER   [44]
A Hexagram of the 7th Month, (AUGUST).

50

TING

INVIGORATING AND CULTIVATING ABLE
PERSONS IN PURSUIT OF NOBLE GOALS.

ABOVE: LI	Fire, Sun	Brilliance, Clarity	Middle Daughter
BELOW: SUN	Wind, Wood	Gentle, Penetrating	Oldest Daughter

6	▬▬▬▬	R		9am - 11am	FIRE
				Brothers, Sisters, Peers	
5	▬▬ ▬	R O		1pm - 3pm	EARTH
				Sons, Daughters, Descendants	
4	▬▬▬▬			5pm - 7pm	METAL
				Wife, Husband, Money, Business	
3	▬▬▬▬	N		5pm - 7pm	METAL
				Wife, Husband, Money, Business	
2	▬▬▬▬	S		9pm - 11pm	WATER
				Officials, Bosses, Troublemakers	
1	▬▬ ▬			1am - 3am	EARTH
				Sons, Daughters, Descendants	

House: LI, 3rd Position; FIRE   [43]
A Hexagram of the 5th Month, (JUNE).

The nourishment of CHING, #48, for the betterment of all brings about revolution and change to remove the corruption as expressed by KO, #49. Persons producing noble changes and revolution are honored in TING, #50, which further cultivates improvement. Improvement is set into motion in CHEN, #51, as awe inspiring and profound forces.

51   CHEN

SHOCKING AND PROFOUND POWER
AROUSES AWE, AS DOES THUNDER.

ABOVE: CHEN   Thunder   Movement, Arousing   Oldest Son
BELOW: CHEN   Thunder   Movement, Arousing   Oldest Son

Line		Marks	Time	Element	Relations
6	▬▬ ▬▬	S N	7pm 9pm	EARTH	Wife, Husband, Money, Business
5	▬▬ ▬▬		3pm - 5pm	METAL	Officials, Bosses, Troublemakers
4	▬▬▬▬		11am - 1pm	FIRE	Sons, Daughters, Descendants
3	▬▬ ▬▬	O	7am - 9am	EARTH	Wife, Husband, Money, Business
2	▬▬ ▬▬	N	3am - 5am	WOOD	Brothers, Sisters, Peers
1	▬▬▬▬	R N	11pm - 1am	WATER	Fathers, Mothers, Ancestors

House: CHEN, 1st Position; WOOD   PURE   [39]
A Hexagram of the 9th Month, (OCTOBER).

52   KEN

STOPPING AND REMAINING STILL IN THE
APPROPRIATE TIME BRINGS NO HARM.

ABOVE: KEN   Mountain   Stillness, Silence   Youngest Son
BELOW: KEN   Mountain   Stillness, Silence   Youngest Son

Line		Marks	Time	Element	Relations
6	▬▬▬▬	R S	3am - 5am	WOOD	Officials, Bosses, Troublemakers
5	▬▬ ▬▬		11pm - 1am	WATER	Wife, Husband, Money, Business
4	▬▬ ▬▬	N	7pm - 9pm	EARTH	Brothers, Sisters, Peers
3	▬▬▬▬	O N	3pm - 5pm	METAL	Sons, Daughters, Descendants
2	▬▬ ▬▬	N	11am - 1pm	FIRE	Fathers, Mothers, Ancestors
1	▬▬ ▬▬		7am - 9am	EARTH	Brothers, Sisters, Peers

House: KEN, 1st Position; EARTH   PURE   [40]
A Hexagram of Months 1—3. (FEBRUARY—APRIL).

The improvement nourished in TING, #50, is brought into motion as the shocking and profound power of CHEN, #51. Thunderous and awesome power needs to be checked and kept still at appropriate times, as in KEN, #52. From such stillness there again comes the gradual and developing progress of CHIEN, #53.

53   CHIEN

GRADUAL PROGRESS AND DEVELOPMENT
FOR GROWTH WHEN OBEDIENT.

ABOVE: SUN   Wind, Wood   Gentle, Penetrating   Oldest Daughter
BELOW: KEN   Mountain   Stillness, Silence   Youngest Son

Line		Time	Element	Relation
6	O	5am - 7am	WOOD	Officials, Bosses, Troublemakers
5	R N	9am - 11am	FIRE	Fathers, Mothers, Ancestors
4	N	1pm - 3pm	EARTH	Brothers, Sisters, Peers
3	S N	3pm - 5pm	METAL	Sons, Daughters, Descendants
2	R N	11am - 1pm	FIRE	Fathers, Mothers, Ancestors
1		7am - 9am	EARTH	Brothers, Sisters, Peers

House: KEN, 8th Position; EARTH   SPIRITS RETURN   [64]
A Hexagram of the 12th Month, (JANUARY).

54   KUEI MEI

ABANDONING INCORRECT ATTITUDES AND
RE-ADAPTING PREVENTS MISFORTUNE.

ABOVE: CHEN   Thunder   Movement, Arousing   Oldest Son
BELOW: TUI   Lake, Marsh   Joyous, Cheerful   Youngest Daughter

Line		Time	Element	Relation
6	O N	7pm - 9pm	EARTH	Fathers, Mothers, Ancestors
5	R	3pm - 5pm	METAL	Brothers, Sisters, Peers
4		11am - 1pm	FIRE	Officials, Bosses, Troublemakers
3	S	1am - 3am	EARTH	Fathers, Mothers, Ancestors
2		5am - 7am	WOOD	Wife, Husband, Money, Business
1	N	9am - 11am	FIRE	Officials, Bosses, Troublemakers

House: TUI, 8th Position; METAL   SPIRITS RETURN   [63]
A Hexagram of the 8th Month, (SEPTEMBER).

The appropriate stillness and silence of KEN, #52, gradually gives way to the progress and development represented by CHIEN, #53. As development is gradual, so is agreement and subordination, and KUEI MEI, #54, follows. Agreement and subordination require great compromise by all, but when accomplished, the greatest moments of FENG, #55, occur.

55 FENG

WITH PROSPERITY AND ABUNDANCE OF THE
GREATEST MOMENT PREPARE FOR DECLINE.

ABOVE: CHEN   Thunder   Movement, Arousing   Oldest Son
BELOW: LI   Fire, Sun   Brilliance, Clarity   Middle Daughter

Line		Mark	Time	Element	Relations
6	▬▬ ▬▬	N	7pm - 9pm	EARTH	Officials, Bosses, Troublemakers
5	▬▬ ▬▬	R S	3pm - 5pm	METAL	Fathers, Mothers, Ancestors
4	▬▬▬▬▬		11am - 1pm	FIRE	Wife, Husband, Money, Business
3	▬▬▬▬▬	N	9pm - 11pm	WATER	Brothers, Sisters, Peers
2	▬▬ ▬▬	O N	1am - 3am	EARTH	Officials, Bosses, Troublemakers
1	▬▬▬▬▬	N	5am - 7am	WOOD	Sons, Daughters, Descendants

House: K'AN, 6th Position; WATER   [28]
A Hexagram of the 5th Month, (JUNE).

56 LU

TRAVELING BRINGS VULNERABILITY AND
DIFFICULTY WHICH MUST BE RESOLVED.

ABOVE: LI   Fire, Sun   Brilliance, Clarity   Middle Daughter
BELOW: KEN   Mountain   Stillness, Silence   Youngest Son

Line		Mark	Time	Element	Relations
6	▬▬▬▬▬		9 am - 11am	FIRE	Brothers, Sisters, Peers
5	▬▬ ▬▬	R	1pm - 3pm	EARTH	Sons, Daughters, Descendants
4	▬▬▬▬▬	O	5pm - 7pm	METAL	Wife, Husband, Money, Business
3	▬▬▬▬▬	N	3pm - 5pm	METAL	Wife, Husband, Money, Business
2	▬▬ ▬▬	N	11am - 1pm	FIRE	Brothers, Sisters, Peers
1	▬▬ ▬▬	S	7am - 9am	EARTH	Sons, Daughters, Descendants

House: LI, 2nd Position; FIRE   [28]
A Hexagram of the 3rd Month, (APRIL).

The agreement and subordination of KUEI MEI, #54, represents compromise, and so follow the greatest moments of FENG, #55. Such greatness and abundance are sure to shake the dwelling, and the result is found in the traveling of LU, #56. When wandering and traveling there is the submission to the gentle penetration of SUN, #57.

57   SUN

GENTLE, PENETRATING, MOVEMENT AND
OBEDIENTLY ADAPTING TO CIRCUMSTANCES.

ABOVE: SUN   Wind, Wood   Gentle, Penetrating   Oldest Daughter
BELOW: SUN   Wind, Wood   Gentle, Penetrating   Oldest Daughter

Line			Time	Element	Relation
6	▬▬▬▬▬	S	5am - 7am	WOOD	Brothers, Sisters, Peers
5	▬▬▬▬▬	R N	9am - 11am	FIRE	Sons, Daughters, Descendants
4	▬▬ ▬▬	N	1pm - 3pm	EARTH	Wife, Husband, Money, Business
3	▬▬▬▬▬	O N	5pm - 7pm	METAL	Officials, Bosses, Troublemakers
2	▬▬▬▬▬		9 pm- 11pm	WATER	Fathers, Mothers, Ancestors
1	▬▬ ▬▬		1am - 3am	EARTH	Wife, Husband, Money, Business

House: SUN, 1st Position; WOOD   PURE   [38]
A Hexagram of the 7th Month, (AUGUST).

58   TUI

JOY AND CHEERFULNESS ENCOURAGE
PROGRESS AND ATTAINMENT.

ABOVE: TUI   Lake, Marsh   Joyous, Cheerful   Youngest Daughter
BELOW: TUI   Lake, Marsh   Joyous, Cheerful   Youngest Daughter

Line			Time	Element	Relation
6	▬▬ ▬▬	S N	1pm - 3pm	EARTH	Fathers, Mothers, Ancestors
5	▬▬▬▬▬	R N	5pm - 7pm	METAL	Brothers, Sisters, Peers
4	▬▬▬▬▬		9pm - 11pm	WATER	Sons, Daughters, Descendants
3	▬▬ ▬▬	O	1am - 3am	EARTH	Fathers, Mothers, Ancestors
2	▬▬▬▬▬	R	5am - 7am	WOOD	Wife, Husband, Money, Business
1	▬▬▬▬▬	N	9am - 11am	FIRE	Officials, Bosses, Troublemakers

House: TUI, 1st Position; METAL   PURE   [37]
A Hexagram of months 7—9. (AUGUST—OCTOBER).

The traveling and wandering of LU, #56, finds solace in the gentle and penetrating influence of SUN, #57. Such solace manifests in the joy, cheerfulness, and encouragement expressed in TUI, #58. Such joy and satisfaction are dissipated and yield to divorce and dissolution, and the scattering of HUAN, #59, follows.

59   HUAN

SCATTERING EXPOSES THE INFERIOR AND
ALLOWS REASSEMBLY OF THE SUPERIOR.

ABOVE: SUN   Wind, Wood   Gentle, Penetrating   Oldest Daughter
BELOW: K'AN   Water, Rain   Danger, Abysmal   Middle Son

Line		Markers		Time	Element	Relationships
6	▬▬▬			5am - 7am	WOOD	Fathers, Mothers, Ancestors
5	▬▬▬	R S N		9am - 11am	FIRE	Brothers, Sisters, Peers
4	▬ ▬	N		1pm - 3pm	EARTH	Sons, Daughters, Descendants
3	▬ ▬			11am - 1pm	FIRE	Brothers, Sisters, Peers
2	▬▬▬	O		7am - 9am	EARTH	Sons, Daughters, Descendants
1	▬ ▬			3am - 5am	WOOD	Fathers, Mothers, Ancestors

House: LI, 6th Position; FIRE   [27]
A Hexagram of the 5th Month, (JUNE).

60   CHIEH

LIMITATION AND REGULATION PROVIDES
PROGRESS WHEN NOT EXCESSIVELY APPLIED.

ABOVE: K'AN   Water, Rain   Danger, Abysmal   Middle Son
BELOW: TUI   Lake, Marsh   Joyous, Cheerful   Youngest Daughter

Line		Markers		Time	Element	Relationships
6	▬ ▬	N		11pm - 1am	WATER	Brothers, Sisters, Peers
5	▬▬▬	R N		7pm - 9pm	EARTH	Officials, Bosses, Troublemakers
4	▬ ▬	O N		3pm - 5pm	METAL	Fathers, Mothers, Ancestors
3	▬▬▬			1am - 3am	EARTH	Officials, Bosses, Troublemakers
2	▬▬▬			5am - 7am	WOOD	Sons, Daughters, Descendants
1	▬▬▬	S N		9am - 11am	FIRE	Wife, Husband, Money, Business

House: K'AN, 2nd Position; WATER   [27]
A Hexagram of the 6th Month, (JULY).

The joy, pleasure, and satisfaction of TUI, #58, are brought down through dissipation—yielding to the divorce and dissolution of HUAN, #59. The division and separation must be contained by limits and regulation which are found in CHIEH, #60. When so regulated and understood, the inner truth of Chung Fu, #1, is found.

61   CHUNG FU

SINCERITY FROM WITHIN THE HEART
ADVANCES RELATIONSHIPS WITH OTHERS.

ABOVE: SUN   Wind, Wood   Gentle, Penetrating   Oldest Daughter
BELOW: TUI   Lake, Marsh   Joyous, Cheerful   Youngest Daughter

6	▬▬▬▬		5am - 7am WOOD
			Officials, Bosses, Troublemakers
5	▬▬▬▬ R N		9am - 11am FIRE
			Fathers, Mothers, Ancestors
4	▬▬ ▬▬ S N		1pm - 3pm EARTH
			Brothers, Sisters, Peers
3	▬▬ ▬▬		1am - 3am EARTH
			Brothers, Sisters, Peers
2	▬▬▬▬		5am - 7am WOOD
			Officials, Bosses, Troublemakers
1	▬▬▬▬ O N		9am - 11am FIRE
			Fathers, Mothers, Ancestors

House: KEN, 7th Position; EARTH   SPIRITS DEPART   [27]
A Hexagram of the 10th Month, (NOVEMBER).

62   HSIAO KUO

GENTLE BEHAVIOR PREDOMINATES AND
SMALL ENDEAVORS WORK ADVANTAGEOUSLY.

ABOVE: CHEN   Thunder   Movement, Arousing   Oldest Son
BELOW: KEN   Mountain   Stillness, Silence   Youngest Son

6	▬▬ ▬▬ N		7pm - 9pm EARTH
			Fathers, Mothers, Ancestors
5	▬▬ ▬▬ R		3pm - 5pm METAL
			Brothers, Sisters, Peers
4	▬▬▬▬ S		11am - 1pm FIRE
			Officials, Bosses, Troublemakers
3	▬▬▬▬ N		3pm - 5pm METAL
			Brothers, Sisters, Peers
2	▬▬ ▬▬ R N		11am - 1pm FIRE
			Officials, Bosses, Troublemakers
1	▬▬ ▬▬ O		7am - 9am EARTH
			Fathers, Mothers, Ancestors

House: TUI, 7th Position; METAL   SPIRITS DEPART   [28]
A Hexagram of the 12th Month, (JANUARY).

The limits, regulations, and restrictions of CHIEH, #60, dissolve, introducing inner truth, sincerity, and insight as CHUNG FU, #61, which mankind knows within itself. With such knowledge the small grows and passes to the great as HSIAO KUO, #62. And afterward it seems that things are done, as expressed by CHI CHI, #63.

63   CHI CHI

ENDEAVORS ARE ACCOMPLISHED. AFTER COMPLETION ONLY LESSER ORDER FOLLOWS.

ABOVE: K'AN   Water, Rain   Danger, Abysmal   Middle Son
BELOW: LI   Fire, Sun   Brilliance, Clarity   Middle Daughter

Line		Markers	Time	Element
6	— —	O N	11pm - 1am	WATER
			Brothers, Sisters, Peers	
5	——	N	7pm - 9pm	EARTH
			Officials, Bosses, Troublemakers	
4	— —	N	3pm - 5pm	METAL
			Fathers, Mothers, Ancestors	
3	——	S N	9pm - 11pm	WATER
			Brothers, Sisters, Peers	
2	— —	R N	1am - 3am	EARTH
			Officials, Bosses, Troublemakers	
1	——	N	5am - 7am	WOOD
			Sons, Daughters, Descendants	

House: K'AN, 4th Position; WATER   [64]
A Hexagram of the 9th Month, (OCTOBER).

64   WEI CHI

ENDEAVORS ARE YET UNDONE. WITH SINCERE EFFORTS FOR COMPLETION ORDER FOLLOWS.

ABOVE: LI   Fire, Sun   Brilliance, Clarity   Middle Daughter
BELOW: K'AN   Water, Rain   Danger, Abysmal   Middle Son

Line		Markers	Time	Element
6	——	O	9am - 11am	FIRE
			Brothers, Sisters, Peers	
5	— —	R	1pm - 3pm	EARTH
			Sons, Daughters, Descendants	
4	——		5pm - 7pm	METAL
			Wife, Husband, Money, Business	
3	— —	S	11am - 1pm	FIRE
			Brothers, Sisters, Peers	
2	——		7am - 9am	EARTH
			Sons, Daughters, Descendants	
1	— —		3am - 5am	WOOD
			Fathers, Mothers, Ancestors	

House: LI, 4th Position; FIRE   [63]
A Hexagram of the 10th Month, (NOVEMBER).

The small within society grow and seize advantage, passing as the great, as stated in HSIAO KUO, #62. Thus, things are accomplished and are represented by CHI CHI, #63. But when things are completed, they are also beginning again as WEI CHI, #64, which will eventually be accomplished, in CHI CHI, which will again produce the state of being undone, #64. The cycle has no beginning or end, only change, and so King Wen closed the interpretation of the "Book of Changes."

STEP 3: THE I CHING PROPHESIZES

STEP 3 provides the I CHING prophesy translated and interpreted as a Twentieth-Century Occidental rendering.

The Worksheet, from Step 2, should now contain the following:
— The composite description of the Present/Recent Past Hexagram—translated as "Pen Kua."
— The changing lines, if any, and, The composite description of the Future Hexagram—translated as "Shih Kua."

The Hexagrams in Step 3 are located by referencing the number derived in Step 2 to the number appearing in the Upper Left Corner, Left Page, throughout this Step.

The following evaluations are simply condensed as:
PRESENT/RECENT PAST ——▶ CONTROLLING LINE ——▶ FUTURE

The I CHING was written from the standpoint that a "Superior Person" would be consulting it for advice. When seeking predictions about others or situations the references to "YOU" or "YOUR" should be re-applied as "HE, SHE, IT" and "HIS, HERS, ITS, THEIRS", etc., as appropriate.

Remember that Good Fortune can be undermined with careless and reckless attitudes and poorer prophesies can be rendered favorable by re-adapting with correct attitudes. Write commentaries and notes you believe to be important on the Worksheet.

EVALUATION OF THE PRESENT/RECENT PAST. Read and study the Title, Depiction, and Theme of the Present/Recent Past Hexagram while relating to the associated illustration. Associate the commentaries of the Prophesy with the subject of your question. Continue by relating the applicable separate Prophesies to the subject of your question. In some cases they will be direct, in other cases, indirect. For example, Travel may have to be related with Business and Moving to derive the full meaning of the Prophesy. The descriptive material begins with CH'IEN, #1, on page 82, and continues through all 64 Hexagrams in the Orderly Sequence, ending on page 209.

EVALUATION OF THE CHANGING LINES. When more than one line is changing, consider situations to be progressively unstable in direct proportion to the number of lines actually changing. Exercise more than your usual caution in your personal affairs when Danger or Peril are indicated, and pay particular attention to your vulnerability in the circumstances relating to your question.

When evaluating the Changing Lines note that they all relate to the Theme of the Hexagram as modifications. With experience the Player will also be able to relate the Personification of a Line successfully. For example, in a recent situation an individual Player, working for a troublesome and possibly incompetent boss, asked the question "Should I change jobs?" The Oracle responded with a Changing (and Controlling) Line relating to an Official, Boss, or Troublemakers. When the Hexagrams were also evaluated the response of the Orcale, in essence, was "No. Soon your boss will be replaced, bringing a more suitable situation." Within 3 weeks the company's home office replaced the manager—the employee was spared the agony of looking for new employment and found the new circumstances very favorable.

Each of the Changing Lines should be read, then establish the Controlling Line as specified below.

ESTABLISHMENT OF THE CONTROLLING LINE. The Controlling Line isolates the changing circumstances with a governing influence. After reading the Changing Line(s) establish and emphasize the Controlling Line from the number of Lines changing as follows:

— ZERO LINES CHANGING. Consider the Present/Recent Past Hexagram as representing a constancy relative to the time reference you had in mind when consulting the I CHING. There is no separate Controlling Line in this instance. This Hexagram is also the Future Hexagram. Proceed to the Evaluation of the Future Hexagram.

— ONE LINE CHANGING. Consider the Present/Recent Past, then evaluate the single Changing Line. This is the Controlling Line. The method of Yarrow Stick manipulation presented in this publication will always produce one, and only one, Changing Line which is also the Controlling Line. Proceed to the Evaluation of the Future Hexagram.

— TWO LINES CHANGING. Consider the Present/Recent Past, then read both of the Changing Lines, but evaluate the prophesy based upon the UPPER Changing Line. This UPPER Changing Line is the Controlling Line and is the heavenly influence upon mankind. Proceed to the evaluation of the Future Hexagram.

— THREE LINES CHANGING. Consider the Present/Recent Past, then read all three of the Changing Lines, but evaluate the prophesy based upon the MIDDLE Changing Line. This MIDDLE Changing Line is the Controlling Line and represents mankind between the influences of heaven and earth. Proceed to the Evaluation of the Future Hexagram.

— FOUR LINES CHANGING. Read the Present/Recent Past, then read the two UNCHANGING Lines of the Future Hexagram and evaluate the prophesy based upon the LOWER Unchanging Line. This LOWER Unchanging Line of the Future is the Controlling Line and the heavenly influences have passed to earthly influences upon mankind. The prophesy is now more greatly influenced by the Future, and the Present is clearly moving to the Recent Past. Proceed to the Evaluation of the Future Hexagram.

— FIVE LINES CHANGING. Read the Present/Recent Past, then read and evaluate the prophesy based upon the single UNCHANGING Line of the Future Hexagram. This Unchanging Line of the Future is the Controlling Line. The prophesy is now decidedly influenced by the Future, and the Present is regarded as the Recent Past. Proceed to the Evaluation of the Future Hexagram.

— SIX LINES CHANGING. Read the Present/Recent Past, but base the entire Prophesy upon the Evaluation of the Future Hexagram. There is no separate Contolling Line in this instance. This situation is unusually profound and the two most profound cases are:

— CH'IEN, #1, changing completely to K'UN, #2. A perfectly developed character is indicated, and you can expect to provide significant and beneficial effects to mankind in the most worldly sense.

— K'UN, #2, changing completely to CH'IEN, #1. A powerful and permanent change in character which will lead to accomplishment of goals normally considered impossible, but you can also expect losses in personal relationships.

EVALUATION OF THE FUTURE HEXAGRAM. Read and study the Title, Depiction, and Theme of the Future Hexagram while relating to the associated illustration. This Future will be indicative of the Time reference associated with the original question and is portrayed as a static situation. Again, this descriptive material begins on page 82 with CH'IEN, #1.

Associate the commentaries of the Prophesy with the subject of your question. Continue by relating the applicable separate Prophesies to the subject of your question. Remember that these commentaries represent the transition into the future and that the Present/Recent Past has undergone the transition as specified by the Controlling and Changing Lines.

If you have chosen to include the "Inner" or Motivational Hexagram reference (referred to as "Hu Kua")—and obtained as the bracketed number of the Hexagram composite in Step 2—the brief description in Step 2 of this Hexagram should suffice for most Players. But more serious Players may choose to evaluate the prophesy more deeply from the descriptions of the derivation of the prophesies in this Step. When doing so, this Hexagram is not associated with any of the Changing Lines, and denotes internal motivating influences and NOT a "Middle" or transitory state, as do the Changing Lines. More serious attention to the "Hu Kua" is given in our **I CHING, The Advanced Techniques** publication.

Players using the Program associated with this publication will note that the upper portion of the display screen contains the Theme of the Present/Recent Past, the center of the screen—in reversed display—contains the Controlling Line, and the lower portion displays the Theme text of the Future Hexagram.

Write down any comments considered important on the worksheet. You will now have accumulated enough information to evaluate the fundamental response of the I CHING Oracle. For example:

Good Fortune ——▶ Continuing with Caution ——▶ Good Fortune;
is indicative of an affirmative or "YES" answer.

Progress ——▶ No Action Furthers ——▶ Wait;
is indicative of "Not now, but possibly later."

Advantage ——▶ Being Obstructed ——▶ Misfortune;
is indicative of a negative or "NO" answer.

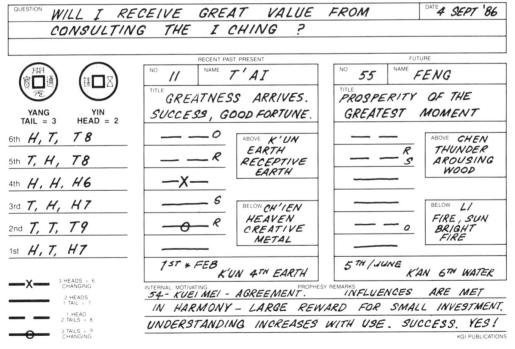

I CHING WORKSHEET

QUESTION: WILL I RECEIVE GREAT VALUE FROM CONSULTING THE I CHING ?

DATE: 4 SEPT '86

YANG TAIL = 3   YIN HEAD = 2

6th H, T, T8
5th T, H, T8
4th H, H, H6
3rd T, H, H7
2nd T, T, T9
1st H, T, H7

3 HEADS = 6 CHANGING
2 HEADS 1 TAIL = 7
1 HEAD 2 TAILS = 8
3 TAILS = 9 CHANGING

RECENT PAST, PRESENT

NO. 11   NAME: T'AI

TITLE: GREATNESS ARRIVES. SUCCESS, GOOD FORTUNE.

— — O
— — R
—X—
——— S
—O— R
———

ABOVE K'UN EARTH RECEPTIVE EARTH

BELOW CH'IEN HEAVEN CREATIVE METAL

1ST ∗ FEB K'UN 4TH EARTH

FUTURE

NO. 55   NAME: FENG

TITLE: PROSPERITY OF THE GREATEST MOMENT

———
— — R S
———
———
— — O
———

ABOVE CHEN THUNDER AROUSING WOOD

BELOW LI FIRE, SUN BRIGHT FIRE

5TH/JUNE K'AN 6TH WATER

INTERNAL MOTIVATING PROPHESY REMARKS
54- KUEI MEI - AGREEMENT. INFLUENCES ARE MET IN HARMONY - LARGE REWARD FOR SMALL INVESTMENT. UNDERSTANDING INCREASES WITH USE. SUCCESS. YES!

KGI PUBLICATIONS

The Player should now proceed to Step 4, Elementary Analysis of the Trigrams, or, if satisfied with individual understanding of the Prophesy, terminate or begin anew with another question or consultation. Remember, the first response from the I CHING Oracle to a particular question is the intuitive answer being sought. Repeatedly asking the same question will produce different results with no consequential meaning, although such effort will ultimately confirm the Prophesy by progressive logical deduction.

If terminating at this point, remember to wrap the I CHING material and place it in a high place as your expression of sincerity.

The following explanation of the published contents of Step 3 are included for reference.

THE HEXAGRAM NUMBER. This is the same number explained in Step 2 and is derived from the Orderly Sequence of the Hexagrams by King Wen. The Player will find this number consistent in nearly all publications, and especially Occidental publications.

THE HEXAGRAM. The Hexagram which corresponds to the Number in the Orderly Sequence is displayed for reference. The primary attributes of the two Trigrams, "ABOVE" and "BELOW," immediately follow to enhance the understanding of the Natural situation represented.

THE ORIENTAL CHARACTER. The Oriental Character for the Hexagram is displayed as it is most commonly represented. In many cases evolutionary changes over the preceeding 5000 years have provided modifications to the ancient character, and meanings defy or contradict current definitions. Our presentation of the character is presented as a cultural enhancement, not as a strict definition.

Players seeking strict definitions are directed to linguistics texts for such purposes as they are beyond the scope of this publication. We have chosen the term "Oriental Character," even though the actual rendering is specifically Chinese—asking the Player to note that in spite of the many dialects of Chinese, the characters remain essentially the same, and that the Japanese character, in most instances, is also the same. Latter day Mainland China versions are also essentially the same, but do contain abbreviations in the form of the character which were not used in antiquity.

THE NAME OF THE HEXAGRAM. The Name, also described in Step 2, is our modification of the "Wade-Giles" system of Romanization and is the most common representation in Occidental texts. The same spelling of a Name frequently occurs and the correct phonetics and meaning are dependent upon the dialect being employed, the use within a sentence, and the form of the Character. The Character itself truly separates one Name from another and the Name displayed is only a reasonable phonetic representation for each Hexagram. We have not prepared a pronunciation guide, as they generally seem quite bizarre to the Occidental Player and provide no further enlightenment unless the Player is familiar with Oriental language systems, as well as a particular dialect. Texts with pronunciation guides which concentrate on particular dialects are available.

THE TITLE OF THE HEXAGRAM. Briefly described in Step 2, this Title is the composite meaning of the Hexagram as it relates to the Character and the elements of the prophesy. Confucius is reputed to have added the "Symbol" to the I CHING. While this Title is often close to the translation of the Symbol for any individual Hexagram, this Title is not intended as a portrayal of the Symbol. This publication does not contain the translated Symbol as it is often cryptic and vague from its passage through the centuries.

THE ILLUSTRATION. The illustrations for each Hexagram, which we have included within the text of step 3, are the results of the fine efforts of Artist/Illustrator Ken C. Yang, and provide a visualization of the Theme of each Hexagram. These illustrations have been thoroughly researched and meticulously prepared as authentic renderings of antiquity, as is the method of preparation. The individual illustrations, for each of the 64 Hexagrams, are original artwork and relate to translation of the ancient text of I CHING from an artist's perspective.

Although other renderings have been made available to us, we have chosen to include this original work as it is strictly based on each Hexagram represented and is free from hidden meanings, such as "little rabbits hiding in the grass."

This is also consistent with the interpretations of this material. "Hidden meanings," examples, and parables, while entertaining, do not contribute meaningfully to Occidental Players in the 20th Century, and have not been included in this publication.

THE DEPICTION. The Depiction, all formed as "..... is depicted as ...." refers directly to the Illustration associated with the Hexagram and functions as a caption. This caption is styled to the Theme of the Hexagram which follows on the next page. Again, the "Symbol" may closely relate to this depiction but they are not intended as equivalencies.

THE THEME OF THE HEXAGRAM. The Theme of the Hexagram, all formed as "...... is a Time ... characterized by (with) ...", is the interpreted and expanded definition of the ancient text. The "Time" represented is not specific to hours, days, or years but instead relates to the circumstances the Hexagram represents.

This Theme may be most closely aligned with the "Judgments" of other texts but there is no attempt of replication because, again, the Judgments which have been passed down through the centuries are often vague and cryptic.

When evaluating a consultation, the circumstances implied by the Theme—in both the Present/Recent Past and Future tense, with the operation of the Controlling Line—consider the I CHING's response a portrayal of positions with respect to the Universal Order, or Tao.

The Themes and the Titles within this publication have been translated and interpreted together, and the Theme provides the Player with a deeper understanding of the circumstances implied by the Hexagram.

The characterization, "... characterized with ... ", provides insight to what the Player may expect in the Time of a particular Hexagram—such as Good Fortune, Progress, Success, Danger, Misfortune, etc.

Warnings contained within the Hexagram are conveyed within the Theme, as are some expanded explanations. Other comments have been added which may be of general interest in relating to the Hexagram.

This publication does not provide the literal translation of the portion frequently referred to as the "Judgment" because the finality represented by the word is inconsistent with the teachings of I CHING, and it is frequently occluded with the "Image," which is commented on further under the heading of "The Description of the Hexagram."

THE PROPHESIES. The Prophesies relate to specific and frequent topics about which the I CHING is consulted. Although all elements of the I CHING's response form the Prophesy, the term "Prophesies" here relates to specific human endeavors and interests related to the Theme. The following sub-paragraphs provide generalized, but not detailed, explanations of the derivation of the Prophesies. In some cases the description will be obvious, particularly when compared with the contents of Step 4, but frequently are derived from Line positions, the internal influences (Hu Kua), and the future movement as expressed by the Orderly Sequence. Each Hexagram is derived individually, and this text is not intended to present the entire derivations of the 64 Hexagrams.

— LUCK and WISHES are derived from the Theme in the most generalized sense.

— LOVE is derived from the manifestation of the interpersonal relationships represented by the Hexagram, and leads directly to Marriage, which is the naturally assumed coupling in this publication.

— MARRIAGES are derived from the consideration of the Personification of the Lines, particularly 2 and 5; the operation of the Subject Line and Trigram (in Step 2 marked "S") with respect to the Object (marked "O"); the Ruling Line (marked "R"); as well as the Theme.

— CHILDREN, when relating to their sex, is derived by comparing the total Yang (male) influence with the total Yin (female). Other comments are included as particular traits or behavior are indicated within the Hexagram.

— PREGNANCY, when relating to sex, is derived from the internalized Yang-Yin comparisons. Significant comments are added when they are suggested by the I CHING.

— SICKNESS—the most difficult of all to understand—when relating to recovery, is derived from the Position of the House in conjunction with the moving trend of the Hexagram. When relating to ailments, the attributes of the Subject Hexagram are considered, but biased with internal representations as well as the physical form of the Hexagram. Answers regarding health require careful consideration as the operation of one part of the body will affect others and symptoms may not obviate the cause. When questions are asked regarding the health of others, greater emphasis should be given to the attributes of the "Object" Trigram, as charted on pages 220 to 221 of Step 4.

— MISSING PEOPLE, when relating to location, are primarily derived from the "Object" Trigram, with lesser significance on the "Subject" Trigram as, generally, the question implies that the Subject is trying to locate the Object. The "Hu Tien," page 217, Step 4, provides an easy visualization of positioning. Note also that the Hu Tien also equates the South to Front, West to Right, North to Rear, East to Left, etc., which could also be applied. When relating situations, the Theme and the physical construction of the Hexagram are considered. For example:

 O (OTHER)

Such an arrangement would indicate that the Object is in the middle of the Trigram K'AN, representing Danger. Hence there is the certain implication that the Object is in Danger.

There may be other influences which suppress danger, and others which promote danger, and further details are topics in the **I CHING, The Advanced Techniques** material.

When considering Missing People, also read the comments relating to Missing Things. They are derived in a similar manner but Missing Things are considered to be closer at hand.

— MISSING THINGS commentaries are derived similarly as Missing People, and the "Missing Thing" is considered the Object, with the Subject searching for it—but the Object is considered to be closer at hand, located in proximity (Front, Right, Rear and Left as expressed by the Hu Tien), and considered more possessive in nature than are Persons. For example:

 O (OTHER)

Such an arrangement would indicate that the Missing item is low and covered by something else. There may be, however, other influences which specifically reorient the strict interpretation. The Lower Trigram, SUN, suggests Front-Left or South-East from the Hu Tien, Step 4.

When answers relating to Missing Things are considered, the preceeding paragraph on relating to Missing People should be considered, since the derivations are occasionally identical, but always similar.

— MOVING is derived, generally, from the Theme of the Hexagram, especially as it relates to the commentary described as "Time" and the advantageousness of "Great Undertakings" and "Crossing the Great Water" (which appears in the literal translation of the ancient text). This ancient phrase has not been literally translated in this publication and originally related to the crossing of the Yellow River in China, considered a difficult task. The I CHING equates one's ability and preparedness for such tasks with this phrase.

— LOANS are derived from the Theme, but particular emphasis is placed on how the lines which are Personified as "Wife, Husband, Money, Business" are positioned within the Hexagram.

— BUSINESS Ventures are derived from: the Theme of the Hexagram; how the lines which are Personified as "Wife, Husband, Money, Business" are positioned within the Hexagram; and the interactions of the Upper and Lower Trigrams. Business Ventures, Loans, and Marriages have similar commentaries, but are isolated to the particular topic, for this reason.

— JOBS are derived from the Theme of the Hexagram, with particular consideration given to the position of the Subject Line as it relates to its position within the Hexagram as a whole.

— The MARKET is derived from the Theme of the Hexagram, but great emphasis is placed upon its movement within the Orderly Sequence. The inference as to the Market being low or high has been avoided because "low" and "high" tend to relate to the opinions of the individual Player. The trend, however, has been included. When seeking answers regarding individual Stocks, associate the movement indicated by the Market with the individual Stock.

Remember that in some cases the question asked of the I CHING may involve analysis of more than one descriptive Prophesy, and that the detailed derivation of each of the 64 Hexagrams is not presented above. Weather has been omitted, but the Player will find the weather attributes charted in Step 4 for each of the Trigrams, and with some practice will be able to accurately predict weather patterns or situations as well.

THE CHANGING LINES. The Lines are arranged in the same "Bottom-Up" order in which the Hexagrams are displayed. The order of presentation is conventional, as "6th Line, Nine, Undivided"; "5th Line, Six, Divided", etc. Nine represents the Old Yang moving to Yin, and six represents the Old Yin moving to Yang, as explained earlier in Step 1.

The characteristics of Instinct (or Intuition), Aspirations (or Goals and Desires), Individual (or Self-Interest), Social (or Social-Interest), Authority, and Wisdom are noted at the top of each Line. These represent the progressive perfections in the character of an individual as defined by the ancient masters.

CHANGING LINE REPRESENTATION

The impact of the Line upon the Hexagram as a whole is displayed at the far right. Constraint: Lines 1 and 6, are the beginning and ending constraints of the Theme of the Hexagram. Significant: Lines 2 and 5, will contain the most significant aspects of the individual Hexagram. Variant: Lines 3 and 4, most often vary the Theme as a whole, as Lines 3 and 4 also represent the transition from the Lower Trigram to the Upper Trigram. As a guideline for the individual Lines:

— Line 1: the beginning of the Theme or "Time" of the Hexagram which will generally be seen as following from the Theme of the preceding Hexagram in the Orderly Sequence. Beginning struggles, difficulties, and education are found on this Line. This Line does not generally represent poor fortune, but rather instructions for behavior in the Time indicated by the Hexagram.

— Line 2: advancing within the Theme of the Hexagram, portrays goals and aspirations as producing generally favorable prophesies.

— Line 3: self-interest—and in general conflict with the Upper Trigram—generally portrays unfavorable prophesies or turmoil.

— Line 4: in antiquity, represented the minister of the higher authority of Line 5. Its duty was to serve the social order as well as the higher authority. When this degree of servitude is achieved, this line represents good fortune, but less so when not achieved or when the conflict with the Lower Trigram (Line 3) is very great.

— Line 5: in antiquity, represented the high authority of the king or emperor. When this Line is associated with justice and characteristics of noble leadership, it represents good fortune and success. This Line will be either strong or yielding, as appropriate to the circumstances, and nearly always favorable.

— Line 6: wisdom, when appropriately acquired and used, will find the Line favorable, otherwise not so. This is also the ending of the Theme or "Time" of a particular Hexagram, and represents the transition into the succeeding Hexagram in the Orderly Sequence.

The correlations between the Earthly influences (Lines 1 and 4); the Human influences (Lines 2 and 5); and the Heavenly influences (Lines 3 and 6) will also contribute to or detract from the favorableness of any given line.

THE DESCRIPTION OF THE HEXAGRAM. The Hexagram is described beginning with the positions of the two Trigrams. These are associated with either natural phenomena, such as Sun over Earth, or characteristics such as Joy within Devotion. These representations are carried forward from antiquity and are intended to explain the derivation of the Theme of any particular Hexagram.

The positions and relationships of the Ruling Lines are contained within the Description as they generally amplify the character of the Hexagram. Ruling Lines convey the governing character of the Hexagram with, normally, positive attributes, and most normally fall on the 5th Line as the middle line of the Upper Trigram, and associated with authority. Next, they will most frequently fall on the 2nd Line, the middle line of the Lower Trigram, or together with the 5th. The physical composure of the Hexagram will often dictate an alternative Line. For example PO, #23, Splitting Apart, finds the Ruling Line as the 6th, which is the remaining strong force holding everything together. These overriding physical composures will also frequently dictate more than one Ruling Line.

By equating the Ruling Line with the characteristic of the Line—Instinct, Aspirations, Individual, Society, Authority and Wisdom—the Player will also find the particular characteristics driving the Theme of the Hexagram. By equating the Ruling Line with the Personification (explained in Step 2), the Player will find insight into particular interpersonal relationships influencing his or her own life.

The Subject, and occasionally the Object, of the Hexagram are noted within the Description. These are derived from ancient tables which also produced the "House" and "Position" (see Step 2). In addition to representing a particular Line, they also represent a particular Trigram and are always separated by three lines. The Subject, or "Self," can be most closely associated with the Player who is consulting the Oracle while the Object, or "Other," is closely removed but still associated with the Prophesy. Greater insight in interpersonal relationships will also be found by evaluating these Lines, when Changing, with their respective Personifications from Step 2.

Other comments relative to the construction or description of the Hexagram are also included when they convey particular significance. The description closely aligns with the "Image" described in other texts, but his publication makes no effort to portray the Image, due again to its cryptic nature and the occlusion with the meanings of the "Judgment."

1

ABOVE: CH'IEN
HEAVEN
Creative
Firmness

BELOW: CH'IEN
HEAVEN
Creative
Firmness

乾

CH'IEN

THE HEAVENLY PRIMAL FORCE OF CREATIVE
POWER AND FIRMNESS, MAKING STRONG.

CH'IEN is depicted as man learning from the behavior of Heavenly Dragons. Eastern Dragons, unlike destructive Western Dragons, are full of Energy, with the attributes of Powerful and Perfect Conduct, Justice, and Wisdom. These Dragons are born in the formation of clouds and CH'IEN is associated with great origins.

CH'IEN is a Time associated with Creative Power and Supreme Wisdom, characterized with Great Success and Good Fortune. All is expected to succeed as you wisely strengthen your character and express concern in the proper times.

PROPHESIES

LUCK is extremely good and WISHES come true, but don't let arrogance overtake you. LOVE succeeds when selfish motives are abandoned. MARRIAGES are marked with the stubborness of two powerful forces. Healthy male CHILDREN that require discipline are indicated. If PREGNANT, expect a boy.

SICKNESS could be severe and related to strokes, brain damage, or broken bones, but proper care will probably restore health.

MISSING PEOPLE, North to West, are difficult to find. MISSING THINGS can be found by searching high. MOVING should be delayed for now.

LOANS are granted, but don't be careless with the proceeds. BUSINESS Ventures are profitable, but don't expand too quickly. JOBS with promotions are indicated, fulfilling ambitions. A high MARKET is indicated, a good time to sell.

CHANGING LINES

6th　　　　9　　　▰▰▰　　　**WISDOM**　　　**CONSTRAINT**

You are in danger of failure through abusive use of power or by attempting to exceed your full potential. This will lead you away from others who have respected and supported you until now.

5th　　　　9　　　▰▰▰　　　**AUTHORITY**　　　**SIGNIFICANT**

Your situation is in complete accord with the natural order. Seeking wise advice promotes even further the success you have already attained.

4th　　　　9　　　▰▰▰　　　**SOCIAL**　　　**VARIANT**

Your talents can be applied in more than one way. By choosing the best time and opportunity to apply these talents you will avoid any mistakes.

3rd　　　　9　　　▰▰▰　　　**INDIVIDUAL**　　　**VARIANT**

Working diligently at your job, and later refining improvements in your character, frees you from error and brings the respect of others.

2nd　　　　9　　　▰▰▰　　　**ASPIRATIONS**　　　**SIGNIFICANT**

Consulting with someone knowledgable on the subject of your question, or forming a partnership with someone possessing talents you lack, produces certain success.

1st　　　　9　　　▰▰▰　　　**INSTINCT**　　　**CONSTRAINT**

Your true potential is now hidden, but growing. It is not a time to act, but one of continuing to plan. Success comes by being alert to, and acting at, the right time.

DESCRIPTION

Heavenly principles, ABOVE, are met with Heavenly principles BELOW, intensifying the Creative Power and Firmness each Trigram represents. Most significant about this Hexagram is that all lines are powerful. The single Ruling Line, 5th, possesses the attributes of Creative Power, Firmness, Moderation, and Justice— the power of Heaven in perfection. The Subject of the Hexagram, 6th Line, contains the warning: with such a powerful position, and the success it represents, it can destroy itself by abuse or arrogance without the due exercise of wisdom.

2

ABOVE: K'UN
EARTH
Receptive
Natural

BELOW: K'UN
EARTH
Receptive
Natural

坤

K'UN

THE EARTHLY PRIMAL FORCE OF NATURAL
STRENGTH, RECEPTIVENESS AND SERVICE.

K'UN is depicted as a Mare of Great Strength, roaming boundlessly through the fields of Earth in tireless pursuit of worthwhile goals. All that is in or on the Earth is within the domain of K'UN.

K'UN is a Time when Natural Strength and Receptiveness are at their highest, characterized by Great Success, furthered by persistence to reach goals. Following, sometimes yielding, are qualities associated with Natural Strength, as is boundless energy to achieve worthwhile goals.

PROPHESIES

LUCK remains stable and WISHES come true by patiently pursuing them. Love is very successful when each understand the relationship. MARRIAGES are good, with only occassional disturbances. Healthy female CHILDREN are foreseen. If PREGNANT, expect a girl.

SICKNESS is mild, related to the stomach, and will be easily overcome with proper care.

MISSING PEOPLE, South to West, are easily found. MISSING THINGS are found by searching low or outside in the yard. MOVING should be delayed, and going to colder climates is not advised.

LOANS are granted, but not easily. BUSINESS Ventures remain essentially the same. JOBS come, but only after several interviews. The MARKET is sure to rise, indicating a time to buy.

CHANGING LINES

6th 6 — — **WISDOM** **CONSTRAINT**

Aggressively forcing conflicts with allies or superiors causes losses on both sides, but you must expect the defeat.

5th 6 — — **AUTHORITY** **SIGNIFICANT**

With conservative and refined conduct in discharging your responsibilities you can expect great achievements with good fortune.

4th 6 — — **SOCIAL** **VARIANT**

Things have come to a standstill. By yielding to a more reserved position you'll not be criticized, nor will you be praised, but you can expect activity to begin again.

3rd 6 — — **INDIVIDUAL** **VARIANT**

Don't seek recognition for work now; let others have the fame. Complete all your tasks now as if preparing for the future.

2nd 6 — — **ASPIRATIONS** **SIGNIFICANT**

The natural order is advancing everything. Likewise, your own advance requires little effort.

1st 6 — — **INSTINCT** **CONSTRAINT**

Your successes are being threatened by increasing signs of misfortune. Your certain preparation in dealing with the inevitable is required at this time.

DESCRIPTION

Earthly principles, ABOVE, are met with Earthly principles, BELOW, intensifying the Natural Strength and Receptiveness each Trigram represents. Although this Hexagram is composed of all weak lines it portends Great Success, particularly when equated with humanitarian ideals. The single Ruling Line, 2nd, suggests serving as opposed to leading. The Subject of the Hexagram, 6th Line, serves as a warning to avoid attempts to ascend to leadership roles that are not the place of K'UN.

3

ABOVE: K'AN
WATER, RAIN
Danger
Abysmal

BELOW: CHEN
THUNDER
Movement
Arousing

CHUN

THE DIFFICULTIES ASSOCIATED WITH NEW BEGINNINGS AND THE BIRTH OF LIFE.

CHUN is depicted as a child representing new life and beginnings filling the void between the man and woman.

CHUN is a Time associated with Difficulties in New Beginnings and Birth of Life, characterized by advances toward Great Success when not acting rashly or blindly. Best results come from help gathered along the way. The Chinese character itself represents "grass trying to grow," and translates as "collect" or "store up".

PROPHESIES

LUCK is poor, but improving, and WISHES are not realized for a long time. LOVE requires much attention and time to become successful. MARRIAGES are troubled with much quarreling. Several male CHILDREN are indicated. If PREGNANT, expect a boy.

SICKNESS is severe and prolonged—it's nature is not clear but could relate to the liver. A full recuperation is eventually seen.

MISSING PEOPLE, North to East, may perish if not found quickly. MISSING THINGS will probably never be seen again. MOVING invites disaster.

LOANS should be renegotiated at a later date. BUSINESS Ventures are characterized by difficulties requiring much time and effort to resolve. JOBS are not plentiful now. The MARKET is fluctuating, with hints of devastating effects.

CHANGING LINES

| 6th | 6 | | WISDOM | CONSTRAINT |

You have allowed the difficulties to defeat you. This is not a time for self-pity, but for recognition that New Beginnings are evolving, though still not mature.

| 5th | 9 | | AUTHORITY | SIGNIFICANT |

Your plans are not receiving the support required. Advancing with small projects is advantageous, but great projects invite disaster.

| 4th | 6 | | SOCIAL | VARIANT |

Gathering the correct help in overcoming difficulties brings progress and advancement.

| 3rd | 6 | | INDIVIDUAL | VARIANT |

You are continuing to pursue something you believe in, but without proper guidance. Stop, and alter your goals, or face failure and humiliation.

| 2nd | 6 | | ASPIRATIONS | SIGNIFICANT |

Difficulties are increasing. Unexpected help should be refused, as it only increases your commitments. Holding to your original plan will, after a long period of time, restore order.

| 1st | 9 | | INSTINCT | CONSTRAINT |

Pausing now to consider difficult issues and gather help is advantageous, while blindly rushing ahead gets you nowhere.

DESCRIPTION

The Rain and Danger, ABOVE, is falling with the Thunder and Movement, BELOW. The air is filled with rain and thunder which eventually clears. Rain provides enrichment for new life and thunder relieves tension from the air. Of the two Ruling Lines, 1st and 5th, the 1st is an appointed helper, and the 5th is the authority appointing the helper. The Subject of the Hexagram, 2nd Line, shows difficulties, with long periods of time before finally achieving success. This is one of the Four Hexagrams representing Difficulty; the others are 29, 39, and 47.

4

ABOVE: KEN
MOUNTAIN
Stillness
Silence

BELOW: K'AN
WATER, RAIN
Danger
Abysmal

MENG

YOUTHFUL FOLLY AND INNOCENCE ARE
EXCUSED WHEN LEARNING AND DEVELOPING.

MENG is depicted as youthful students learning and developing under the tutelage of a wise master.

MENG is a Time associated with the awkwardness of Youth and Innocence in the immature form, characterized by seeking knowledge and wisdom to produce Success. "Beginner's Luck" is suggested, as all turns out well in spite of one's inexperience. The warning of this Hexagram is that the patience of the masters can be quickly exhausted when one is insincere.

PROPHESIES

LUCK isn't too bad now, but don't count on it, and WISHES come true when advice is followed. LOVE is fanciful now and does not last long. MARRIAGES need the help of counselors if they are to succeed. Male CHILDREN are indicated. If PREGNANT, expect a boy.

SICKNESS is related to the spleen or the blood system with possibility of contagion, however, there is improvement when prescriptions of a doctor are followed.

MISSING PEOPLE, North to East, are hard to find. MISSING THINGS can't be seen, and much searching will be required to find them. MOVING should be delayed until later.

LOANS cannot be expected now, but there is some hope in trying. BUSINESS Ventures are troubled and require outside help. JOBS offered now are not correct for your career. The MARKET should be avoided now; settle for more secure investments.

CHANGING LINES

6th　　　**9**　　　▬▬▬▬▬　　　**WISDOM**　　　**CONSTRAINT**

There is no advantage in continuing to punish yourself for mistakes. Learn from your mistakes and avoid repeating them in the future. Be patient, better times will appear.

5th　　　**6**　　　▬▬　▬▬　　　**AUTHORITY**　　　**SIGNIFICANT**

Sincerely and humbly seeking wise advice or knowledge brings certain success. Be warned, however, that if advice is sought too often, it will no longer be extended.

4th　　　**6**　　　▬▬　▬▬　　　**SOCIAL**　　　**VARIANT**

Your continued engagement in youthful folly and playfulness when serious concern is required will bring nothing but humiliation.

3rd　　　**6**　　　▬▬　▬▬　　　**INDIVIDUAL**　　　**VARIANT**

Pursue what you believe in. You are in danger of being swayed by opportunistic persons or situations offering no real advantage.

2nd　　　**9**　　　▬▬▬▬▬　　　**ASPIRATIONS**　　　**SIGNIFICANT**

Your responsibilities include the enlightenment of the underdeveloped. By showing kindly tolerance of the innocent you will experience success.

1st　　　**6**　　　▬▬　▬▬　　　**INSTINCT**　　　**CONSTRAINT**

Avoid any temptations to use excessive discipline with the innocent or underdeveloped, but do not fail to use the correct degree of discipline in restoring order.

DESCRIPTION

The Water, BELOW, comes forth at the base of the Mountain, ABOVE, as a refreshing spring. The flowing water trickles in several directions before it begins to flow in one. Of the two Ruling Lines, 2nd and 5th, the 2nd is a capable teacher, and the 5th is the authority honoring the teacher. The Subject of the Hexagram, 4th Line, lies where the spring has issued from the base of the mountain—the source of innocence. Uncertain progress is excused, sometimes encouraged, but without innocence this awkwardness is not tolerated.

5

ABOVE: K'AN
WATER, RAIN
Danger
Abysmal

BELOW: CH'IEN
HEAVEN
Creative
Firmness

HSU

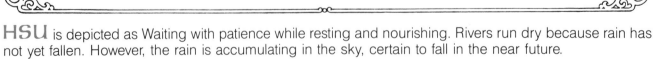

PATIENTLY WAITING AND WORKING TOWARD
A BETTER TIME. RESTING AND NOURISHING.

HSU is depicted as Waiting with patience while resting and nourishing. Rivers run dry because rain has not yet fallen. However, the rain is accumulating in the sky, certain to fall in the near future.

HSU is a Time of Patiently Waiting (not idle hoping) while Working Toward a Better Time, characterized with sincere efforts bringing Success, perseverence bringing Good Fortune, and the accumulation of Strength bringing the ability to undertake new and ambitious projects. Indicated are varying degrees of adversity—from inconvenience to danger—which reinforce the need of patience.

PROPHESIES

LUCK is poor now, but improving, and WISHES come true if held and worked toward. LOVE, without patience and honesty, or if rushed, fails. MARRIAGES are troubled now, but with patience improve. CHILDREN come late in life, are mostly male, and eventually bring happiness. If PREGNANT, expect a boy.

SICKNESS is now severe and is related to the gastrointestinal tract, blood system, or possibly the brain, and improves only with proper and prolonged convalescence.

MISSING PEOPLE, North to Northwest, are safe but take a long time to find. MISSING THINGS can be found later. MOVING is not advised now.

LOANS are eventually approved. BUSINESS Ventures should not aspire to small profits now but should be preparing for greater profits later. JOBS will be granted later; continue patiently trying. The MARKET is sluggish now, but will be improving.

CHANGING LINES

6th	6	▬▬ ▬▬	WISDOM	CONSTRAINT

The danger has brought disaster. Further waiting is pointless. If you accept the help that comes your way now, you will ultimately benefit. But for now, expect disagreement or conflict.

5th	9	▬▬▬▬	AUTHORITY	SIGNIFICANT

Even with peril all about, a relaxed and peaceful composure can bring you good fortune as you persevere toward your goals without haste.

4th	6	▬▬ ▬▬	SOCIAL	VARIANT

You are in an extremely dangerous position and aggressive action promises certain harm. Remain steadfast in your original pursuits and fate will take you from the danger.

3rd	9	▬▬▬▬	INDIVIDUAL	VARIANT

Your exposure to danger is clear and you are vulnerable. Plan your every move with caution.

2nd	9	▬▬▬▬	ASPIRATIONS	SIGNIFICANT

In this difficult time you can expect disagreement and unrest. Staying calm will silence blame and criticism, ultimately bringing good fortune.

1st	9	▬▬▬▬	INSTINCT	CONSTRAINT

In spite of the discomfort you now feel, remain patient and nurture strength as long as possible for improvement. Such patience will keep you free of error.

DESCRIPTION

The Creative Power and Firmness, BELOW, in the face of Danger, ABOVE, wisely waits. The rain is in heaven, but is not yet falling, indicating impending better times. The single Ruling Line, 5th, continually influences the period of Waiting with correct behavior, nurturing the Strength below (or within) as would a brother or sister. The subject of the Hexagram, 4th Line, is, however, in the deepest part of danger, further suggesting the wisdom in Patience, while Resting and Nourishing for the better times ahead. This is one of the Four Hexagrams representing Nourishment; the others are 27, 48, and 50.

6

**ABOVE: CH'IEN
HEAVEN**
Creative
Frimness

**BELOW: K'AN
WATER, RAIN**
Danger
Abysmal

訟

SUNG

DISAGREEMENTS AND LAWSUITS. CONFLICTS
AND OPPOSITION ARE MET AND RESOLVED.

SUNG is depicted, naturally, as the two opposing parties in the presence of the arbitrator.

SUNG is a Time when anger leads to Conflict, especially as a Civil Lawsuit or Tort, characterized by obstruction of sincerity by devious cunning. Good Fortune can be achieved with wisdom and caution. Seeking wise advice brings improvement. There is none of the unity required to begin great undertakings at this time. The significance of compromise and the wisdom of not fighting to the bitter end are important.

PROPHESIES

LUCK is bad for everything, and WISHES do not come true. LOVE fails because one of you lacks sincerity. MARRIAGES are into or close upon divorce. CHILDREN, mostly boys, are drawn into conflicts between the parents. If PREGNANT, expect a boy.

SICKNESS may be very serious, relating to the kidneys, blood, or brain. Stop smoking, your lungs may be in jeopardy.

MISSING PEOPLE, North to West, are in danger and need to be found quickly. MISSING THINGS have been taken; don't expect to find them. MOVING plans should be abandoned.

LOANS are not granted. BUSINESS Ventures show losses due to incorrect management. JOBS are not available. The MARKET is too unstable to be correctly speculated now.

CHANGING LINES

6th   **9**   ▬▬▬▬   **WISDOM**   **CONSTRAINT**

The conflict is fought to the bitter end. It appears that you win, but you lose respect. Gains, without merit, are lost immediately.

5th   **9**   ▬▬▬▬   **AUTHORITY**   **SIGNIFICANT**

You have proven yourself correct and righteous in the conflict before an arbitrator. Expect great success and a favorable ending to the conflict.

4th   **9**   ▬▬▬▬   **SOCIAL**   **VARIANT**

The opposing forces are unequal and you realize that the conflict cannot be resolved. Withdrawing, changing your attitude and letting the matter solve itself, brings eventual good fortune.

3rd   **6**   ▬▬ ▬▬   **INDIVIDUAL**   **VARIANT**

A difficult conflict, but with virtuous determination and by maintaining your position, you can expect good fortune. If you go too far, expect nothing.

2nd   **9**   ▬▬▬▬   **ASPIRATIONS**   **SIGNIFICANT**

You are inferior to the opposition. Quit the conflict now to preclude harm to yourself and associates.

1st   **6**   ▬▬ ▬▬   **INSTINCT**   **CONSTRAINT**

By dropping the conflict in the beginning you will experience some criticism, but ultimately good fortune.

DESCRIPTION

The Strength, ABOVE, increases and bears more pressure on the Danger, BELOW, forcing it to sink lower into devious cunning. The discord and disagreement increases between the two. The 5th Ruling Line shows a just and authoritative arbitrator capable of resolving the disputes fairly, while all other lines quarrel. The Subject of the Hexagram, 4th Line, represents the stronger, but not necessarily the more correct, force.

A clear distinction is made between this hexagram and SHIH HO, #21, which addresses criminal justice.

ABOVE: K'UN
EARTH
Natural
Receptive

BELOW: K'AN
WATER, RAIN
Danger
Abysmal

SHIH

ARMY, STRENGTH STORED IN A MASS OF
PEOPLE. ORGANIZATION AND LEADERSHIP.

SHIH is depicted as the Army, which embraced the whole society. The younger, strong men were employed as warriors, the women maintained the battlements, and children or the infirm managed supplies. The capable leader was able to organize and motivate all these forces to bear upon an enemy.

SHIH is a Time when Organization and Leadership are required to direct the efforts of a Strong Potential, particularly as a large group of people, characterized by capable and trustworthy Leadership producing Success, or victory.

PROPHESIES

LUCK is not favorable now, and WISHES do not come true. LOVE is not successful because there are too many other things to do now. MARRIAGES are poor, as each partner concentrates too greatly upon their own priorities. Several female CHILDREN are seen. If PREGNANT, expect a girl.

SICKNESS is severe, but improving, and relates to the kidneys, abdomen, or blood system. Don't ignore minor illnesses.

MISSING PEOPLE, South to West, will fall to danger if not found quickly. MISSING THINGS, being used up, will not be found. MOVING plans require careful consideration.

LOANS are not granted because the funds are not available. BUSINESS Ventures are in serious trouble if without effective leadership. JOBS are not available, but there is much work to do at home. The MARKET is unstable, trying to adapt to the times.

CHANGING LINES

6th   6   ▬▬ ▬▬   **WISDOM**   **CONSTRAINT**

To achieve success and union, place authority with capable and motivated people. Lesser persons will only abuse the authority and power issued to them.

5th   6   ▬▬ ▬▬   **AUTHORITY**   **SIGNIFICANT**

A vicious and unprovoked attack organizes all together in self-defense. Leadership must be strong and experienced to achieve success—otherwise expect disaster.

4th   6   ▬▬ ▬▬   **SOCIAL**   **VARIANT**

Your wisdom of retreating or withdrawing to a secure position when confronted with a superior force produces no error.

3rd   6   ▬▬ ▬▬   **INDIVIDUAL**   **VARIANT**

Ineffective delegation produces too many and too poorly-motivated persons in leadership capacities. When such persons are so assigned, expect defeat and disaster.

2nd   9   ▬▬▬▬   **ASPIRATIONS**   **SIGNIFICANT**

Knowing the needs of the people will allow you to properly organize and motivate them. Expect honor and success without needless waste of resources.

1st   6   ▬▬ ▬▬   **INSTINCT**   **CONSTRAINT**

You must provide the proper organization and discipline to establish order at the beginning—otherwise expect disaster.

DESCRIPTION

The Natural Strength, ABOVE, represents a "mass of humanity," with the Danger, BELOW, and more specifically, within. Thus danger within a mass of people, ARMY, is derived. Both Ruling Lines, 2nd and 5th, are indicative of the availability of both strong and weak leadership potential. The strong, 2nd, is further identified as having been delegated the official capacity by the weak, 5th. The Subject of the Hexagram, 3rd line, sits at the top of danger, and forewarns of defeat due to poor and ineffective organization and leadership.

8

ABOVE: K'AN
WATER, RAIN
Danger
Abysmal

BELOW: K'UN
EARTH
Natural
Receptive

PI

THE GROUP IS UNITED AND HELD TOGETHER
WITH SINCERE AND LOYAL RELATIONSHIPS.

PI is depicted as a group of horsemen, displaying union to reach common goals, in this case, travel.

PI is a Time to Form and Hold Unions Together with Sincerity and Loyalty between persons with similar goals and aspirations. It is characterized with Good Fortune when these associations are faithfully entered. The prophesy warns that we must have sincere motives when joining—even reexamining the decision to join—and then remaining loyal after joining. Excessive hesitation in joining may find the group gone or filled when the decision to join is delayed too long.

PROPHESIES

LUCK is favorable, and WISHES come true with the help of others. LOVE is successful; when the partners are faithful. MARRIAGES are typified by good fortune and harmony. Several healthy CHILDREN of both sexes are seen. If PREGNANT, expect a boy.

SICKNESS, having been serious, is now improving and relates to the abdomen, kidneys, or regions in the lower back.

MISSING PEOPLE, in the North, are safe and can be found easily. MISSING THINGS can be found when you get help. MOVING is very advantageous now.

LOANS are granted but may require a co-signer. BUSINESS Ventures, particularly partnerships, are successful when quickly jumping ahead of the competition. JOBS are available to those who do not hesitate. The MARKET will begin a rally in which you should participate.

CHANGING LINES

6th   **6**   ▬▬ ▬▬   **WISDOM**   **CONSTRAINT**

Your hesitation or indecision has served as a poor beginning. No guidance comes to you, and you can expect an unfortunate end with restraints.

5th   **9**   ▬▬▬▬   **AUTHORITY**   **SIGNIFICANT**

Wise leadership provides choices without fear and requires no submission. Continuing in this manner, you can expect good fortune.

4th   **6**   ▬▬ ▬▬   **SOCIAL**   **VARIANT**

Openly and faithfully following the authority or the ideals of the group will bring you success and good fortune.

3RD   **6**   ▬▬ ▬▬   **INDIVIDUAL**   **VARIANT**

Allying yourself with a group whose interests and goals are not the same as yours promises sadness with no success.

2nd   **6**   ▬▬ ▬▬   **ASPIRATIONS**   **SIGNIFICANT**

Joining groups which share your interests and goals brings good fortune and success.

1st   **6**   ▬▬ ▬▬   **INSTINCT**   **CONSTRAINT**

Your honest and sincere efforts attracts others to you. The inspiration you provide cements the relationships, and unexpected good fortune follows.

DESCRIPTION

The Water or Danger, ABOVE, flows downward into, and is absorbed by, the Naturally Strong and Receptive Earth, BELOW. Thus, a natural unity is formed between these two elements. The single Ruling Line, 5th, is the strong authority in natural accord with the 2nd Line regarding human affairs. It likewise is the binding force for all the remaining weak lines. The Subject of the Hexagram, 3rd Line, contains a warning against uniting for evil or with evil elements.

9

ABOVE: SUN
WIND, WOOD
Gentle
Penetrating

BELOW: CH'IEN
HEAVEN
Creative
Firmness

小畜

**HSIAO
CH'U**

A SMALL, WEAK FORCE RESTRAINING A POWERFUL AND VITAL FORCE.

HSIAO CH'U is depicted as a weak authoritive force which governs with the restraint of decree rather than motivation and encouragement, as would the strong. However, early stages of education generally require this type of disciplinary restraint.

HSIAO CH'U is a Time, although temporary, when weak forces can maintain Restraint and Authority over Powerful and Vital Forces, characterized by the use of gentle (friendly) persuasion to Progress or Succeed in Small Matters. Neither the weak nor the obstructions will yield to force now, even though it appears that they should.

PROPHESIES

LUCK is not good now, but, after a short time, becomes better, and WISHES will not be realized right now. LOVE does not succeed and could lead to tragedy. MARRIAGES are troubled because the husband may have allowed himself to become henpecked. CHILDREN, mostly girls, require discipline. If PREGNANT, expect a girl.

SICKNESS relates to the heart, lungs, or breathing system, with a possibly of venereal disease. Good health returns when the causes are eliminated.

MISSING PEOPLE are not far away and have probably concealed themselves as lovers would. MISSING THINGS are closer than you imagine, possibly in your purse or pocket. MOVING arrangements fail.

LOANS are being obstructed or denied by a woman. BUSINESS Ventures are now hindered by temperamental individuals. JOBS do not come through and one should consider additional study. The MARKET is making no progress now.

CHANGING LINES

6th   9   ▬▬▬▬▬   WISDOM   CONSTRAINT

Your progress is halted for the time being, so enjoy your accumulations. Not knowing when to stop, or proceeding with improper conduct, will bring you disaster.

5th   9   ▬▬▬▬▬   AUTHORITY   SIGNIFICANT

By sincerely and honestly working for the betterment of all, the others join you, advancing both as individuals and as a group.

4th   6   ▬▬ ▬▬   SOCIAL   VARIANT

With honesty and sincere effort you can correctly maintain order in difficult and frightening situations in which you find yourself.

3rd   9   ▬▬▬▬▬   INDIVIDUAL   VARIANT

Failure to realize that obstacles to your ambitions were too great, has brought you humiliation and loss of dignity, but not a disaster that cannot be overcome.

2nd   9   ▬▬▬▬▬   ASPIRATIONS   SIGNIFICANT

Despite your desire to succeed, obstacles to your ambitions are too great. Returning to your original position, as others have done before you, eventually brings good fortune.

1st   9   ▬▬▬▬▬   INSTINCT   CONSTRAINT

Your ambitions are greater than your abilities or desires to succeed. Returning to your original position eventually brings good fortune.

DESCRIPTION

The Wind, ABOVE, as a Gentle force, blows across the Heaven, BELOW, preventing the Creative Power and Firmness from ascending as would be expected. A strong Ruling Line, 5th Line, provides honest and loyal cooperation with the weak 4th, which is restraining all other powers. This weak restraining force is also the Object of this Hexagram. The Subject of the Hexagram, 1st Line, is powerful, but has too many obstructions (the strong 2nd and 3rd Lines) which prevent its rise as a force against the weak force of the 4th Line.

10

ABOVE: CH'IEN
HEAVEN
°Creative
Firmness

BELOW: TUI
LAKE, MARSH
Joyous
Cheerful

履

LU

CONSIDERATE CONDUCT WITH RESPECT
TOWARDS OTHERS. TREADING PROPERLY.

LU is depicted as one stepping on a tiger's tail. The tiger is easily irritated and capable of severe reprisal. Behavior alone will determine whether such a bold action will promote Success or invite Disaster.

LU is a Time when Considerate Conduct and Respect Towards Others is emphasized (as it is an enduring virtue), characterized with Progress and Success when proper etiquette and concern are shown. Failures in this conduct are expected to bring reprisals. Here it is easy to know what is correct—but difficult to do what is correct.

PROPHESIES

LUCK is good when the surrounding danger is understood, and WISHES come true when they are not rushed or forced. LOVE needs much careful effort to succeed. MARRIAGES can succeed when behavioral obstructions are resolved. Energetic female CHILDREN are indicated. If PREGNANT, expect a girl.

Without proper care, SICKNESS can become extremely serious, and relates to the head, brain, or lungs. Maladies involving coughing are indicated, as are sexual disorders.

MISSING PEOPLE, West to North, could fall to danger if not found now. MISSING THINGS are concealed among other things. MOVING will probably bring difficulties now.

LOANS have little hope of being granted. BUSINESS Ventures are endangered by the competition and require much effort to correct. JOBS are being sought by many, and are difficult to obtain. The MARKET will be moving slightly higher before falling.

CHANGING LINES

6th   9   ▬▬▬▬   WISDOM   CONSTRAINT

Judge the benefit and consequence of your own behavior in the past. Rectifying errors and continuing that which is correct will provide your future path to great good fortune.

5th   9   ▬▬▬▬   AUTHORITY   SIGNIFICANT

Your position is advantageous and may become more so, but stubbornness and obstinacy will place you in peril. And if any obstinacy continues, you can expect disaster.

4th   9   ▬▬▬▬   SOCIAL   VARIANT

Understanding obstacles which may be encountered, and carefully planning to resolve them when encountered, eventually brings you success.

3rd   6   ▬▬ ▬▬   INDIVIDUAL   VARIANT

Your attempts to battle your way into a position exceeding your abilities has provoked disaster.

2nd   9   ▬▬▬▬   ASPIRATIONS   SIGNIFICANT

Keeping free of entanglements and controversy, frees you from their associated difficulties. Expect good fortune.

1st   9   ▬▬▬▬   INSTINCT   CONSTRAINT

Your situation is safe from danger, and you can advance according to your original conduct or plan without mistake.

DESCRIPTION

The Joyous Lake, BELOW, lies open and honest under the Heaven, ABOVE. Movement of both of these Trigrams is upward and the Pleasant, but lesser, force is seen to tread upon (or follow), the powerful force. The single Ruling Line, 5th, is shown as persevering in the presence of the other strong forces as Respect for others, lest they retaliate against abusive behavior. The Subject of the Hexagram is also the 5th Line.

11

ABOVE: K'UN
EARTH
Natural
Receptive

BELOW: CH'IEN
HEAVEN
Creative
Firmness

T'AI

PEACE, HARMONY. THE BAD DEPARTS, THE
GREAT ARRIVES. SUCCESS, GOOD FORTUNE.

T'AI is depicted as greatness arrived in all things. The heavens are cleared of winter storms, mankind turns to production, commerce, and social harmony. The earth comes forth with new growth as nature produces the first blossoms.

T'AI is a Time when circumstances and relationships are Peaceful, Harmonious and Productive and Greatness Arrives while Lesser Influences Depart. It is characterized by Success and Good Fortune having arrived of their own accord, rather than by force or power. The lesser influences are likewise departing. Such is nature's preparation for spring.

PROPHESIES

LUCK is supremely favorable, and WISHES come true beyond your expectations. LOVE—particularly new love—flourishes. MARRIAGES are particularly peaceful and harmonious. CHILDREN of both sexes are peaceful and harmonious, but they must not be spoiled. If PREGNANT, expect a girl.

SICKNESS is rapidly passing, and probably relates to the head, abdomen, intestines, or lungs. Prepare for allergies.

MISSING PEOPLE, in Westerly directions, move farther away, fall in love or marry, but are not hard to find. MISSING THINGS, once concealed, show up unexpectedly. MOVING brings fatigue and disorder.

LOANS are secured with ease. BUSINESS Ventures succeed and sales climb. JOBS in large companies are plentiful, but don't expect managerial positions. The MARKET is broadening and lowering, don't invest blindly.

CHANGING LINES

6th   **6**   ▬▬ ▬▬   **WISDOM**   **CONSTRAINT**

Harmony has fallen to disorder. Any action you take adds to the disorder. Be patient and adjust to the new circumstances.

5th   **6**   ▬▬ ▬▬   **AUTHORITY**   **SIGNIFICANT**

As the lowly submits to the mighty, so must the mighty submit to the lowly. The leader is truly the servant. When you are in accord, expect great good fortune.

4th   **6**   ▬▬ ▬▬   **SOCIAL**   **VARIANT**

You may now preserve harmony in associations with others by minimizing financial issues and expressing sincere concern.

3RD   **9**   ▬▬▬▬   **INDIVIDUAL**   **VARIANT**

Harmony is being replaced with increasing difficulty. With caution, understanding, and planning during such a change, you will suffer no setback.

2nd   **9**   ▬▬▬▬   **ASPIRATIONS**   **SIGNIFICANT**

Even in harmony, keeping order can be difficult. Maintain order by being tolerant of others, administering fair and impartial justice, and remaining alert to the circumstances.

1st   **9**   ▬▬▬▬   **INSTINCT**   **CONSTRAINT**

Working in peace and harmony with those around you brings success and advancement.

DESCRIPTION

The Earth, ABOVE, descends and the Heaven, BELOW, rises. The two primal forces meet in perfect Harmony and Peace. Living things bloom and prosper, and the new spring is being prepared. Of the two Ruling Lines, 2nd and 5th, the 2nd discharges duties from the authority, and in the 5th the authority discharges responsibilities relative to its subordinates. There is a special union in peace and harmony, even though the Lines appear to be out of natural order. The Subject of the Hexagram, 3rd Line, is at the height of the Arriving Greatness (from the bottom) and the "Bad" is seen Departing from the top, 6th Line.

ABOVE: CH'IEN
HEAVEN
Creative
Firmness

BELOW: K'UN
EARTH
Natural
Receptive

否

P'I

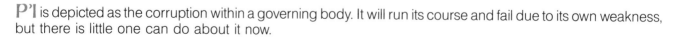

ENDURING DISORDER, STAGNATION. LESSER
INFLUENCES ARRIVE. THE GREAT DEPARTS.

P'I is depicted as the corruption within a governing body. It will run its course and fail due to its own weakness, but there is little one can do about it now.

P'I is a Time of Disorder, Stagnation, and Decay as Greatness Departs and Lesser Influences Arrive, characterized by the need to Endure this Disordered time by refusing to associate with Lesser Influences. Unpleasantness now, but with proper care disaster can be avoided. Best expressed as a "grin and bear it" time. Shameful acts bring humiliation. Gossip and slander abound.

PROPHESIES

LUCK, forget it, and the only WISH that you can hope for is that you successfully endure this time. LOVE fails as the interests of each partner move further apart. MARRIAGES are troubled with quarrels based upon distorted viewpoints. Quiet and gentle female CHILDREN are indicated. If PREGNANT, expect a girl.

SICKNESS worsens and is related to the abdomen, intestines, or possibly the head. Check for cancer, and, if a woman, check for uterine problems.

MISSING PEOPLE are moving further away in Westerly directions and don't want to be found. MISSING THINGS are destroyed and lost forever. MOVING invites too many difficulties to be practical now.

LOANS are not granted. BUSINESS Ventures look good on the outside, but are rife with internal chaos. JOBS, if found, bring unhappiness. The MARKET shows no hope; put your money into savings accounts.

CHANGING LINES

6th   9   ▬▬▬▬   **WISDOM**   **CONSTRAINT**

Your diligent efforts have overcome the decay. Expect happiness and particularly peaceful relationships with your colleagues.

5th   9   ▬▬▬▬   **AUTHORITY**   **SIGNIFICANT**

You have succeeded in restoring order, but if you fail to be doubly cautious against the return of the causes of disorder, this success perishes.

4th   9   ▬▬▬▬   **SOCIAL**   **VARIANT**

You can now begin improving upon the disorder. Your opinions and advice attracts others, as helpers, also desirous of clearing the disorder.

3rd   6   ▬▬ ▬▬   **INDIVIDUAL**   **VARIANT**

Inferior persons are failing in the responsibilities they have undertaken and their shame is growing. Stand back and avoid being swept into their downfall.

2nd   6   ▬▬ ▬▬   **ASPIRATIONS**   **SIGNIFICANT**

Inferior persons, now in official capacity, delight in the prolific decay and corruption. You will suffer, but do not join. Withdraw and preserve your ideals—they will be needed later.

1st   6   ▬▬ ▬▬   **INSTINCT**   **CONSTRAINT**

In spite of the apparent successes of inferior persons, you can expect good fortune by moving away from the inferior environment, which cannot endure.

DESCRIPTION

The Heaven, ABOVE, rises while the Earth, BELOW, descends. Although these Trigrams look well ordered, the two forces have actually moved apart and are unable to accomplish anything. The weak is replacing the strong. The single Ruling Line, 5th, is working to overcome the disorder or standstill, but the lines are working out of accord. The Subject of the Hexagram, 3rd line, is seen as the leader of the Lesser Influences bringing shame and humiliation, while the Greatness, 6th line, is Departing at the top.

13

ABOVE: CH'IEN
HEAVEN
Creative
Firmness

BELOW: LI
FIRE, SUN
Brilliance
Clarity

同人

T'UNG
JEN

FELLOWSHIP AND PEACEFUL UNION AMONG
COLLEAGUES. PROGRESS, SUCCESS.

T'UNG JEN is depicted as camaraderie among those joined together at a common meeting place.
The Chinese character is translated as "same person."

T'UNG JEN is a Time of Peaceful Unions or Associations between Colleagues of similar interests, characterized by their ability, when so united, to produce Progress and Success. This group is presented as pre-existent (unlike PI, Hexagram #8, wherein groups are formed), and has already restored order, with success. Great projects can now be undertaken by such a group. Such Peaceful Union (Fellowship), while capable of producing Progress and Success, can also bring mistrust from self-interest.

PROPHESIES

LUCK is good when you respect the opinions of others, and WISHES come true as if by magic. LOVE is very successful. MARRIAGES are happy and good with sincere companionship. Strong male children are indicated. If PREGNANT, expect a boy.

SICKNESS is improving and relates to the lungs, breathing system, or heart. A severe warning is issued against smoking. Your sight is diminishing—expect glasses or stronger prescriptions.

MISSING PEOPLE return from the Northwest. MISSING THINGS, especially valuables, need to be found quickly or they will be spent or traded off by another. MOVING is favorable now—friends help.

LOANS, even large loans, are granted. BUSINESS Ventures are generally good, but selfish interests interfere. JOBS are available but there is much competition for positions. The MARKET will increase dramatically—a good time to invest.

CHANGING LINES

6th   **9**   ▬▬▬▬   **WISDOM**   **CONSTRAINT**

Even though your objectives have not been met, you should remain true to them and continue in their pursuit. Regret not, a greater time is near.

5th   **9**   ▬▬▬▬   **AUTHORITY**   **SIGNIFICANT**

A correct association is being hindered by strong opposition. Persistence to effect this union will succeed and restore order.

4th   **9**   ▬▬▬▬   **SOCIAL**   **VARIANT**

In resolving difficulties, do not use an outright attack. Expect good fortune, however, by abandoning overly aggressive means of enforcement and resorting to peaceful solutions.

3rd   **9**   ▬▬▬▬   **INDIVIDUAL**   **VARIANT**

You will experience no advantage in opposing stronger elements. Your interests are best served by planning for the better times ahead.

2nd   **6**   ▬▬ ▬▬   **ASPIRATIONS**   **SIGNIFICANT**

To improve yourself, you will have to go beyond your group, as away to college. Remaining with the group is easier, but will bring later regrets from not having made such an improvement.

1st   **9**   ▬▬▬▬   **INSTINCT**   **CONSTRAINT**

With honesty and openness between all, you and your colleagues now advance without error.

DESCRIPTION

The Fire or Sun, BELOW, rising into the Heaven, ABOVE, is a natural and peaceful association. Both Ruling Lines, 2nd and 5th, form a natural and harmonious association. The weak 2nd yields to all the powerful lines, and the powerful 5th corresponds with the 2nd. The Subject of the Hexagram, 3rd Line, has brought Good Fortune, but also the seeds of mistrust, affecting interpersonal relationships.

14

ABOVE; LI
FIRE, SUN
Brilliance
Clarity

BELOW: CH'IEN
HEAVEN
Creative
Firmness

大有

TA YU

POSSESSION OF VIRTUE AND STRENGTH
PRODUCES PROGRESS AND SUCCESS.

TA YU is depicted as the community striving for and accomplishing the common benefit. The Chinese character translates as "Great Havings."

TA YU is a Time of Abundant Possession of Virtue and Strength (of character in particular), characterized by Great Success and Good Fortune. The social union is in complete accord, and all common good is achieved. Gentle and unselfish leadership guides responsive and capable helpers to Progress and Success.

PROPHESIES

LUCK is very favorable, and WISHES come true, but are spoiled if taken for granted. LOVE succeeds, but may be destroyed by arrogance. MARRIAGES are harmonious and gentle, a helpful wife is seen as being of great benefit to the husband. Strong male CHILDREN requiring discipline are indicated. If PREGNANT, expect a girl.

SICKNESS is rapidly improving, and related to the lungs or head. Fevers are indicated, as is tuberculosis.

MISSING PEOPLE, in the South, must be found quickly or they go further away. MISSING THINGS are high, but not hidden. MOVING is favorable when all your tasks have been completed.

LOANS come easily as your collateral is excellent. BUSINESS Ventures succeed with teamwork. JOBS are plentiful to those willing to work diligently. The MARKET is rising and very active.

CHANGING LINES

6th   9   ▬▬▬▬▬   WISDOM   CONSTRAINT

Your virtuous conduct brings respect and benefit as if from heaven. All endeavors succeed and you can expect good fortune.

5th   6   ▬▬ ▬▬   AUTHORITY   SIGNIFICANT

Your sincerity will tend to motivate others but you must assert your leadership ability to achieve progress or good fortune.

4th   9   ▬▬▬▬▬   SOCIAL   VARIANT

Abundant accumulation must be conserved and properly used. Without waste, or boastful pride, you will experience no loss.

3RD   9   ▬▬▬▬▬   INDIVIDUAL   VARIANT

The sharing of accumulated wealth for the common good is advantageous and brings advance. Lesser persons hoard and are not to be trusted.

2nd   9   ▬▬▬▬▬   ASPIRATIONS   SIGNIFICANT

Accumulate and use only what is due to you. Acting without greed or excesses allows you to advance without blame or criticism.

1st   9   ▬▬▬▬▬   INSTINCT   CONSTRAINT

Wealth is accumulating. Your only danger is arrogance or insensitivity toward others.

DESCRIPTION

The Fire or Sun, ABOVE, high in the Heaven, BELOW, shows Great Brilliance and Clarity. This radiant light conveys the image of Possession to the Greatest Degree. The single Ruling Line, 5th, is seen as yielding to all the power and receiving the place of great honor. Thus, this Line is not considered weak. Humility stands in the presence of Great Possession (Strength) as a supreme virtue. The Subject of this Hexagram, 3rd Line, is clearly placed in the midst of Virtue and Strength.

15

ABOVE: K'UN
EARTH
Natural
Receptive

BELOW: KEN
MOUNTAIN
Stillness
Silence

CH'IEN

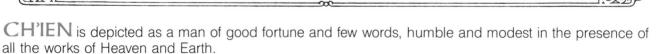

MODEST BEHAVIOR GREATENS GOOD FORTUNE.
SUCCESS MUST NOT BRING ARROGANCE.

CH'IEN is depicted as a man of good fortune and few words, humble and modest in the presence of all the works of Heaven and Earth.

CH'IEN is a Time when Modest or Silent behavior prevails, charcterized by Good Fortune already in Possession and becoming Greater when not ostentatiously displayed or arrogantly flaunted. Words are seen as having little effect on mankind, but one's deeds are visible far and wide. The Occidental idea of embarrassment or meagerness needs to be shaken off to understand this high virtue.

PROPHESIES

LUCK is very favorable, don't flaunt it, and WISHES come true. LOVE is blissful and endures. MARRIAGES are happy, as each know and respect the other's viewpoints. Peaceful CHILDREN of both sexes are seen. If PREGNANT, expect a boy.

SICKNESS is not severe, and relates to the organs in the lower part of the body (torso). Poisoning, possibly food poisoning, may produce vomitting or diarrhea. Women should check for uterine problems.

MISSING PEOPLE, North to East, return when not chased—don't worry. MISSING THINGS are concealed under something, and probably hidden high. MOVING can be undertaken without difficulty, unless rushed.

LOANS are granted when reasonable requests are made. BUSINESS Ventures succeed when firmly directed, but needless or rushed expansion will defeat the success. JOBS, particularly ones working with the earth, are plentiful. The MARKET is indicating a fortunate rise coming soon.

CHANGING LINES

| 6th | 6 | ▬▬ ▬▬ | WISDOM | CONSTRAINT |

Your modesty in behavior has been misunderstood as weakness. Enforcement and strict discipline, with proper regard towards others, is required. Correctly apply your energies now.

| 5th | 6 | ▬▬ ▬▬ | AUTHORITY | SIGNIFICANT |

A time has arisen to take a disciplinary action. Such action, when not excessively applied, wins support and promotes success.

| 4th | 6 | ▬▬ ▬▬ | SOCIAL | VARIANT |

Modesty is not a rendering of weakness nor an excuse for hesitation. Firm action now, free of arrogance towards others, furthers your endeavors.

| 3rd | 9 | ▬▬▬▬▬ | INDIVIDUAL | VARIANT |

You are now recognized with respect and as an individual of particular merit and virtue. You can expect success through to completion with good fortune.

| 2nd | 6 | ▬▬ ▬▬ | ASPIRATIONS | SIGNIFICANT |

Your modest and disciplined behavior is seen by all in the quality of your efforts. Expect good fortune, with much help from others.

| 1st | 6 | ▬▬ ▬▬ | INSTINCT | CONSTRAINT |

With modest and disciplined behavior, you can now expect your greatest undertakings to be successful.

DESCRIPTION

The Mountain or Stillness, BELOW, lies within the Earth, ABOVE. Everyone knows that the Mountain stands above the Earth, but here the Mountain is shown as Silently withdrawing into the Earth, hence Modesty. Natural Character is so Great that it has no need to display or flaunt itself. The single Ruling Line, 3rd, is the only clear light at the top of the Mountain. Power is passed to all the lesser lines. Normally the 3rd Line is not favorable, but here Modesty works Great Success. The Subject of the Hexagram, 5th line, indicates Modesty, but not weakness, in authority.

16

ABOVE: CHEN
THUNDER
Movement
Arousing

BELOW: K'UN
EARTH
Natural
Receptive

豫

YU

ENTHUSIASM AS THE JOINING OF ENERGY AND DEVOTION IN NEW UNDERTAKINGS.

YU is depicted as the delegated leader embarking out on a new campaign with loyal and obedient support. The campaign need not be military or aggressive, but is represented as a New Beginning.

YU is a Time of Energy, Devotion, and Obedience while Moving Naturally, characterized by advantage in New Undertakings. Spring is Nature's New Beginning as it breaks away from Winter's restrictions. Movement along paths of least resistance are the natural ways of movement suggested. This Hexagram warns of not getting carried into a frenzy with enthusiasm.

PROPHESIES

LUCK cannot be fully relied upon, and WISHES only come true by faithfullly working toward them. LOVE succeeds when the opinions of others are considered. MARRIAGES are good as they mature, but the bliss of matrimony should be remembered and not sought. Active CHILDREN of both sexes are indicated, although one may be lame or partially crippled. If PREGNANT, expect a boy.

SICKNESS is not too severe and relates to an abdominal area. There is a particular caution of alcohol abuse leading to liver diseases.

MISSING PEOPLE, probably in the East, are moving further away, and becoming more difficult to find. MISSING THINGS are not where you thought you lost them and difficult to find. MOVING is very favorable now.

LOANS are granted when applications are made carefully. BUSINESS Ventures succeed only when energies are properly channeled to produce useful work. JOBS show some promotion, but not what was expected. The MARKET is tending to rise, but is variable. A true gamble.

CHANGING LINES

6th 6 — — WISDOM CONSTRAINT

Enthusiasm has given way to delirium. You can still return to safety by recognizing reality and following ways not filled with illusions.

5th 6 — — AUTHORITY SIGNIFICANT

Accept the talents and capabilities of others. Delegate to the strong and enthusiastic to continue undertakings.

4th 9 ——— SOCIAL VARIANT

Approaching the undertaking of your honest desire with enthusiasm and loyally following it through to the end, brings attainment.

3rd 6 — — INDIVIDUAL VARIANT

Understanding that unrealistic desires will not be realized, in spite of your enthusiasm, will lead you away from regret.

2nd 6 — — ASPIRATIONS SIGNIFICANT

Discern the difference between reality and illusion. Thus mature pursuit, not blind enthusiasm, will bring good fortune.

1st 6 — — INSTINCT CONSTRAINT

Your excessive ambition and determination to get ahead is working against you. Expect disaster.

DESCRIPTION

The Energy of Thunder, ABOVE, with Movement across the Earth, BELOW, joins with Natural Strength and Devotion to produce Enthusiasm. The season for New Undertakings is represented and this is a Hexagram of the 2nd Month, MARCH, with the Spring Equinox approaching. The single Ruling Line, 4th, is a Minister in whom authority has been vested. All remaining broken lines Obey and Yield to the 4th Ruling Line. The Subject of the Hexagram, 1st Line, is in the position of New and Enthusiastic Beginning.

17

ABOVE: TUI
LAKE, MARSH
Joyous
Cheerful

BELOW: CHEN
THUNDER
Movement
Arousing

隨

SUI

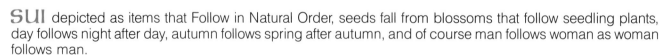

FOLLOWING NATURE'S WAY, AS AUTUMN
DOES SPRING, LEADS TO GREAT SUCCESS.

SUI depicted as items that Follow in Natural Order, seeds fall from blossoms that follow seedling plants, day follows night after day, autumn follows spring after autumn, and of course man follows woman as woman follows man.

SUI is a Time of Following the Natural Order, characterized by Great Success when in natural accord. Autumn follows Spring, Spring follows Autumn—this is nature's perpetual cycle. The Movement represented by Following must be done with Joy and Pleasure to realize the Great Success indicated.

PROPHESIES

LUCK is favorable, and WISHES come true when they are not forced. LOVE is very successful. MARRIAGES are good when the husband is not too demanding. CHILDREN of both sexes are indicated and relationships are in harmony with their parents. If PREGNANT, expect a girl.

SICKNESS is improving slowly, but general health may be slowly declining and probably relates to the digestive tract, lungs, or sexual organs.

MISSING PEOPLE are moving, probably from East to West, and are difficult to find. MISSING THINGS are concealed with other items, but can be found with much searching. MOVING is favorable now, when sufficiently planned.

LOANS will eventually be approved. BUSINESS Ventures break even by imitating the competition. JOBS come when tirelessly pursued. The MARKET is gradually declining from a previous high.

CHANGING LINES

6th 6 ▬▬ ▬▬ **WISDOM** **CONSTRAINT**

What you have achieved is also the result of the efforts of those who have followed and helped you. Failure to remain true to them brings disorder and decay.

5th 9 ▬▬▬▬ **AUTHORITY** **SIGNIFICANT**

Your sincere pursuit of high ideals wins the confidence of others and brings good fortune.

4th 9 ▬▬▬▬ **SOCIAL** **VARIANT**

Your motives are suspect by the one you are following. Remove this doubt by clearly demonstrating that your intentions are not ulterior. Otherwise, expect disaster.

3rd 6 ▬▬ ▬▬ **INDIVIDUAL** **VARIANT**

Abandoning lesser influences and steadfastly striving to higher ideals will bring you the advance you seek.

2nd 6 ▬▬ ▬▬ **ASPIRATIONS** **SIGNIFICANT**

When you choose to follow lesser goals, you can see the great opportunities departing.

1st 9 ▬▬▬▬ **INSTINCT** **CONSTRAINT**

Your position is changing; follow the new order without anger. Expanding your horizons and meeting new people brings success.

DESCRIPTION

Pleasure or Joy, the Lake, ABOVE, with Movement, Thunder, BELOW, (within the Lake). Movement with Joy is defined as the Natural Following. Here the Older (BELOW) is seen as following the Younger (ABOVE), as Autumn follows Spring. It should be remembered that Spring also follows Autumn. Both Ruling Lines, 1st and 5th, are each strong, but subordinate to and follow the weaker lines directly above. The Subject of the Hexagram, 3rd Line, is likewise following the strong. Only the 2nd and 4th Lines represent an incorrect following.

18

ABOVE: KEN
MOUNTAIN
Stillness
Silence

BELOW: SUN
WIND, WOOD
Gentle
Penetrating

蠱

KU

PREPARE IN ADVANCE. ELIMINATE THE
DECAY AND REBUILD, COMPLETING SWIFTLY.

KU is depicted as the Repair of material or natural Decay by all. The Chinese character is symbolized as legendary venomous insects in a bowl—Decay that needs to be corrected.

KU is a Time for Eliminating the Causes of and Repairing Decay with both Pre-planning and Swift Completion, characterized by Great Progress, Success, and the ability for Great Undertakings. There is also an implication of guilt, because Decay has been allowed to happen.

PROPHESIES

LUCK has been poor, but is now improving, and WISHES tend to not come true. LOVE is poor as mutual concern is not shown. MARRIAGES are troubled, but can be repaired when the partners recognize and correct faults. Troublesome CHILDREN of both sexes are seen needing discipline. If PREGNANT, expect a girl.

SICKNESS is bad now, but with medical attention, complete recuperation is possible. Indicated are diseases that affect more than the originally afflicted organ, such as hepatitis. Hereditary problems are also indicated.

MISSING PEOPLE have moved much, but are now probably in Easterly directions and are ashamed to return on their own. MISSING THINGS have been moved, are probably broken and underneath something else. MOVING can be undertaken when planned carefully.

LOANS to repair damage may be granted, but expect no others. BUSINESS Ventures require strict guidance to succeed. JOBS are available now, but don't last long —find another. The MARKET suggests a good time to invest.

CHANGING LINES

6th　　9　　▬▬▬▬▬　　**WISDOM**　　**CONSTRAINT**

You are correctly credited for having repaired the decay, but don't accept the promotion offered at this time. Greatness and promotion are approaching, but your time has not yet arrived.

5th　　6　　▬▬　▬▬　　**AUTHORITY**　　**SIGNIFICANT**

Your strength in overcoming faults, particularly your own, is admired. You can expect help and fulfillment of your goals.

4th　　6　　▬▬　▬▬　　**SOCIAL**　　**VARIANT**

The decay has been caused by your inability to correct faults. Proceeding—when the faults remain—brings further misfortune.

3rd　　9　　▬▬▬▬▬　　**INDIVIDUAL**　　**VARIANT**

The decay has been caused by neglect in the past. Overzealous efforts to correct faults will bring you minor regret and embarassment, but you can ultimately expect forgiveness.

2nd　　9　　▬▬▬▬▬　　**ASPIRATIONS**　　**SIGNIFICANT**

The decay has been caused by weakness requiring correction. Proceed gently, or you may do more harm than good.

1st　　6　　▬▬　▬▬　　**INSTINCT**　　**CONSTRAINT**

The decay has been caused by neglect in the past. When correcting this decay you will be in peril, but expect good fortune upon completion.

DESCRIPTION

The Wind, Gentleness, BELOW, with Stillness, Mountain, ABOVE, is indicative of Stagnation and Decay as the Gentle Obedience below is stopped by the Unyielding Stillness above. The Wind is scattered at the base of the Mountain—vegetation is destroyed and seeds are scattered. The single Ruling Line, 5th, succeeds in overcoming the Decay with its yielding nature. The Subject of the Hexagram, 3rd Line, bears a warning against overzealous correction of Decay, but here the cause is just and forgiveness is also present.

ABOVE: K'UN
EARTH
Natural
Receptive

BELOW: TUI
LAKE, MARSH
Joyous
Cheerful

LIN

GREATNESS APPROACHES WITH
WELL-DEVELOPED LEADERSHIP.

LIN is depicted as Greatness Approaching, seen here as a caravan bringing newness, interest, and activity. The caravan, like all successful undertakings, requires capable leadership to stay together and arrive at or accomplish goals as planned.

LIN is a Time of Approaching Greatness with Leadership capable of motivating and inspiring, characterized by Great Progress and Success. This Progress or Success endures for a long time, but not forever. This Hexagram offers the warning to prepare for and recognize the changing circumstances.

PROPHESIES

LUCK is favorable and improving, and WISHES come true, but do not last forever. LOVE is not too favorable now, but with careful attention could improve. MARRIAGES are characterized with long-lasting harmony and improvement. Gentle and obedient CHILDREN of both sexes are indicated, but do not pamper or spoil them. If PREGNANT, expect a girl.

SICKNESS is becoming less severe, and relates to the organs of the lower part of the body, such as the digestive or urinary tracts, Even the feet may be affected. Gout is strongly suggested.

MISSING PEOPLE, probably South to West, are returning on their own, or are letting you find them. MISSING THINGS, probably dropped when traveling, can be found with help. Moving should not be attempted now.

LOANS are granted, but difficulty is seen in paying them back. BUSINESS Ventures are quite good, particularly when low cost inventory is bought for future sales. JOBS are available, but within one year you will lose the position either by promotion or termination—your effort will determine which. The MARKET is rising, but slowly. Consider buying.

CHANGING LINES

6th   6   ▬▬ ▬▬   **WISDOM**   **CONSTRAINT**

With honesty and generosity towards others, your advance is associated with good fortune without error. Expect a time to contemplate and improve further.

5th   6   ▬▬ ▬▬   **AUTHORITY**   **SIGNIFICANT**

Your wisdom in selecting others to help you advance produces certain good fortune.

4th   6   ▬▬ ▬▬   **SOCIAL**   **VARIANT**

Your position is perfect for advance. Seeking help at this time insures no error in progress.

3rd   6   ▬▬ ▬▬   **INDIVIDUAL**   **VARIANT**

Insincere or idle flattery is incapable of inspiring or motivating—expect no advance. Correcting your approach will lead you from this error.

2nd   9   ▬▬▬   **ASPIRATIONS**   **SIGNIFICANT**

Strong opposition requires tough and determined leadership, in addition to inspiration and motivation. Such an approach brings good fortune, but some will be uncomfortable with these tactics.

1st   9   ▬▬▬   **INSTINCT**   **CONSTRAINT**

Leadership roles always require inspiration and motivation of others to secure progress. Advancing with the ability to inspire and motivate others will bring you good fortune.

DESCRIPTION

The Joyous, Lake, BELOW, lies within Devotion, Earth, ABOVE. Leadership, Joyfully Devoted and Obedient to the natural order is an inspiration to others. Such leadership is able to accomplish much with little apparent effort. Both Ruling Lines, 1st and 2nd, due to their position and upward movement, represent the Approach of Greatness. (Greatness Arrives in T'AI, Hexagram #11.) The Subject of the Hexagram, 2nd Line, is Leading the Approach, as January leads to Spring.

20

ABOVE: SUN
WIND, WOOD
Gentle
Penetrating

BELOW: K'UN
EARTH
Natural
Receptive

KUAN

OBSERVATION OF THE CONDITIONS AND
CONTEMPLATION FOR IMPROVEMENT.

KUAN is depicted as the governors observing the toil and efforts of the populace for future improvement.

KUAN is a Time for Observations of Conditions, particularly on Earth, or below, from a vantage point, characterized by Contemplation for Improvement in methods. It is not a significant time for action, and fortunes don't significantly increase or decrease. However, analyses of conditions now, pave the way for enduring hardships and creating advancement in the future.

PROPHESIES

LUCK is becoming less favorable, and WISHES should be delayed until later. LOVE isn't too bad, but can't be rushed. MARRIAGES can expect future difficulties, solvable when working together. CHILDREN of both sexes are indicated. They may have difficulties in their personal lives or health. If PREGNANT, expect a girl.

SICKNESS is getting worse, and relates to the abdominal area, digestive tract, or nervous system. Don't ignore seemingly minor maladies, such as the flu.

MISSING PEOPLE, in Southerly directions, seem to vanish, and are all but impossible to find. MISSING THINGS are deeply concealed, buried, or possibly stolen. MOVING leads to disaster if undertaken now.

LOANS are not granted now, nor for quite awhile. BUSINESS Ventures face growing difficulties, which can be corrected with the proper effort. JOBS are sparse; wait for the right opportunity. The MARKET is or will be falling; consider selling.

CHANGING LINES

6th　　　　**9**　　▬▬▬▬▬▬　　**WISDOM**　　　　**CONSTRAINT**

As you examine others you are likewise examined. Correct faults and expect times of judgment to follow.

5th　　　　**9**　　▬▬▬▬▬▬　　**AUTHORITY**　　　　**SIGNIFICANT**

Self-examination is required to insure favorable effects upon others from your efforts. In this way, you can maintain or correct your conduct as necessary.

4th　　　　**6**　　▬▬▬　▬▬▬　　**SOCIAL**　　　　**VARIANT**

When contemplating all the circumstances, both the favorable and unfavorable will be exposed. You can continue to advance when you direct your efforts toward the favorable effects.

3rd　　　　**6**　　▬▬▬　▬▬▬　　**INDIVIDUAL**　　　　**VARIANT**

Observe and contemplate for improvement. Your action now should be limited to adjusting yourself to the current circumstances.

2nd　　　　**6**　　▬▬▬　▬▬▬　　**ASPIRATIONS**　　　　**SIGNIFICANT**

Egotistical or self-serving interests are narrow and obscured viewpoints. Contemplate changing if you plan to advance or work with others.

1st　　　　**6**　　▬▬▬　▬▬▬　　**INSTINCT**　　　　**CONSTRAINT**

Responding without understanding only serves persons of no particular worth. Contemplation and understanding of issues will save you from this humiliation.

DESCRIPTION

The Gentle Wind, ABOVE, blows across the Receptive Earth, BELOW—hence Traveling and Observing the Conditions upon the Earth (Below) with Contemplation for Improvement. Both Ruling Lines, 5th and 6th, are strong and have a grand view of all that is below, and can offer advice for improvement in earthly affairs. The Subject of the Hexagram, 4th Line, is on the threshold of (just below) greatness. In this Hexagram the lesser influences are ascending, but not yet relevant. August/September, but not yet Autumn.

21

ABOVE: LI
FIRE, SUN
Brilliance
Clarity

BELOW: CHEN
THUNDER
Movement
Arousing

噬嗑

SHIH
HO

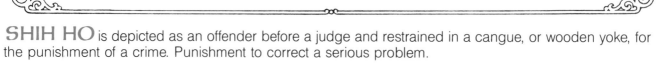

BITING THROUGH, TENACIOUSLY WORKING TO
CORRECT SERIOUS PROBLEMS SUCCEEDS.

SHIH HO is depicted as an offender before a judge and restrained in a cangue, or wooden yoke, for the punishment of a crime. Punishment to correct a serious problem.

SHIH HO is a Time for the Administration of Justice and appropriate Punishment for Reform, characterized by Progress, when Punishment is legally and correctly applied. Here the lips of the mouth cannot meet until the obstruction between them is "bitten through," or adequately resolved. Though the circumstances may be unpleasant, these are necessary actions, defined by the laws of society.

PROPHESIES

LUCK is particularly poor now, and WISHES have only the slightest chance of success with much tenacity. LOVE is being interfered with from an outside influence and is not successful. MARRIAGES are highly troubled and require substantial reform if they are to survive. CHILDREN of both sexes are seen, but with problems requiring much attention. If PREGNANT, expect a girl.

SICKNESS may be prolonged and require professional treatment to cure. It relates to something taken in through the mouth—alcohol or drug abuse, food poisoning settling into the stomach or intestines, or even throat cancer.

MISSING PEOPLE, East to South, may be in jail, fleeing to avoid some unpleasantness, or in need of help from the police. MISSING THINGS have been stolen. Reporting these to the police may result in their return and catching the thief. MOVING plans are obstructed, but can be accomplished with diligent effort and professional help.

LOANS are not going to be granted. BUSINESS Ventures are troubled, particularly with statutory difficulties, such as tax payments, which can be overcome with resolute effort. JOBS require removal of obstructions to succeed. The MARKET is active and rising. An unconventional approach, however, will probably produce the greatest profit.

CHANGING LINES

6th   9   WISDOM   CONSTRAINT

Your failure to respond to the need for reform invites certain disaster, while correction of deficiencies restores order, union, and freedom.

5th   6   AUTHORITY   SIGNIFICANT

Your weakness or leniency in resolving difficult situations is evident. Seeking capable help in meeting responsibilities brings reform without blame.

4th   9   SOCIAL   VARIANT

Powerful oppositions now require reform. Strong and decisive action, without excesses, will secure the reform desired. Expect good fortune.

3rd   6   INDIVIDUAL   VARIANT

A disagreeable or harmful action is now required to correct or reform a spoiled element. Expect some failure or disappointment, but reform in the end.

2nd   6   ASPIRATIONS   SIGNIFICANT

Correction or reform now requires a deep committment. Tenaciously applying efforts toward correction keeps you free from error.

1st   9   INSTINCT   CONSTRAINT

Expect restraint from past errors by a force serving your own interests. Accepting this restraint frees you from further errors or mistakes.

DESCRIPTION

The Sun, Brilliance, ABOVE, with Thunder, Movement, BELOW, represents a higher Authority over lower Movement. More clear, however, is the explanation of "Biting Through" when this Hexagram is compared to #27, "Mouth", and shows something in the mouth which must be bitten through, or taken care of, even though the circumstances may be unpleasant. The single Ruling Line, 5th, represents yielding to a higher power to advance further. The Subject of the Hexagram is also in the 5th Line. All this combines to indicate how the laws of society are made and enforced.

22

ABOVE: KEN
MOUNTAIN
Stillness
Silence

BELOW: LI
FIRE, SUN
Brilliance
Clarity

PI

OUTWARD BEAUTY PROVIDES NO
GUARANTEE OF INNER CONTENTS.

PI is depicted as outward beauty and grace, but there is no indication of inner virtues or motives.

PI is a time when Outward Beauty provides No Guarantee of Inner Contents—and pursuit of the outward beauty may lead to disappointment and regret from not having examined the inner contents. PI is, however, characterized with Success when issues are analytically scrutinized. An obscuration is implied by this Hexagram and all the facts necessary to make great decisions are not evident.

PROPHESIES

LUCK appears favorable, but is really troubled, and WISHES, providing they are not too ambitious, come true. LOVE is being hampered by vanity. MARRIAGES are in peril of splitting up as the concern of the community is not foremost. CHILDREN of both sexes are indicated, but they will experience unfulfilling lives. If PREGNANT, a girl is slightly favored.

SICKNESS will become grave without the proper care, and relates to the blood system and its organs, such as the heart, kidneys, liver, or spleen. Chronic ailments can be expected.

MISSING PEOPLE, North to East, return on their own, or a friend tells you where they are. MISSING THINGS are mixed with other things, but not too far away. MOVING for short distances can be accomplished without difficulty.

LOANS, in small amounts, will be granted. BUSINESS Ventures are endangered when quality is sacrificed for the sake of visual appearances. JOBS are available, but don't get in over your head. Consider the fine arts. The MARKET is apparently strong, but without careful research your investments could be in serious jeopardy.

CHANGING LINES

6th   **9**   ▬▬▬▬▬   **WISDOM**   **CONSTRAINT**

All outward appointments are abandoned to perfect inner virtue. You can expect to undertake upcoming tasks without mistake.

5th   **6**   ▬▬ ▬▬   **AUTHORITY**   **SIGNIFICANT**

Perfecting inner virtue may deprive you of outward beauty or appointments. Expect to be misunderstood, but also expect joy and good fortune in the end.

4th   **6**   ▬▬ ▬▬   **SOCIAL**   **VARIANT**

Suspicions and doubt may result from overly elegant outward appearances, even though inner virtue and motives are correct.

3rd   **9**   ▬▬▬▬▬   **INDIVIDUAL**   **VARIANT**

Your outward beauty or appearance attracts others to you in a complementary manner, but maintain your inner virtue if you expect good fortune.

2nd   **6**   ▬▬ ▬▬   **ASPIRATIONS**   **SIGNIFICANT**

By evaluating situations based on outward appearances, you can expect to misunderstand the situations as they actually are.

1st   **9**   ▬▬▬▬▬   **INSTINCT**   **CONSTRAINT**

Your abilities and virtues are adequate for your advancement. You can abandon elegant appointments and still expect to continue favorably.

DESCRIPTION

The Silence, Mountain, ABOVE, covers the Brilliance, Fire, BELOW. The Brilliance shines around the base of the Mountain, making it more beautiful, but what is within cannot be seen and there is no true indication of the favorableness—or unfavorableness—which lies inside. Of the two Ruling Lines, 2nd and 6th, the 2nd carries a warning against following outward beauty without the presence of inner virtue, while the 6th follows its own inner virtue without any regard to outward beauty. The Subject of the Hexagram, 1st Line, is seen as abandoning outward beauty, or vanity, to "walk" on the path of inner virtue.

23

ABOVE: KEN
MOUNTAIN
Stillness
Silence

BELOW: K'UN
EARTH
Natural
Receptive

PO

DETERIORATION AND BREAKING APART
AS THE INFERIOR BECOMES DOMINANT.

PO is depicted as the Deterioration and Breaking Apart of natural and man-made objects, with obvious danger in Movement (Travel) at this time.

PO is a Time of Enduring Deterioration and Breaking Apart, characterized by no advantage in any movement. Now is a time to develop character while this disorder runs its course. There is no implication to shirk responsibilities, but rather the wisdom of knowing when your energy, in spite of your desires, cannot be usefully applied. The Hexagram itself shows a splitting apart, from the bottom up, and is held together by only the top.

PROPHESIES

LUCK is very poor now, and WISHES will not come true. LOVE does not succeed as each person goes their separate way without regard for the other. MARRIAGES are in eminent danger of ruin, but there is some small hope of salvation if the difficulties can now be endured. CHILDREN are not likely, but when present, expect difficulties in life, and possibly shortened lives. If PREGNANT, expect a girl and take precaution against a miscarriage.

SICKNESS is severe, with little hope of recovery. Physical damage to the body is seen as burns, beatings, broken bones, etc. Abdominal ailments, such as peritonitis, can be expected.

MISSING PEOPLE are very likely near death or dead, and no location can reasonably be determined, underscoring the difficulty in finding them. MISSING THINGS, destroyed or broken, should be forgotten and replaced with new items later. MOVING should not even be considered now as any attempts bring disaster.

LOANS may be granted for reconstruction later, are but hopeless now. JOBS are not available now, and don't attempt to relocate for employment. BUSINESS Ventures may be salvaged in receivership, but plan on their collapse. The MARKET could wipe you out. Place your assets in highly liquid investments such as gold or silver.

CHANGING LINES

6th   **9**   ▬▬▬▬   **WISDOM**   **CONSTRAINT**

The evil has destroyed itself and collapsed. Only good works remain in setting right the conditions. Support comes as you lead this return from devastation.

5th   **6**   ▬▬ ▬▬   **AUTHORITY**   **SIGNIFICANT**

The inferior is voluntarily seeking reform and guidance from beyond their ranks. You have a favorable opportunity to restore order and secure advantage. Carefully observe the circumstances.

4th   **6**   ▬▬ ▬▬   **SOCIAL**   **VARIANT**

The inferior has inflicted disaster to the full extent it is capable. You cannot prevent calamity now. Work on plans for rebuilding.

3rd   **6**   ▬▬ ▬▬   **INDIVIDUAL**   **VARIANT**

You have an opportunity to break with the inferior. Do so silently. You will be opposed, but in the end you will experience no mistake or blame.

2nd   **6**   ▬▬ ▬▬   **ASPIRATIONS**   **SIGNIFICANT**

The inferior has seized power. Expect severe, even bodily, attack and loss of allies. Any action on your part now degenerates misfortune into disaster.

1st   **6**   ▬▬ ▬▬   **INSTINCT**   **CONSTRAINT**

The inferior has begun to rise. You can expect attack by slander and stealth. Wait it out. The opposition is too powerful, and counter-attack will bring misfortune.

DESCRIPTION

The Stillness, Mountain, ABOVE, has settled over the Receptive, Earth, BELOW. Stillness is Received and forward movement ceases. Deterioration and Breaking Apart are prevalent. The lesser, or inferior, influences are dominant and driving out the only remaining superior influence. The single Ruling Line, 6th, is the remaining strong element in this Splitting Apart. As this Line departs, the collapse occurs. The Subject of the Hexagram, 5th Line, does show the weak striving for, and succeeding in, improvement.

24

ABOVE: K'UN
EARTH
Natural
Receptive

BELOW: CHEN
THUNDER
Movement
Arousing

復

FU

NATURAL RETURN FROM ERROR AND
CORRECTION OF FAULTS BRINGS ADVANTAGE.

FU is depicted as a welcome return of newness, or youth, from times of disorder.

FU is a Time of Natural Return from Error and Correction of Faults, characterized by newness and advantage in movement in any direction. As with anything new, nurturing and rest must be allowed so strength can develop. The return is natural, without force, and must be made with sincerity. This Return comes after a long period of disorder.

PROPHESIES

LUCK is neither good nor bad, and WISHES, when held for awhile, come true. LOVE is succeeding, but its effects are as yet unseen. Don't rush, be sincere and honest. MARRIAGES indicate that reconciliation or remarriage has a strong chance of success. Mostly male CHILDREN will properly develop when devoted concern is given in their youth. If PREGNANT, expect a boy.

SICKNESS, not too severe, improves with proper rest and convalesence, and relates to the abdominal area. Crutches, splints, broken legs, and foot problems are also seen.

MISSING PEOPLE, South to West, return unexpectly or are found with unexpected ease. MISSING THINGS are found easily. Even broken things can be repaired. MOVING will be favorable now.

LOANS are granted, but not immediately. BUSINESS Ventures, when new, are very risky. Existing ventures offer great chances for success, but must not be rushed. JOBS are abundant, but don't rush—take time to choose the right one. The MARKET will be rising; a good time to buy.

CHANGING LINES

6th   **6**   ▬▬ ▬▬   **WISDOM**   **CONSTRAINT**

Perpetuating your faults brings defeat from within and failure in your works. Without correction, expect severe and enduring hardships—with correction, a new sense of freedom.

5th   **6**   ▬▬ ▬▬   **AUTHORITY**   **SIGNIFICANT**

Self-examination and confession may be required to correct faults. Such honesty will free you from blame or guilt.

4th   **6**   ▬▬ ▬▬   **SOCIAL**   **VARIANT**

Correcting faults may take you away from the company you are with, and likewise remove you from peril.

3rd   **6**   ▬▬ ▬▬   **INDIVIDUAL**   **VARIANT**

In correcting faults wavering decisions will place you in peril. Resolute decisions prevent uncertainty, freeing you from guilt.

2nd   **6**   ▬▬ ▬▬   **ASPIRATIONS**   **SIGNIFICANT**

Correcting faults, particularly one's own, requires self-discipline. Set aside your pride and quietly correct faults. Expect good fortune.

1st   **9**   ▬▬▬▬   **INSTINCT**   **CONSTRAINT**

Correcting faulty or harmful plans, before they are implemented or go too far, will keep you free of guilt. Expect great good fortune.

DESCRIPTION

The Movement, Thunder, BELOW, within the Receptive, Earth, ABOVE, is seen as a force not yet powerful enough to reach its heavenly position. Although it is a return of the new, it still requires rest and nurturing to attain great power. The single Ruling Line, 1st, is a powerful new rising force and is also the Subject of the Hexagram. Here a Natural Return without force or coercion is represented, and development begins anew. Also shown is the addition of light, or lengthening of days, after the winter solstice.

25

ABOVE: CH'IEN
HEAVEN
Creative
Firmness

BELOW: CHEN
THUNDER
Movement
Arousing

无妄

WU
WANG

THE UNEXPECTED APPEARS EVEN WITH
HONEST AND SINCERE EFFORTS.

WU WANG is depicted as Honest and Sincere effort associated with natural toil. The "Unexpected" relates to the 3rd line, as the theft of a cow or ox unexpectedly occurs.

WU WANG is a Time of Natural Order with Honest and Sincere effort, characterized by Progress when not spoiled by the Unexpected. When circumstances are in order Progress is expected, even though Unexpected misfortune can appear. Unlike the expected Spring thunderstorms, there now appears the Unexpected thunderstorm of late summer, with its ability to damage the coming harvest.

PROPHESIES

LUCK is favorable, and WISHES come true—but both carry some unexpected misfortune. LOVE is successful with sincerity and patience, but don't come on too strong. MARRIAGES, mostly happy, can be upset by unexpected gossip. Difficulties could be improved with a short separation. Mostly male CHILDREN, seemingly old for their ages, still require discipline. If PREGNANT, expect a boy.

SICKNESS tends to drag on with unexpected relapses. Worry and improper care worsen conditions. Head or brain related problems can be expected—but the unexpected, such as appendicitis, is highly likely.

MISSING PEOPLE, in Easterly directions, are difficult to find, but will suddenly surprise you. MISSING THINGS, up high, will unexpectedly reappear—be patient. MOVING is favorable when not forced or rushed.

LOANS will be granted. Make sure you can pay them off. BUSINESS Ventures are generally favorable, but avoid excessive ambitions. JOBS are offered, but so are sudden terminations. The MARKET is fairly steady, consider holding, even though selling is slightly favored now.

CHANGING LINES

6th   **9**   ▬▬▬▬   **WISDOM**   **CONSTRAINT**

Any action now, no matter how honest or sincere, produces calamity. Wait out this time; greater times are near at hand.

5th   **9**   ▬▬▬▬   **AUTHORITY**   **SIGNIFICANT**

Unexpected misfortune has come upon you through no fault of your own. Remain sincere without worry. The circumstances readjust, and this time passes naturally.

4th   **9**   ▬▬▬▬   **SOCIAL**   **VARIANT**

Continuing with honest and sincere efforts brings you to your goals without mistake. Don't, however, proceed without caution. Unexpected misfortune can ruin your gains.

3rd   **6**   ▬▬ ▬▬   **INDIVIDUAL**   **VARIANT**

Honest and sincere efforts unexpectly meet with calamity. Your loss is another's gain. You can also expect to be falsely accused.

2nd   **6**   ▬▬ ▬▬   **ASPIRATIONS**   **SIGNIFICANT**

Taking care of tasks at the proper time, without regard to future reward, brings you advantage.

1st   **9**   ▬▬▬▬   **INSTINCT**   **CONSTRAINT**

Your actions are recognized as honest and sincere—expect good fortune.

DESCRIPTION

The Thunder, Movement, BELOW, rolls through the Heaven, Creative Power, ABOVE. This is a natural order as the thunder obeys the heavenly law. Honesty and Sincerity proceed from this natural order. Both Ruling Lines, 1st and 5th, are powerful elements. The Subject of the Hexagram, 4th Line, is positioned at the base of Creative Power. The Movement through Heaven suddenly and Unexpectedly appears as audible Thunder and visible lightning, then moves on to another place. For centuries this Hexagram has confused scholars, and the Chinese characters have been interpreted both as Sincerity and the Unexpected.

26

ABOVE: KEN
MOUNTAIN
Stillness
Silence

BELOW: CH'IEN
HEAVEN
Creative
Firmness

大畜

TA
CH'U

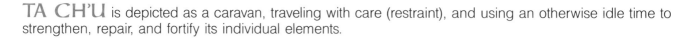

GREAT RESTRAINT PROVIDES GREAT SAVING,
ACCUMULATING STRENGTH AND WEALTH.

TA CH'U is depicted as a caravan, traveling with care (restraint), and using an otherwise idle time to strengthen, repair, and fortify its individual elements.

TA CH'U is a Time of Great Restraint and Accumulation of Strength and Wealth, characterized by Good Fortune and the Undertaking of Great Tasks. Strengthening occurs at a time of restriction, and can include minor repairs, preventative maintenance, or just allowing interest to accrue in banks.

PROPHESIES

LUCK is poor now, but will be improving, and WISHES come true only when you work at them. LOVE is not very good now but can work out. MARRIAGES have some deep seated problems needing attention if the marriages are to survive. CHILDREN, mostly male, are troublesome to parents, but are industrious and finally succeed. If PREGNANT, expect a boy.

SICKNESS will be improving, and is related to fatigue, such as with lumbago, backache, hemorrhoids, or constipation. Fatigue may also cause accidents and broken bones while working.

MISSING PEOPLE, in Northerly directions, have involved themselves in other endeavors. While not hiding, they are still difficult to find. MISSING THINGS are close and underneath something large. MOVING is favorable, but take care along the way to insure that everything is in proper or working order before leaving.

LOANS are not needed now, but will be granted if requested. BUSINESS Ventures face difficulty. Success is most likely when traveling for business reasons, such as in sales. JOBS take time, but good positions are offered. The MARKET is steady—hold investments or keep money in banks. An upward trend is indicated later.

CHANGING LINES

6th   9   ▬▬▬▬   WISDOM   CONSTRAINT

The restraint and oppression are over. Your accumulated strength or wealth can now be used to progress. Good fortune will be enhanced by strengthening character and nurturing virtue.

5th   6   ▬▬   ▬▬   AUTHORITY   SIGNIFICANT

Your precautions against significant difficulties preclude the difficulties from impeding your progress. Expect good fortune with unexpected blessings.

4th   6   ▬▬   ▬▬   SOCIAL   VARIANT

Your foresight in preventing problems in the beginning (before they arise) provides great good fortune.

3rd   9   ▬▬▬▬   INDIVIDUAL   VARIANT

Your advancement comes through hard work and the cooperation of circumstances, or other people, all pulling in the same direction. Plan ahead with contingencies for meeting with obstacles.

2nd   9   ▬▬▬▬   ASPIRATIONS   SIGNIFICANT

Your progress is being impeded by a force you have no control over. Stopping now will bring no criticism, but proceeding invites disaster.

1st   9   ▬▬▬▬   INSTINCT   CONSTRAINT

Many obstacles put your advance in danger. Self-restraint, as halting or desisting, frees you from this peril.

DESCRIPTION

The Creative Power, Heaven, BELOW, is restrained by the Stillness, Mountain, ABOVE. This Great Restraint, or restraint of the great, allows Accumulation of Power and Wealth, as the spending of these attributes is naturally restricted. Both Ruling Lines, 5th and 6th, represent authority and wisdom providing Restraint. The Subject of the Hexagram, 2nd line, is in the midst of the Accumulating Greatness. Great Restraint is also shown as the weak 4th and 5th Lines restricting the remaining powerful Lines.

27

ABOVE: KEN
MOUNTAIN
Stillness
Silence

BELOW: CHEN
THUNDER
Movement
Arousing

頤

I

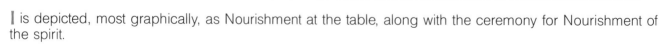

INVIGORATE AND CULTIVATE THE GROWING
AS DOES THE MOUTH PROVIDE NOURISHMENT.

I is depicted, most graphically, as Nourishment at the table, along with the ceremony for Nourishment of the spirit.

is a Time for Invigorating and Cultivating Growth by Nourishing virtue and spirit, as well as the body. It is characterized by Good Fortune, particularly when temperance and frugality are employed along with Nourishment. One is also called to view, as an example, the behavior of others who possess these virtues, but warnings against jealousy and envy are also issued.

PROPHESIES

LUCK is poor, becoming worse when boasting, and WISHES come true gradually with continued effort in making them happen. LOVE may be upset by a deceitful or boastful partner. MARRIAGES have some discord now, but harmony can be restored by refusing to argue and, instead, seeking the truth. CHILDREN, of both sexes tend to be quiet with marginal health, and shouldn't be pampered. If PREGNANT, expect a boy.

SICKNESS can become very grave, and relates to the stomach, liver, or intestines. The cause is seen as coming through the mouth; pay careful attention to your diet, treat ailments as soon as they appear.

MISSING PEOPLE, in Easterly directions, are probably very ill, and can be found by searching. MISSING THINGS have been enclosed within something else, but are not hard to find. MOVING should be delayed for now.

LOANS will be granted later, but not now. BUSINESS Ventures have been damaged by a competitor's slander or libel. A good public relations program can turn the tide. JOBS can be found, but should be considered temporary as a better opportunity comes later. The MARKET is indicating a good time to buy and hold.

CHANGING LINES

6th   **9**   ▬▬▬▬   **WISDOM**   **CONSTRAINT**

Assuming responsibility for the cultivation of others is grave and hazardous, but you now have the ability for great undertakings and can expect good fortune.

5th   **6**   ▬▬ ▬▬   **AUTHORITY**   **SIGNIFICANT**

Being conscious of your deficiencies and seeking help from superior forces allows you progress and good fortune. But your position is still too weak for great undertakings.

4th   **6**   ▬▬ ▬▬   **SOCIAL**   **VARIANT**

Remaining alert and responding to the needs of others brings no blame and further cultivates your own growth—expect good fortune.

3rd   **6**   ▬▬ ▬▬   **INDIVIDUAL**   **VARIANT**

A poor association, which you believed to be correct, is now bringing you misfortune. This uncultivated influence, or neglect, will burden any action you take for a long time to come.

2nd   **6**   ▬▬ ▬▬   **ASPIRATIONS**   **SIGNIFICANT**

Your position is weak, and continuing to seek help from sources incorrect for your interests brings misfortune.

1st   **9**   ▬▬▬▬   **INSTINCT**   **CONSTRAINT**

Even though your needs are fulfilled you find yourself envious or jealous of others. This lack of personal self-esteem will bring you criticism and misfortune.

DESCRIPTION

The Movement, Thunder, BELOW, is at the base of Stillness, the Mountain, ABOVE. Here can be seen the Arousing energy to Invigorate and Cultivate Growth. More significantly this Hexagram resembles and is represented as an "Open Mouth." Thus Nourishment is implied, particularly for Growth in character as well as life forms. Both Ruling Lines, 5th and 6th, are in "high places" or with high ideals. The Subject of the Hexagram, 4th Line, at the base of Stillness, provides advice of temperance in speech, eating, drinking, and behavior in general.

28

ABOVE: TUI
LAKE, MARSH
Joyous
Cheerful

BELOW: SUN
WIND, WOOD
Gentle
Penetrating

大過

TA
KUO

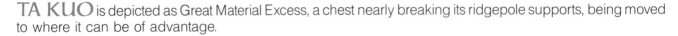

GREAT BEHAVIOR OR MATERIAL EXCESSES PREDOMINATE, EXPECT UNUSUAL CHANGE.

TA KUO is depicted as Great Material Excess, a chest nearly breaking its ridgepole supports, being moved to where it can be of advantage.

TA KUO is a Time of Excesses requiring change, such as use or distribution, characterized by acting with Excessively Great and Unusual Behavior in producing Success. The Great and Unusual Behavior here serves to preserve or promote Success. For example: a king turns over reign of his kingdom to an able minister, where usually the regal heir would be his son. This Hexagram also contains the warning that unused excesses may produce collapse.

PROPHESIES

LUCK is unfavorable, and WISHES are too ambitious to be achieved. LOVE will not be working out well. MARRIAGES can be troubled, and divorce threatens if the relationship becomes too routine. Mostly male CHILDREN need to be well disciplined, or else they end up in trouble. If PREGNANT, expect a boy.

SICKNESS tends to become severe, and swelling is indicated. Spinal or lung problems dominate, but dietary problems relating to excesses are also warned against.

MISSING PEOPLE, South to East, are ill and need help, but are difficult to find. MISSING THINGS have been moved or carried away, and may never be seen again. MOVING should be undertaken only when absolutely necessary.

LOANS will not be granted. BUSINESS Ventures face difficulties as inventories build and sales are neglected. Inflation is also indicated. JOBS in unskilled trades are available, but skilled jobs are rare. The MARKET indicates a definite time to sell.

CHANGING LINES

6th   **6**   ▬▬ ▬▬   **WISDOM**   **CONSTRAINT**

Your bold advance in attempting to resolve hardships, without the necessary strength, has brought misfortune. But you will not be criticized for having tried.

5th   **9**   ▬▬▬▬   **AUTHORITY**   **SIGNIFICANT**

You have entered into an unusual situation, offering nothing but the possibility of humiliation. Expect no progress and yield authority to those more capable than yourself.

4th   **9**   ▬▬▬▬   **SOCIAL**   **VARIANT**

You are faced with important responsibilities and decisions. Do your best and seek help, if necessary. But in securing good fortune avoid help from selfish or self-serving interests.

3rd   **9**   ▬▬▬▬   **INDIVIDUAL**   **VARIANT**

Your stubbornness is driving away the support you had counted on, leaving you weakened. Expect misfortune.

2nd   **9**   ▬▬▬▬   **ASPIRATIONS**   **SIGNIFICANT**

You have entered into an unusual association, bringing new and fresh ideas and restoring lost hopes. Expect progress and advantage in every way.

1st   **6**   ▬▬ ▬▬   **INSTINCT**   **CONSTRAINT**

You are carrying more responsibility and tasks than you are capable of handling. Careful delegation to others will allow all to advance without mistake.

DESCRIPTION

The Pleasant, Lake, ABOVE, spills over the Gentleness, Wood, BELOW. This typifies the Predominance, or Preponderance, of Great Excesses as Pleasant Lake waters rise on the banks and cover the Woods and Trees. This condition of overflow has resulted from storing, then adding even more, without consuming. The Hexagram itself acutely portrays the excesses as four strong lines, held up by two weaker ends. Both Ruling Lines, 2nd and 4th, indicate that a transition, expressly by movement, will be or is occurring. The Subject of the Hexagram, 4th line, is seen as shoring up the Excess, preventing its collapse.

29

ABOVE: K'AN
WATER, RAIN
Danger
Abysmal

BELOW: K'AN
WATER, RAIN
Danger
Abysmal

坎

K'AN

PERSISTENCE SUCCESSFULLY OVERCOMES
DIFFICULTIES AND HARDSHIPS.

K'AN is depicted as a Persistent individual, setting out to overcome Difficulty and Hardship with Danger all about.

K'AN is a Time of Difficulty and Hardship where journeys through life are bound by Danger and Peril, characterized by Successfully overcoming Difficulty and Hardship with Persistently high ideals and working toward the benefit of all things. This beneficial contribution includes teaching of others, as well as increasing your own knowledge. The Chinese character symbolizes a bank or ridge, indicating a Perilous place which leads further downwards.

PROPHESIES

LUCK is truly self-made now, and WISHES only come true when you diligently work at them. LOVE is troubled as the partners are too deceptive. MARRIAGES are in certain danger of failure, and require great compromise by both parties for any chance of success. CHILDREN, mostly male, have difficulties all through life and can be best prepared with substantial education. If PREGNANT, expect a boy.

SICKNESS tends to be severe and dangerous, with liver, kidney, and urinary tract ailments. Beware of alcohol abuse.

MISSING PEOPLE, in the north, have probably been kidnapped, pressed into hiding and submission, and may be impossible to find. MISSING THINGS have been stolen and recovery is unlikely. MOVING should not be considered now.

LOANS, probably not to be granted now, may end in default. BUSINESS Ventures are being seriously jeopardized internally, such as with embezzlement, employee theft, or neglect. JOBS are hopeless now—wait until a later time. The MARKET is erratic—a good time to stay out and rest at home.

CHANGING LINES

6th   6   � merchant   **WISDOM**   **CONSTRAINT**

You are now at the mercy of the difficulties and hardships surrounding you. Expect them to place severe restraints upon you for a considerable time to come.

5th   9   ▬▬▬▬   **AUTHORITY**   **SIGNIFICANT**

Concentrate on overcoming the difficulties and hardships one at a time. Such effort at this time will save you from error, but don't bother yourself with new endeavors.

4th   6   ▬▬ ▬▬   **SOCIAL**   **VARIANT**

You are able to work on solutions to the hardships with a strong ally. Honest exchange of the nature of the difficulties will lead you away from error.

3rd   6   ▬▬ ▬▬   **INDIVIDUAL**   **VARIANT**

The peril is equally great, whether you advance or withdraw. Attempts to overcome difficulties are now met with failure—better to wait until circumstances improve.

2nd   9   ▬▬▬▬   **ASPIRATIONS**   **SIGNIFICANT**

Hardships must be endured. Small endeavors will bring you small success, but no sweeping reform of the situation.

1st   6   ▬▬ ▬▬   **INSTINCT**   **CONSTRAINT**

Callous disregard for the peril of your situation serves only to bring misfortune from any action.

DESCRIPTION

The Danger, Water, BELOW, is reinforced by Danger, Water, ABOVE. In this Hexagram, Water travels downward in the presence of Danger. The Hexagram consequently represents the Deep, Depths, Abysmal, or Pit. Also, like Water, this travel terminates at a calm, peaceful place benefiting all things. Both Ruling Lines, 2nd and 5th, are strong influences, but only the 5th is in a position of easy deliverance from the peril. The Subject of the Hexagram, 6th Line, is in peril of being overtaken by its own misdeeds, but by clinging to reform, it can eventually ascend out of the Pit, or Hardship.

30

ABOVE: LI
FIRE, SUN
Brilliance
Clarity

BELOW: LI
FIRE, SUN
Brilliance
Clarity

LI

CLINGING TO SINCERITY AND HONESTY
BRINGS ASCENT AND ENLIGHTENMENT.

LI is depicted as the Brilliance of the Sun, illuminating and enlightening, as the affairs of mankind increase in importance.

LI is a Time of Clinging and perpetuating the Brilliance of individual character and striving to Enlighten mankind, characterized with Success when one persists with this goal and Good Fortune follows when one finds inner peace. As Fire Clings and Rises so does Sincerity and Honesty. Darkness, shadows, and ignorance are cleared away with this particular brilliance.

PROPHESIES

LUCK is favorable when not abused, and WISHES, even ambitious wishes, come true. LOVE succeeds when time is taken to dispel mistrust and suspicion. MARRIAGES are harmonious and will endure. Many female CHILDREN are seen, highly intelligent and active, although sometimes too shrewd. If PREGNANT, expect a girl.

SICKNESS will be severe and prolonged, but recuperation is seen. Ailments relate to the heart and blood system. Fevers, contagious maladies, and diminished sight are also indicated.

MISSING PEOPLE, in the South, are easily found and have been influenced to stay away. MISSING THINGS don't turn up right away, so use something else. Paper and wood may be lost forever. Thieves confess, and stolen things are returned. MOVING is favorable when not rushed and carefully planned.

LOANS are granted, but require considerable patience. BUSINESS Ventures improve when plans are made for the future, but profits are low now. JOBS can be found, and relatives, particularly parents, help. Make sure your application is correct. The MARKET is favorable and rising. Holding and buying are recommended.

CHANGING LINES

6th 9 ——— WISDOM CONSTRAINT

You must now destroy evil with strong action to restore order. You must also use care to spare the innocent from punishment to prevent chaos.

5th 6 — — AUTHORITY SIGNIFICANT

Strong influences are filling you with anxiety and apprehension. If you can adjust with a gentle and yielding attitude, you can expect good fortune.

4th 9 ——— SOCIAL VARIANT

Sudden and reckless activity rapidly consumes itself. Your efforts will not be regarded as beneficial or long lasting.

3rd 9 ——— INDIVIDUAL VARIANT

Endeavors have come to an end. Seek the joy and contentment of your achievements. Melancholiness over mistakes will only bring you misfortune.

2nd 6 — — ASPIRATIONS SIGNIFICANT

You have been surrounded with rare harmony and opportunity. Remain free of arrogance and inwardly confident and seize this opportunity which provides great good fortune.

1st 9 ——— INSTINCT CONSTRAINT

A confused beginning is indicated. Proceeding with careful consideration and detailed plans will keep you free from error.

DESCRIPTION

The Brilliance, Fire, BELOW, is doubly Brilliant from the Brilliance, Fire, ABOVE. Fire Ascends and the Brilliance is made more Brilliant—all the darkness is Enlightened. This Enlightenment is portrayed as Honesty and Sincerity. Both Ruling Lines, 2nd and 5th, are weak lines to be influenced—as if Clinging to the power on either side. The Subject of the Hexagram, 4th Line, marks a period of Enlightened transistion. This Hexagram is also the transistion from Earthly and Heavenly importance (Section I of the I CHING) to emphasis on the affairs of Humanity (Section II of the I CHING).

31

ABOVE: TUI
LAKE, MARSH
Joyous
Cheerful

BELOW: KEN
MOUNTAIN
Stillness
Silence

咸

HSIEN

NATURAL INFLUENCE WITHOUT DESIGNS OR SCHEMES FORMS SINCERE RELATIONSHIPS.

HSIEN is depicted as the wooing and mutual attraction of young lovers—here on the pleasant mountain lake.

HSIEN is a Time when Natural Influences prevail in Forming Relationships without Designs or Schemes, characterized by Success and Contentment. The Chinese character used for HSIEN is translated as "all" or "together," but is a modification of KAN or "feeling," where the heart has been taken out and given without ulterior motive.

PROPHESIES

LUCK is favorable, and WISHES come true when motives are free of guile. LOVE succeeds when courtship and sex are not rushed. MARRIAGES become harmonious as they mature. CHILDREN of both sexes are seen as pleasant and peaceful, living happy lives. If pregnant, expect a girl.

SICKNESS endures, but does not cause much pain or discomfort, and relates to the mouth, lungs, or chest, and is seen as contagious. Sexual problems or maladies of the sexual organs, such as V.D., are also highly likely. Proper care brings recuperation.

MISSING PEOPLE, probably in the West, but possibly in the North, can be found easily and in the company of another. MISSING THINGS can be found in something else and probably wet. MOVING, when slowly and carefully done, is favorable.

LOANS, in small amounts, are granted. BUSINESS Ventures are reasonably successful and new projects or products can be undertaken. JOBS are available, but resumes and interviews must be convincing. The MARKET is steadily improving—a good time to invest.

CHANGING LINES

6th   6   ▬▬ ▬▬   WISDOM   CONSTRAINT

Chatter and gossip suggest insincerity. Your influence is now minimal or ineffective. To endure slander quietly set out and complete your own tasks.

5th   9   ▬▬▬▬▬   AUTHORITY   SIGNIFICANT

Your convictions are sincere, but your goals are trivial—your influence is ineffective. Expect no advance, but you also remain free of any regret.

4th   9   ▬▬▬▬▬   SOCIAL   VARIANT

Remaining uncertain or unsettled restricts any influence you can now apply. Changing to a decisive and consistent demeanor will free you of regret and lead to good fortune.

3rd   9   ▬▬▬▬▬   INDIVIDUAL   VARIANT

Remaining under the influence of others will bring you regret and humiliation. Return to actions based upon your own natural instincts.

2nd   6   ▬▬ ▬▬   ASPIRATIONS   SIGNIFICANT

Overly anxious efforts to influence a situation will bring you trouble. Wait. Capable help will arrive and the situation will turn favorable.

1st   6   ▬▬ ▬▬   INSTINCT   CONSTRAINT

Influences you now apply are ineffective. Your intentions may be sincere, but the situation is more complex than you are aware of, so wait and observe.

DESCRIPTION

The Joyous, Lake, ABOVE, rests upon the Stillness, Mountain, BELOW. This natural and peaceful combination relates Influence and Sincerity. The Natural Relationship represented is a young lady and young man in courtship. The two Ruling Lines, 4th and 5th, represent different perspectives. The 4th Line signifies the Sincerity within the heart, and the 5th Line, the strength of the back or shoulders. The Subject of the Hexagram, 3rd Line, is at the height of Stillness and Peace, but can be adversely influenced by the weak, below. Section II of the I CHING begins here, and themes now concentrate on human affairs.

32

ABOVE: CHEN
THUNDER
Movement
Arousing

BELOW: SUN
WIND, WOOD
Gentle
Penetrating

恆

HENG

CONTINUED CONSIDERATION AND SINCERITY PRESERVES NATURAL RELATIONSHIPS.

HENG is depicted as a mature marital relationship, with the husband and wife diligently resolving issues together.

HENG is a Time for Continuing Consideration and Sincerity to Preserve Natural Relationships, characterized by consistent Progress and Success. Futher advantage is found in moving toward goals as a particular team. This Relationship brings no regret, and is seen as a mature marriage where each partner can adapt to and support the needs of the other.

PROPHESIES

LUCK is very favorable, and WISHES come true in a natural manner. LOVE is especially harmonious. MARRIAGES meet with continued success and are even admired by others. CHILDREN of both sexes are peaceful, with unusual learning abilities. If PREGNANT, expect a boy.

SICKNESS regresses, but is long lasting and relates to the liver. Problems with speech, legs, or feet are suggested, as is multiple sclerosis.

MISSING PEOPLE, in Easterly directions, are moving around a lot and are difficult to find. MISSING THINGS are in some forgotten place, but will reappear eventually. MOVING is not as favorable as maintaining residence and sinking "roots" into the original community.

LOANS are granted easily. BUSINESS Ventures are successful when tried and true methods or endeavors are pursued. The untried should be avoided. JOBS are available, particularly in technical trades. The MARKET will be declining—consider selling.

CHANGING LINES

6th   **6**   ▬▬ ▬▬   **WISDOM**   **CONSTRAINT**

Continued inconsistent efforts filled with anxious energy portrays you as unreliable. Expect relationships to fail with disastrous consequences.

5th   **6**   ▬▬ ▬▬   **AUTHORITY**   **SIGNIFICANT**

Consideration and consistency must also adapt to changing circumstances to preserve relationships. This ability to change and adapt brings good fortune.

4th   **9**   ▬▬▬▬   **SOCIAL**   **VARIANT**

Continuing to pursue relationships which are unnatural for you will bring you nothing.

3rd   **9**   ▬▬▬▬   **INDIVIDUAL**   **VARIANT**

Inconsistent and uncertain efforts raise conflict instead of enduring relationships. No matter how sincere your intent, expect disgrace and humiliation.

2nd   **9**   ▬▬▬▬   **ASPIRATIONS**   **SIGNIFICANT**

With sincerity and consideration you can provide the basis for enduring relationships. Expect remorse to disappear.

1st   **6**   ▬▬ ▬▬   **INSTINCT**   **CONSTRAINT**

Your haste or forceful persuasion in attempting to establish enduring relationships, or results, brings no advantage, and you can expect misfortune.

DESCRIPTION

The Movement, Thunder, ABOVE, is tempered by the Penetrating Gentleness, Wind, BELOW. Both Trigrams also reinforce the constancy associated with wood. The Enduring and Natural Relationship portrayed in this Hexagram is the successful and long lasting marriage. The single Ruling Line, 2nd, represents determination in reaching goals or aspirations, and the willingness to adapt and show consideration. The Subject of the Hexagram, 3rd Line, is at a confused place where the Gentle and Arousing Influences meet.

33

ABOVE: CH'IEN
HEAVEN
Creative
Firmness

BELOW: KEN
MOUNTAIN
Stillness
Silence

TUN

STRENGTH YIELDS AND WITHDRAWS
AS APPROPRIATE TO THE CIRCUMSTANCES.

TUN is depicted as a sage withdrawn from the lesser influences and improving inner character for future service.

TUN is a Time of Yielding to lesser forces and Withdrawing, or retreating, into secure and possibly isolated positions, characterized by Progress and Advantage in small matters. The Withdrawal is neither from fear nor hatred of the lesser elements, but rather a recognition of their inevitable existence. Lesser principles are now on the rise and forceful action is not effective.

PROPHESIES

LUCK is not particularly good now, and WISHES must be held a long time if they are to be realized. LOVE is being troubled by jealous outside parties. MARRIAGES fall out of harmony, possibly from in-laws moving in. CHILDREN, mostly male, will tend to be disobedient and sickly. If PREGNANT, expect a boy, with difficulties in delivery or a miscarriage.

SICKNESS improves later and relates to chronic ailments affecting major portions of the body. Bone marrow diseases are seen, along with fatigue and loss of energy.

MISSING PEOPLE, in Northerly directions, are withdrawing further—becoming more difficult to find. MISSING THINGS are lost in some large place. MOVING should not be undertaken now.

LOANS will not be granted now. BUSINESS Ventures are troubled with problems relating to employee relations. JOBS will be available later, but are scarce now. The MARKET will be rising later, but will drop first.

CHANGING LINES

6th   **9**   ▬▬▬▬▬   **WISDOM**   **CONSTRAINT**

Your complete withdrawal from troublesome situations brings advantage in every way. Great strength and vigor are indicated.

5th   **9**   ▬▬▬▬▬   **AUTHORITY**   **SIGNIFICANT**

Your withdrawal from troublesome situations is tactfully done and admirable. Friendships and associations are preserved—expect good fortune.

4th   **9**   ▬▬▬▬▬   **SOCIAL**   **VARIANT**

Your withdrawal from troublesome situations can be made without restraint—expect good fortune. Choosing to remain within the troublesome situation, however, brings misfortune.

3rd   **9**   ▬▬▬▬▬   **INDIVIDUAL**   **VARIANT**

Your withdrawal from a troublesome situation is being restrained by your overly-close association with it. Small success can be attained by tactfully avoiding the sources of trouble.

2nd   **6**   ▬▬ ▬▬   **ASPIRATIONS**   **SIGNIFICANT**

Remain firm to your purpose. No advantage will be gained by withdrawing now, as your committment is too deep. Retain any strong support you can find to resolve arising difficulties.

1st   **6**   ▬▬ ▬▬   **INSTINCT**   **CONSTRAINT**

Immediately cease and withdraw your opposition to growing troublesome sources. Your ideals are correct, but you lack the strength for effective opposition. Continuing your opposition brings misfortune.

DESCRIPTION

The Stillness, Mountain, BELOW, is ascending into the Creative Power, Heaven, ABOVE. The strength is being stilled by a natural force. The Hexagram itself shows the 4 strong Lines at the top yielding to 2 weak Lines at the bottom. This is in accord with natural order as summer passes and July yields to August. The Ruling Line, 5th, is strong and authoritative. The Subject of the Hexagram, 2nd Line, portrays the weak becoming (but not yet) dominant and circumstances change. Specific adjustments to the changing circumstances are required.

ABOVE: CHEN
THUNDER
Movement
Arousing

BELOW: CH'IEN
HEAVEN
Creative
Firmness

大壯

TA
CHUAN

GREAT STRENGTH AND POWER INCREASE
BUT CANNOT BE ABUSED OR USED AS FORCE.

TA CHUAN is depicted as a person of great strength with the capacity for either productive good or destructive harm.

TA CHUAN is a Time of the Great becoming stronger, characterized by correct conduct with this power bringing Advantage. As the power is great, so are the warnings against abusive use of power, or using this power as a force against harmony or natural order. The choice of how this power is applied determines Good or Poor Fortune.

PROPHESIES

LUCK can be favorable, and WISHES come true if not forced. LOVE succeeds when consideration towards each other is shown. MARRIAGES remain harmonious when partners consider the pursuits and goals of the other. Mostly stubborn male CHILDREN, requiring discipline, are indicated. If PREGNANT, expect a boy, but not an easy delivery.

SICKNESS relating to the head or lungs such as pneumonia, will be extended by carelessness. Get a good doctor and ignore "magazine remedies."

MISSING PEOPLE, North to West, are far away, hard to find, and stubbornly refuse to return. MISSING THINGS have fallen down into something, possibly seen but unable to be retrieved. MOVING goes well when not too much is attempted.

LOANS will be granted. BUSINESS Ventures are generally favorable, but some projects are stubbornly slowing progress, requiring care or conservation. JOBS are favorable, but require harmonious effort with others. The MARKET looks favorable, but be careful, it is not as good as it looks.

CHANGING LINES

6th   **6**   ▬▬ ▬▬   **WISDOM**   **CONSTRAINT**

Wisely realizing when a situation cannot be overcome by force relieves you of embarassment. Ultimately expect good fortune and easy progress.

5th   **6**   ▬▬ ▬▬   **AUTHORITY**   **SIGNIFICANT**

Circumstances require no stubbornness on your part. Cooperation brings advance without regret.

4th   **9**   ▬▬▬▬   **SOCIAL**   **VARIANT**

Using inner strength without outward force in removing obstacles proves successful. You can expect good fortune without difficulty or remorse.

3rd   **9**   ▬▬▬▬   **INDIVIDUAL**   **VARIANT**

Exercise of excessive strength will lead you into difficulty, which can be prevented by applying only the proper amount of energy to achieve the desired results.

2nd   **9**   ▬▬▬▬   **ASPIRATIONS**   **SIGNIFICANT**

Resistence to advance is giving way. Your efforts, when not abusively applied, are successful. Expect good fortune.

1st   **9**   ▬▬▬▬   **INSTINCT**   **CONSTRAINT**

A reckless and forceful attempt to advance will be bringing you conflict, regret, and misfortune.

DESCRIPTION

The Movement, Thunder, ABOVE, over the Creative Power, Heaven, BELOW, reveals the Great Strength and Power of this Hexagram. The 4 strong Lines are rising, driving out the remaining weakness, or darkness. This is also associated with the Vernal Equinox, when days become longer and vitality increases. The single Ruling Line, 4th, represents leading the advance of the strong. The Subject of the Hexagram, also the 4th Line, is likewise at this leading edge of advance. A clear warning is included, associated with authoritative abuse of this power or a lack of wisdom by using this Power as force.

ABOVE: LI
FIRE, SUN
Brilliance
Clarity

BELOW: K'UN
EARTH
Natural
Receptive

CHIN

PROGRESS AND RECOGNITION FROM
ENLIGHTENED AND VIRTUOUS EFFORTS.

CHIN is depicted as the authority bestowing steeds upon a minister for valuable and virtuous discharge of his assigned responsibilities.

CHIN is a Time of Progress and Recognition from Enlightened and Virtuous Efforts, characterized by Rapid and Easy Advancement with Good Fortune. The Good Fortune associated with this Hexagram comes from the recognition and reward for superior service as opposed to individual handiwork. Care must be taken not to abuse this favorable time by either indifference or greed.

PROPHESIES

LUCK is very favorable, and WISHES come true as motives are virtuous and sincere. LOVE easily succeeds. MARRIAGES are harmonious with rewarding benefits. Mostly female CHILDREN, intelligent and obedient, bring happiness. If PREGNANT, expect a girl.

SICKNESS will become worse and possibly fatal without serious care, and relates to the heart or abdominal area. Drinking problems and stomach ulcers are also indicated.

MISSING PEOPLE, in Southerly directions, are easily found and safe, and return when they're ready. MISSING THINGS can be found, probably in the bottom of a box or chest. You may need a flashlight. MOVING goes well.

LOANS with very favorable rates are granted. You may even be given money. BUSINESS Ventures are particularly good. Enlightened and valuable contributions come spontaneously from business associates. JOBS are favorable with unexpected progress. The MARKET indicates a very good time to buy.

CHANGING LINES

6th   **9**   ▬▬▬▬▬   **WISDOM**   **CONSTRAINT**

Beware of the danger of your high position. Enforcement to correct troublesome elements brings good fortune, but carrying punishment too far brings certain regret.

5th   **6**   ▬▬ ▬▬   **AUTHORITY**   **SIGNIFICANT**

With well-ordered and virtuous effort you have no need of concern for gain or loss. Expect further progress and advantage.

4th   **9**   ▬▬▬▬▬   **SOCIAL**   **VARIANT**

Your efforts lack virtue and are exposed as stealth and greed. Your position is perilous and continuing invites disaster.

3rd   **6**   ▬▬ ▬▬   **INDIVIDUAL**   **VARIANT**

Your efforts bring the trust and support of your associates. Expect advancement with no remorse.

2nd   **6**   ▬▬ ▬▬   **ASPIRATIONS**   **SIGNIFICANT**

Virtuous effort requires sacrifice and toil. Continuing brings good fortune. Unexpected favor or inheritance also follows.

1st   **6**   ▬▬ ▬▬   **INSTINCT**   **CONSTRAINT**

Your efforts and attitudes are correct for advance, but an opening is not yet available. Remain consistent now—the right opportunity and good fortune are soon to follow.

DESCRIPTION

The Brilliance, Sun, ABOVE, shines down upon the Receptive, Earth, BELOW, showing Clarity and Enlightenment. All efforts are clearly seen and deeds show merit or lack of merit. Nothing is hidden. The single Ruling Line, 5th, although weak, progresses and ascends from being seated in the midst of brightness. The Subject of the Hexagram, 4th Line, carries a warning against greed in these very favorable circumstances.

36

ABOVE: K'UN
EARTH
Receptive
Natural

BELOW: LI
FIRE, SUN
Brilliance
Clarity

明夷

MING
I

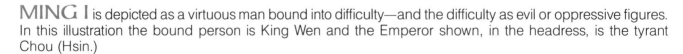

THE DARKENING OF THE LIGHT AS VIRTUE
AND INTELLECT ARE OBSCURED.

MING I is depicted as a virtuous man bound into difficulty—and the difficulty as evil or oppressive figures.
In this illustration the bound person is King Wen and the Emperor shown, in the headress, is the tyrant
Chou (Hsin.)

MING I is a Time when Virtue and Intellect are Obscured by self-serving and jealous interests, characterized by harm or injury, but eventual release from the "dark" time by maintaining one's virtue, character, and the intelligent realization of the dangerous circumstances. The Chinese character symbolizes light (sun and moon) wounded, the light is represented here as virtue and intellect (brilliance).

PROPHESIES

LUCK is very poor now, and WISHES will not come true. LOVE is disastrous. MARRIAGES tend to break-up, mostly due to the interference of outside parties. CHILDREN, if any, are troublesome girls. If PREGNANT, expect a girl, and possibly a stillbirth.

SICKNESS is proceeding toward death and relates to the heart or abdominal area. Only a very strong will to survive will sustain life. Eye problems may lead to blindness.

MISSING PEOPLE, in Southerly directions, are in extreme danger, probably captive, and possibly dead. MISSING THINGS have been deeply covered or buried and should be forgotten. MOVING is very perilous now.

LOANS will not be granted. BUSINESS ventures are in severe danger of being torn apart from external influences. Union difficulties are very likely. JOBS are not granted, probably because of some jealous slander. The MARKET is unfavorable now—investing or holding is not recommended.

CHANGING LINES

6th   **6**   ▬▬ ▬▬   **WISDOM**   **CONSTRAINT**

The opposition has attained great power, but its destructive nature is also exposed. Continuing to proceed carefully is advantageous as the opposition fails.

5th   **6**   ▬▬ ▬▬   **AUTHORITY**   **SIGNIFICANT**

Recognizing the danger and carefully proceeding in the face of the opposition brings advantage.

4th   **6**   ▬▬ ▬▬   **SOCIAL**   **VARIANT**

Deep penetration of your opposition reveals that motives are indeed destructive and dangerous. Escape and complete withdrawal should be undertaken immediately.

3rd   **9**   ▬▬▬▬   **INDIVIDUAL**   **VARIANT**

Your efforts to overcome opposition prove successful, but don't become over-eager in restoring order.

2nd   **6**   ▬▬ ▬▬   **ASPIRATIONS**   **SIGNIFICANT**

Your advance is being impeded by powerful opposition. Expect set-back, but good fortune in the end with the help of another.

1st   **9**   ▬▬▬▬   **INSTINCT**   **CONSTRAINT**

Your advance is being halted by a dangerous force. Expect slander and gossip, but avoid confrontations with your opposition now.

DESCRIPTION

The Brilliance, Sun, BELOW, has descended beneath the Receptive, Earth, Above. The light is obscured, hidden by the earth, and darkness prevails. The two Ruling Lines, 2nd and 5th, maintain the virtue in this difficult time. The 6th Line, however, is portrayed as bringing darkness down upon all the others. The Subject of the Hexagram, 4th Line, warns against getting swept along by bad influences or times. Understanding offers a clear exit from the circumstances.

37

ABOVE: SUN
WIND, WOOD
Gentle
Penetrating

BELOW: LI
FIRE, SUN
Brilliance
Clarity

家人

CHIA
JEN

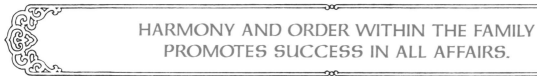

HARMONY AND ORDER WITHIN THE FAMILY
PROMOTES SUCCESS IN ALL AFFAIRS.

CHIA JEN is depicted as each member of the family cooperating and contributing as is fitting to their relationship within the family.

CHIA JEN is a Time of Harmony, Order, and Cooperation between members of a Family or Clan, characterized by Advantage and Good fortune in both internal and external affairs. This is derived from the inner peace and confidence of knowing ones internal affairs are in order, thus allowing proper attention to be applied to other affairs. However, severity in attempting to achieve this order, only works against harmony.

PROPHESIES

LUCK is generally favorable, and WISHES come true when cooperating with other members of a particular group. LOVE is favorable with gentle consideration towards each other. MARRIAGES are harmonious and successful as everyone works toward common goals. Many CHILDREN, of both sexes, are gentle and obedient, requiring little discipline. If PREGNANT, expect a girl.

SICKNESS not severe, improves gradually, relating to the heart or blood system (including the liver or kidneys). Treat the flu immediately and stay in bed; watch out for medical "quacks".

MISSING PEOPLE, South to East, return after a family argument is forgotten or settled—don't worry. MISSING THINGS are close and probably visible—expect to find them. MOVING is not favored—remain where you are.

LOANS will be granted. BUSINESS Ventures are well structured, and profits come with increased sales. JOBS are available and go smoothly, but don't plan on working alone. The MARKET indicates a time to sell. You should only buy futures at low prices.

CHANGING LINES

6th   **9**   ▬▬▬▬▬   **WISDOM**   **CONSTRAINT**

Setting examples with your own honest and sincere efforts toward the goals of the group motivates others—expect good fortune.

5th   **9**   ▬▬▬▬▬   **AUTHORITY**   **SIGNIFICANT**

Authoritive influences are causing anxieties within the group. The motives of the authority favor the group as a whole, and cooperation will bring good fortune.

4th   **6**   ▬▬ ▬▬   **SOCIAL**   **VARIANT**

Working and cooperating to enrich the group as a whole brings all great good fortune.

3RD   **9**   ▬▬▬▬▬   **INDIVIDUAL**   **VARIANT**

Laxity now causes a loss of economy and balance. Stern discipline causes grief, but restores order, and good fortune follows.

2nd   **6**   ▬▬ ▬▬   **ASPIRATIONS**   **SIGNIFICANT**

Maintain your normal duties and responsibilities to attain good fortune. Selfish endeavors bring no advantage now.

1st   **9**   ▬▬▬▬▬   **INSTINCT**   **CONSTRAINT**

Establishing regulations and insuring proper order in the beginning relieves you of later regret. Expect progress.

DESCRIPTION

The Brightness, Fire, BELOW, produces the Gentle Penetrating, Wind, ABOVE. This is a rising influence of Natural Harmony and Order, such as within a well-maintained and regulated Family. Both Ruling Lines, 2nd and 5th, operate as equal partners but with different responsibilities, such as a husband and wife. Emphasized is each member of a family providing harmony and order by acting according to their particular role. The Subject of the Hexagram, 2nd Line, suggests a yielding influence may be required to maintain order, and a warning against severity in regulating order is contained in this Hexagram.

38

ABOVE: LI
FIRE, SUN
Brilliance
Clarity

BELOW: TUI
LAKE, MARSH
Joyous
Cheerful

K'UEI

SEPARATE AND OPPOSED ELEMENTS CAN
SUCCESSFULLY ACHIEVE A COMMON GOAL.

K'UEI is Depicted as two sisters, each with their own opinion, opposed and viewing issues differently, but still of the same family.

K'UEI is a Time when misunderstandings lead to Separation and Opposition even though objectives and goals are commonly shared, characterized by Success in small matters but lacking the unity to achieve great progress or success. This is also a time when, even though disappointment is frequent, differences must be understood. There is no right or wrong implied, and order can be restored.

PROPHESIES

LUCK is not favorable now, and WISHES tend not to come true because of the lack of cooperation. LOVE is being stifled by partners clinging too greatly to their own opinions, MARRIAGES lack harmony as the family tends to quarrel. Few CHILDREN, but of both sexes and prone to disagreement, are seen. If PREGNANT, expect a girl.

SICKNESS does not improve without professional help, and relates to the mouth, throat, or lungs. Continued tension, however, could lead to a heart attack. Your eyesight may need some attention.

MISSING PEOPLE, in the West, are very hard to find, probably because of a family feud. MISSING THINGS have fallen, are broken or covered, and you should not expect to find them. MOVING invites disaster.

LOANS will not be granted. BUSINESS Ventures are being troubled by problems requiring reorganization. JOBS are hard to find and offer no satisfaction. The MARKET is variable—wait for a better time to buy or sell.

CHANGING LINES

6th   **9**   ▬▬▬▬   **WISDOM**   **CONSTRAINT**

You have been isolated by your own misconception of the circumstances. Careful reconsideration removes doubt, and you can expect progress and good fortune.

5th   **6**   ▬▬ ▬▬   **AUTHORITY**   **SIGNIFICANT**

Support from a close association is instrumental in helping you overcome the opposition. Expect easy progress with freedom from error.

4th   **9**   ▬▬▬▬   **SOCIAL**   **VARIANT**

The opposition has left you isolated. Forming an association with others having the same goals and objectives as your own produces successful progress in spite of a perilous position.

3rd   **6**   ▬▬ ▬▬   **INDIVIDUAL**   **VARIANT**

The opposition has become restrictive and punishing. Lay aside your anger. Your course is correct, and order is restored in the end by the triumph of your virtue.

2nd   **9**   ▬▬▬▬   **ASPIRATIONS**   **SIGNIFICANT**

Separated viewpoints or opinions have met in pursuit of a common goal. A proper course, although different, is being followed by each—expect to continue without mistake.

1st   **9**   ▬▬▬▬   **INSTINCT**   **CONSTRAINT**

Opposition or misunderstanding has caused the loss of a close associate. Stay in communication, but don't attempt conversion or change. The disagreement repairs itself naturally.

DESCRIPTION

The Brightness, Fire, ABOVE, rises away from the falling Joyous, Lake, BELOW. Two forces normally capable of producing harmony are moving further apart. This Hexagram also refers to two sisters living in the same house, but of different wills. The two Ruling Lines, 2nd and 5th, act as opposing elements—the yielding 5th and the firm 2nd isolate each other. The Subject of the Hexagram, 4th Line, suggests the avoidance of disagreement rather than perpetuating hostilities.

39

ABOVE: K'AN
WATER, RAIN
Danger
Abysmal

BELOW: KEN
MOUNTAIN
Stillness
Silence

CHIEN

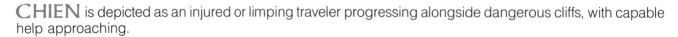

THE DIFFICULTIES ASSOCIATED WITH A PERSONAL RESTRAINT OR INJURY, LIMPING.

CHIEN is depicted as an injured or limping traveler progressing alongside dangerous cliffs, with capable help approaching.

CHIEN is a Time when Difficulties, associated with Personal Restraint or Injury, impede or hinder progress, and is characterized by Good Fortune when persisting to overcome Difficulties—particularly with capable help. This Hexagram is referred to as "limping," and the Chinese character itself symbolizes a "frozen foot."

PROPHESIES

LUCK is mediocre, and WISHES come true only when persisting to make them come true. LOVE does not progress well. MARRIAGES are marked with difficulties which can be overcome, though considerable effort is required. Few CHILDREN, male, are seen, but they don't get along well together and need much help in life. If PREGNANT, expect a boy, but don't expect an easy delivery.

SICKNESS tends to be severe and drags on, eventually improving with proper care, and relates to the kidneys, urinary tract, or rectum. Females can expect uterine problems. Fatigue and loss of energy is indicated. Hearing difficulties are also indicated.

MISSING PEOPLE, in Northerly directions, are injured or disabled, and need help now—find them quickly or lose them forever. MISSING THINGS, probably damaged, can be found by searching low and in a dark place—any damage can be repaired. MOVING is not favored now.

LOANS will only be granted with a co-signer. BUSINESS Ventures experience difficulties, especially relating to finance, which must be patiently worked out. JOBS are not easily obtained, and require the help of another. The MARKET, seemingly low, does not indicate a good time to buy, unless investing in mutual funds.

CHANGING LINES

6th 6 — — WISDOM CONSTRAINT

Your assisting others in overcoming difficulties adds to your own, but you can expect good fortune and satisfaction. Seek sound advice.

5th 9 ——— AUTHORITY SIGNIFICANT

Even though in great difficulty and peril, your sincere efforts to resolve the difficulties bring capable help, almost as rescue.

4th 6 — — SOCIAL VARIANT

Attempting to advance now only brings greater difficulty. Seek capable help before attempting to resolve difficulties now.

3rd 9 ——— INDIVIDUAL VARIANT

Attempting to advance now only brings greater difficulty. Return to or remain in your original position or association to avoid misfortune.

2nd 6 — — ASPIRATIONS SIGNIFICANT

Your duties require the resolution of many difficulties, which are not necessarily your own. Expect to have to struggle in perilous situations, but honor in the end.

1st 6 — — INSTINCT CONSTRAINT

Struggling to overcome difficulties now will only lead to greater difficulties beyond your ability to manage. Wait for a more favorable time.

DESCRIPTION

The Stillness, Mountain, BELOW, faces Danger, Water, ABOVE. This represents Obstacles or Restrictions on either side which must be carefully avoided or overcome. The Water is being restrained by the terrain of the Mountain, but once it overcomes the Obstacles it flows successfully downward. The single Ruling Line, 5th, acts as authority, providing help in resolving the difficulties. The Subject of the Hexagram, 4th line, in the depth of danger, serves as a warning to withdraw from a perilous position.

40

ABOVE: CHEN
THUNDER
Movement
Arousing

BELOW: K'AN
WATER, RAIN
Danger
Abysmal

解

CHIEH

LIBERATION AND LOOSENING OF RESTRAINTS BY TIMELY RESOLUTION OF DIFFICULTIES.

CHIEH is depicted as a prince of antiquity removing a bird of prey, an indication of certain good fortune.

CHIEH is a Time of Liberation from, or the loosening of, Restraints by timely and complete resolution of Difficulties, characterized by the return of order and Good Fortune. Withdrawing from inferior influences is prescribed for personal behavior. Timeliness in resolving difficulties is emphasized in this Hexagram.

PROPHESIES

LUCK is improving, and WISHES come true with attention to time and seizing the opportunity. LOVE is favorable. MARRIAGES return to harmony as difficulties are resolved. Mostly male CHILDREN are adventurous and tend to neglect school but bring happiness after all. If PREGNANT, expect a boy.

SICKNESS improves when care is taken to avoid its causes, and relates to the liver, kidneys, urinary tract, or gall bladder. Digestive ailments are also indicated.

MISSING PEOPLE, East to North, can and should be found quickly, but they won't want to return home. MISSING THINGS cannot be seen, but can be found now. If not found now they will be forgotten with time. MOVING goes very well now.

LOANS will be granted, but several applications may have to be completed. BUSINESS Ventures are improving as obstacles in production or marketing are resolved. Immediate expansion may relieve some restraints. JOBS are becoming more available—keep your eye open for the right opportunity. The MARKET indicates a profitable time to sell.

CHANGING LINES

6th   **6**   ▬▬ ▬▬   **WISDOM**   **CONSTRAINT**

Your swift and complete removal of obstacles eliminates all hardship, producing advantage in every way.

5th   **6**   ▬▬ ▬▬   **AUTHORITY**   **SIGNIFICANT**

Your efforts in resolving difficulties now deliver you from inferior influences. Expect the confidence of others and good fortune.

4th   **9**   ▬▬▬▬▬   **SOCIAL**   **VARIANT**

The source of the difficulty is close at hand and may affect you personally, yet this obstacle must be removed to restore order or build productive relationships.

3rd   **6**   ▬▬ ▬▬   **INDIVIDUAL**   **VARIANT**

Your abilities are not strong enough now to overcome obstacles. The pretense of strength only brings further difficulty and regret.

2nd   **9**   ▬▬▬▬▬   **ASPIRATIONS**   **SIGNIFICANT**

Persistence in resolving the accumulated difficulties brings certain reward and a loosening of restrictions.

1st   **6**   ▬▬ ▬▬   **INSTINCT**   **CONSTRAINT**

No mistake is made as you begin to resolve the difficulties and hardships that have accumulated.

DESCRIPTION

The Movement, Thunder, ABOVE, travels away from the Danger, Water, BELOW. Thunder has brought rain, clearing the air, easing tensions, and loosening restraints. Both Ruling Lines, 2nd and 5th, act with temperance in removing all influences contrary to Harmony and Order. The Subject of the Hexagram, 2nd Line, is strong and quickly restores order—hence the warning to quickly and completely resolve the difficulties.

ABOVE: KEN
MOUTAIN
Stillness
Silence

BELOW: TUI
LAKE, MARSH
Joyous
Cheerful

損

SUN

THE VIRTUE OF INDIVIDUAL DECREASE OR
SACRIFICE FOR THE BENEFIT OF ALL.

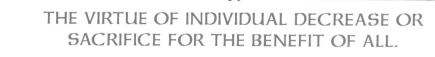

SUN is depicted as the decrease by one from a trio to become the companion of another.

SUN is a Time represented by the Virtue of Individual Decrease or Sacrifice for the Benefit of all, characterized by Freedom from Error and Advantage in every way. Material items are indicated, but more importantly is the individual setting aside anger, wrath, or desire in favor of the common good. The losses or decreases are by choice, or sacrifice, and speak of certain virtue.

PROPHESIES

LUCK is not favorable, and WISHES, of personal natures, do not come true—but do come true when for the benefit of all. LOVE with continued sincerity succeeds. MARRIAGES improve with more attention to joint, or community, effort. CHILDREN, of both sexes, tend to be argumentative and stubborn, but become peaceful as they mature. If PREGNANT, a girl is most likely.

SICKNESS, caused by carelessness, relates to the mouth (breathing or nutrition), and lingers on until proper care is applied. Consequently digestive problems, anemia, or loss of energy can be expected. Smoking suggests emphysema.

MISSING PEOPLE, in Northerly directions, are moving further away and are becoming increasingly difficult to find. MISSING THINGS are hard to find; a step ladder is suggested to help find them. MOVING is favorable with proper planning—don't rush.

LOANS are more likely to have to be made by you, but don't expect them to be granted to you. BUSINESS Ventures face difficulties, possibly relating to employee turnover. Better salaries and benefits may improve conditions for all. JOBS are considered temporary, but with meaningful contribution permanent positions are offered at a later time. The MARKET is indicating a good time to buy, but be wary of cheap stocks.

CHANGING LINES

6th   **9**   ▬▬▬▬   **WISDOM**   **CONSTRAINT**

Your favorable position is furthered by contribution to others within your means. Expect advantage, good fortune, and faithful followers.

5th   **6**   ▬▬ ▬▬   **AUTHORITY**   **SIGNIFICANT**

Releasing pride and accepting the sincere help of others in weak situations works to produce great good fortune.

4th   **6**   ▬▬ ▬▬   **SOCIAL**   **VARIANT**

Quickly recognize your need for capable help, and set aside any shortcomings or faults—such as animosity—to invite the meaningful help you require.

3rd   **6**   ▬▬ ▬▬   **INDIVIDUAL**   **VARIANT**

Releasing excesses to achieve balance and benefit for all preserves trust and order.

2nd   **9**   ▬▬▬▬   **ASPIRATIONS**   **SIGNIFICANT**

You can help others with advice and suggestions for improvement, but assuming their responsibilities is a sacrifice which will bring you disaster.

1st   **9**   ▬▬▬▬   **INSTINCT**   **CONSTRAINT**

Helping others in settling their affairs produces no error, but consider carefully the extent of committment you can make at this time.

DESCRIPTION

The Joyous, Lake, BELOW, decreases by yielding to the Stillness, Mountain, ABOVE. A convection fog or mist evaporates from a lake at the base of a mountain, giving moisture to the living things on earth (on the mountain)—a natural and virtuous order. The single Ruling Line, 5th, benefits from the redistribution represented by this Hexagram. The Subject of the Hexagram, 3rd Line, and the Object, 6th Line, coincide with each other and represent the redistribution. Anger or wrath is decreased to secure the benefit of all.

42

ABOVE: SUN
WIND, WOOD
Gentle
Penetrating

BELOW: CHEN
THUNDER
Movement
Arousing

益

I

INDIVIDUAL ADVANTAGE IS DERIVED FROM THE COMMON BENEFIT IN ITS TIME.

I is depicted as the common wealth being made available by the common body for individual advantage or endeavor when motives are correct.

I is a Time of Individual Advantage derived from accumulated common benefit, such as strength or wealth, characterized by Advantage and Good Fortune, even when undertaking great tasks. It is understood from SUN, #41, that the individual has sacrificed for the common good, and the common body now lends its support to individual endeavor. The expected warnings about selfishness and self-serving interests are issued.

PROPHESIES

LUCK is very favorable, and WISHES come true—even overcoming unfortunate circumstances—when working with others. LOVE succeeds, when free of selfish motives. MARRIAGES are harmonious and endure as joint and community endeavor prevail. CHILDREN, mostly boys, are intelligent and industrious, bringing much happiness. If PREGNANT, expect a girl.

SICKNESS passes quickly with proper care and relates to the internal abdominal organs. Liver problems, however, can be unexpectedly severe.

MISSING PEOPLE, in Easterly directions, are not far off and unexpectedly return or are found. MISSING THINGS, on top of something else, have been moved by someone else and will not be found in the expected manner. MOVING is very favorable now.

LOANS will be granted. BUSINESS Ventures bring success by working together to complete tasks. JOBS are available and favorable. The MARKET indicates a good time to sell or hold.

CHANGING LINES

6th   **9**   ▬▬▬▬   **WISDOM**   **CONSTRAINT**

Showing no consistent regard for others brings their wrath, accompanied with misfortune.

5th   **9**   ▬▬▬▬   **AUTHORITY**   **SIGNIFICANT**

Don't worry about the results of your efforts enriching the others. Your generosity is recognized and returns great good fortune with sincere appreciation.

4th   **6**   ▬▬ ▬▬   **SOCIAL**   **VARIANT**

Your reasoning and advice is clear and honest. Expect advantage from your ability to influence others while working towards the common good.

3rd   **6**   ▬▬ ▬▬   **INDIVIDUAL**   **VARIANT**

You have brought adversity upon yourself, but aid will be granted from common assets when your efforts to restore order are honest and sincere. Expect no blame.

2nd   **6**   ▬▬ ▬▬   **ASPIRATIONS**   **SIGNIFICANT**

By persisting with honesty and sincerity you can expect assistance from common assets to provide you good fortune.

1st   **9**   ▬▬▬▬   **INSTINCT**   **CONSTRAINT**

Common assets for great undertakings are available at this time, if not planned for personal convenience. Such undertakings can now produce great good fortune without criticism.

DESCRIPTION

The Penetrating, Wind, ABOVE, increases the power of the Arousing, Thunder, BELOW. Both strengthen with a common bond. The individual lines are in positions to gain advantage from this common strength, or benefit. This time passes and the opportunity needs to be seized when available. The two Ruling Lines, 2nd and 5th, implement great tasks and bestow benevolence from their corresponding positions. The Subject of the Hexagram, 3rd line, benefits from unfortunate events, but the Object, 6th Line, is met with evil and no gain because motives are purely selfish.

43

ABOVE: TUI
LAKE, MARSH
Joyous
Cheerful

BELOW: CH'IEN
HEAVEN
Creative
Firmness

夬

KUAI

RESOLUTE DECISION TO EXPOSE
AND REMOVE CORRUPTION.

KUAI is depicted as the corrupt being driven away. The waterfall symbolizes both division and danger.

KUAI is a Time of Resolute Decision and Action in Exposing and Removing Corruption, characterized by Advantage in endeavors Following the Elimination of Corruption. The corruption is close at hand, and truthful exposure represents danger, yet the matters must be resolved carefully without excessive zeal or aggressiveness. The elimination of the remaining evil restores order.

PROPHESIES

LUCK looks good, but there is trouble approaching, and WISHES only come true after decisions and action for improvement. LOVE does not succeed, and MARRIAGES are in extreme peril of failure unless decisions are made to eliminate troublesome sources. Mostly male CHILDREN bring trouble later, particularly amongst themselves. If PREGNANT, expect a boy and a difficult delivery.

SICKNESS, if not attended to immediately, will become severe, relating to the breathing system, lungs, or the head. External injuries to the skull are also indicated. Maintaining a good physical condition will be an asset now.

MISSING PEOPLE, in Westerly directions, are in shame and have no desire to return, nor should you expect to find them. MISSING THINGS have fallen and are deeply covered, and you should not plan on finding them. MOVING should not be considered now.

LOANS are not approved. BUSINESS Ventures face administrative problems, and the need for a thorough reorganization is indicated. It may be best to layoff employees and close some facilities, but certainly do not expand. JOBS are possible with determined and sincere efforts. The MARKET indicates a time to sell. Don't be tempted by speculative profits.

CHANGING LINES

6th   6   ▬▬ ▬▬   WISDOM   CONSTRAINT

Expect misfortune and no help from others. Order will only be restored after you remove the corruption.

5th   9   ▬▬▬▬   AUTHORITY   SIGNIFICANT

It may seem a hopeless task to completely remove corruption, but expect success with determined efforts. No error can be found even though you may have had to eliminate close associations.

4th   9   ▬▬▬▬   SOCIAL   VARIANT

Indecision and inner conflict in removing corruption are allowing it to linger. Join with others in removing corruption. Allow yourself to be led.

3RD   9   ▬▬▬▬   INDIVIDUAL   VARIANT

It is not yet time to remove the corruption, and efforts to do so now bring misfortune. Endure this situation, even though you will be misunderstood and criticized.

2nd   9   ▬▬▬▬   ASPIRATIONS   SIGNIFICANT

Remain cautious and alert in your efforts to remove corruption in order to preclude reprisals, or harm from reprisals.

1st   9   ▬▬▬▬   INSTINCT   CONSTRAINT

Your position is not as strong as you believe, and attempts to advance on pride alone will bring regret, embarrassment, and setbacks.

DESCRIPTION

The Pleasant, Lake, ABOVE, has risen over the Creative, Heaven, BELOW, resulting in a careless and unnatural situation requiring resolve, as the lake is in a place it cannot properly be. Here the lake is seen to be in a corrupt position, ready to collapse downward as a cloudburst. The single Ruling Line, 5th, represents the leader of the five strong elements (below) driving out the corruption at the top, and is also the Subject of the Hexagram. The warning, particularly in the 6th Line, is not to allow the evil to persist.

44

**ABOVE: CH'IEN
HEAVEN**
Creative
Firmness

**BELOW: SUN
WIND, WOOD**
Gentle
Penetrating

姤

KOU

**ADVANTAGE IS FOUND BY AVOIDING
STRONG AND INFERIOR TEMPTATION.**

KOU is depicted as the tempting courtesan attracting the traveler as he passes by, while the adversity remains hidden.

KOU is a Time of Avoiding Adversity which would be associated with Strong and Inferior Temptations, and is characterized by advantage when restraint is applied in avoiding these temptations. Sexual contact and meeting is implied, but so is the anguish resulting from a fickle lover. The meeting and temptation occur, but the association should be concluded without involvement since the adversity which could follow is carefully concealed.

PROPHESIES

LUCK is not favorable now, and WISHES come true but bring adversity instead of the anticipated good fortune. LOVE becomes greatly troubled with jealousy. MARRIAGES are not harmonious as too many influences compete. Mostly male CHILDREN are poorly principled and have difficulty getting along together or with the parents, requiring firm discipline. If PREGNANT, expect a girl.

SICKNESS tends to be severe and worsening. The causes need to be avoided and relate to the liver, brain, or lungs. Common temptations of alcohol, drugs, and promiscuous sex must be avoided.

MISSING PEOPLE, West to North, are in love and safe, but still take time to find. MISSING THINGS are close by and can be found by thoroughly searching. MOVING brings many and unimagined hardships.

LOANS are ultimately rejected. BUSINESS Ventures may be jeopardized by some accident, but an exceptional time is seen for a female entrepreneur. JOBS do not turn out as expected. The MARKET looks as if it is a good time to buy, but further drops are indicated.

CHANGING LINES

6th   9   ━━━━━   WISDOM   CONSTRAINT

Forceful action in meeting and overcoming temptation will bring you humiliation, but with sincere effort expect no blame and a return to order.

5th   9   ━━━━━   AUTHORITY   SIGNIFICANT

Advantage will be achieved by allowing your fine qualities to develop inwardly. The inferior and tempting influences withdraw from this advantageous position.

4th   9   ━━━━━   SOCIAL   VARIANT

Your inability to work with others, due to the inferior influences they appear to represent, causes you loss of opportunities—expect misfortune to follow.

3RD   9   ━━━━━   INDIVIDUAL   VARIANT

The inferior temptations are great and difficult to avoid. Remaining aware of the potential for adversity they represent will prevent you from making any great mistakes.

2nd   9   ━━━━━   ASPIRATIONS   SIGNIFICANT

Inferior and tempting influences require restraint and containment. You will experience no error when restraint is applied in a friendly manner.

1st   6   ━━ ━━   INSTINCT   CONSTRAINT

Applying restraint to prevent the growth of inferior influences leads to good fortune, while heedlessly proceeding will bring certain misfortune.

DESCRIPTION

The Gentle, Wind, BELOW, is in contact with the Creative Power, Heaven, ABOVE. The wind is a gentle and penetrating force with certain strength, and moves about the four corners of the earth. The union is tempting, and even seen as sexual contact, but no benefit comes from the union and anguish follows. Both ruling Lines, 2nd and 5th, represent virtue restraining the inferior influences. The Subject of the Hexagram, 1st Line, shows the inferior influence gathering strength and rising.

ABOVE: TUI
LAKE, MARSH
Joyous
Cheerful

BELOW: K'UN
EARTH
Natural
Receptive

萃

TS'UI

GATHERING TOGETHER AS ONE PROMOTES
SUCCESS IN PURSUIT OF COMMON GOALS.

TS'UI is depicted as the gathering together of persons as the water has gathered upon the earth bringing joy and benefit.

TS'UI is a Time of Gathering Together as one for the Pursuit of Common Goals, characterized by Success and Good Fortune. The suitability of obtaining wise advice and great undertakings are also indicated. The gathered, collected, or assembled lot also needs protection from loss, and this Hexagram warns to provide this precaution.

PROPHESIES

LUCK is good and improving, and WISHES come true when they are not selfishly motivated. LOVE is favorable. MARRIAGES are in unusual harmony as the entire family pursues common goals. Mostly female CHILDREN are cheerful and industrious, causing parents little concern. If PREGNANT, expect a girl.

SICKNESS tends to slowly improve when the doctor's advice is followed and relates to the lungs, breathing system, or chest. Expect coughing, bronchitis, or digestive problems as well.

MISSING PEOPLE, in Westerly directions, have joined other groups, are easily found, but only return when they choose to. MISSING THINGS can be found, and have possibly been taken by another. You may need help in recovering them. MOVING goes very well.

LOANS will be granted, but not in great amounts. BUSINESS Ventures experience success as every one works together with the same purpose. JOBS, when working with others, proceed favorably. The MARKET indicates a very good time to buy.

CHANGING LINES

6th   6 ━━ ━━   WISDOM   CONSTRAINT

Remaining aloof from the assembled group offers no satisfaction, but as your goals are also the same you will not be criticized.

5th   9 ━━━━━   AUTHORITY   SIGNIFICANT

Your position of authority within the assembly requires that your actions inspire continuing confidence and trust to promote success without error.

4th   9 ━━━━━   SOCIAL   VARIANT

Gathering others together for the pursuit of common goals and good without selfish regard for your own priorities, produces great success without error.

3RD   6 ━━ ━━   INDIVIDUAL   VARIANT

Hesitation and indecision have provided you no advantage. To advance assemble with those with whom you share common goals. Expect no error, but some regret for the delay.

2nd   6 ━━ ━━   ASPIRATIONS   SIGNIFICANT

Your high ideals and individual sacrifice have attracted others to invite you in assembling together. Joining the others provides you good fortune without error.

1st   6 ━━ ━━   INSTINCT   CONSTRAINT

Confusion and disorder are hindering assembly. If you seek advice and help in gathering together, you can expect to advance without error.

DESCRIPTION

The Joyous, Lake, ABOVE, has gathered as water, upon the Receptive, Earth, BELOW. Water has collected into the lake, bringing benefit and joy to all the surroundings. This is a greatness from the gathering. This greatness must also be protected against loss. Both Ruling Lines, 4th and 5th, represent the moral and human influences which actually perform the act of gathering. The Subject of the Hexagram, 2nd Line, is joining, or assembling with the others—sacrificing some independence to achieve success in pursuit of common goals.

ABOVE: K'UN
EARTH
Receptive
Natural

BELOW: SUN
WIND, WOOD
Gentle
Penetrating

SHENG

OPPORTUNITY TO RISE AND ADVANCE BY ACCUMULATING VIRTUE UNTIL GREAT.

SHENG is depicted as a superior person beginning the ascent of stairs at a ceremonial temple. This ascent represents the accumulation of virtue along the way.

SHENG is a Time of Opportunity associated with Rising and Advancement, and characterized by Great Progress and Success. Seeking wise advice in accumulating virtue furthers such advance. Also contained in this hexagram is a message to be aware when no further ascent or advancement is possible beyond one's abilities.

PROPHESIES

LUCK is very good, and WISHES come true one after another in proper order. LOVE is successful. MARRIAGES are harmonious and become great through time as virtue is accumulated. CHILDREN of both sexes have happy and fulfilling lives, probably bringing honor to parents. If PREGNANT, expect a girl.

SICKNESS improves with careful plans for recuperation, and relates to organs in the lower abdominal area. Digestive problems, which induce vomitting, are also seen, along with a possibility of gout.

MISSING PEOPLE, in Southerly directions, take time to find, and are probably in the company of an elderly woman. MISSING THINGS can be found when looking down into something else, such as a chest or box. MOVING goes well when necessary, but better results can be expected by remaining in a particular area.

LOANS will be granted. BUSINESS Ventures are successful and growing, but don't overextend beyond the current requirements. JOBS are particularly favorable, with promotions. The MARKET indicates a good time to buy and hold.

CHANGING LINES

6th　　　**6**　　━━　━━　　**WISDOM**　　　**CONSTRAINT**

Your attempts to advance further may exceed your abilities and bring loss. Remain content with your present situation.

5th　　　**6**　　━━　━━　　**AUTHORITY**　　　**SIGNIFICANT**

Your goals or desires are being realized as your achievements accumulate. Continue on and expect to enjoy good fortune.

4th　　　**6**　　━━　━━　　**SOCIAL**　　　**VARIANT**

Your talents and virtues are recognized by superiors or authorities. Plan on continued advancement without error and good fortune.

3rd　　　**9**　　━━━━━　　**INDIVIDUAL**　　　**VARIANT**

There are no real obstacles to your advancement. You can proceed without doubt or hesitation, but expect no particular reward.

2nd　　　**9**　　━━━━━　　**ASPIRATIONS**　　　**SIGNIFICANT**

Bringing sincerity and honesty to a situation preserves mutual trust. Expect progress without error.

1st　　　**6**　　━━　━━　　**INSTINCT**　　　**CONSTRAINT**

You can confidently expect the support of superiors. Expect advancement and great good fortune, but don't neglect the accumulation of virtue.

DESCRIPTION

The Penetrating, Wood, BELOW, grows upward, as a tree from within the Receptive, Earth, ABOVE. Ascending is seen as proceeding from the bottom line through to the top, while strength and virtue are accumulated. The single Ruling Line, 5th, is seen as the ascent of virtue with a yielding character promoting good fortune. The Subject of the Hexagram, 4th Line, brings recognition of ascent and accumulation of virtue from others, particularly others in authority.

47

ABOVE: TUI
LAKE, MARSH
Joyous
Cheerful

BELOW: K'AN
WATER, RAIN
Danger
Abysmal

困

K'UN

HONESTY AND BRAVERY WHILE ADAPTING TO
DIFFICULTIES. COMPLAINTS GO UNHEARD.

K'UN is depicted as a superior person adapting to a confinement which suppresses superior talent and virtue. Notice that there is no one to complain to.

K'UN is a Time of Difficulties arising out of exhaustion, depletion, or weariness, and is characterized by Good Fortune when Honestly and Bravely adapting to and resolving the difficulties. Complaints go unheard and arguments provoke disaster at this time. Cheerfulness needs to prevail to prevent the spirit from being defeated.

PROPHESIES

LUCK is poor, and WISHES should be held until better times while cheerfully adapting to the current difficulties. LOVE fails after initial confusion and argument. MARRIAGES are not expected to succeed and endure only with unrelenting effort. CHILDREN of both sexes argue too much between themselves and require direction to find happiness. If PREGNANT, expect a girl.

SICKNESS severe and prolonged, improves only with proper care, and relates to the breathing or respiratory system. The kidneys or urinary tract may also provide particular difficulty. Expect weariness and avoid excessive sexual activity.

MISSING PEOPLE, West to North, are confined or hiding and difficult to find, but may return after a long time. MISSING THINGS should be replaced by something new if needed now, but they will eventually reappear. MOVING should be put off until much later.

LOANS are not granted now. BUSINESS Ventures experience extreme difficulties with depletions of capital and cash, requiring exceptional effort to return to order. JOBS are not favorable now. The MARKET suggests buying, but expect further declines.

CHANGING LINES

6th 6 ▬ ▬ **WISDOM** **CONSTRAINT**

Attempts to advance now, without repentance and correction of past errors, leads nowhere. Nourish your virtue now to provide good fortune when this time of oppression ends.

5th 9 ▬▬▬ **AUTHORITY** **SIGNIFICANT**

The obstacles in reaching your goals are not yet removed, but slowly and carefully proceeding serves your best interests.

4th 9 ▬▬▬ **SOCIAL** **VARIANT**

You will experience some regret from not having provided charitable help earlier, but porviding this help now, eventually brings you advantage.

3rd 6 ▬ ▬ **INDIVIDUAL** **VARIANT**

Adversity has led you to despair. Lamenting and complaining brings misfortune. Gently guide yourself away from your current circumstances.

2nd 9 ▬▬▬ **ASPIRATIONS** **SIGNIFICANT**

Advancement is offered. This is a time to refuse and maintain your position. Accepting brings hardships, even though the fault is not your own.

1st 6 ▬ ▬ **INSTINCT** **CONSTRAINT**

Difficulties arising from confusion will endure for a fairly long time. Cheerfully adapting to the circumstances now is your best course of action.

DESCRIPTION

The Abysmal, Water, BELOW, with the Joyous, Lake, ABOVE. The water is below the lake and in the depths. The lake is empty. This is a difficult state, particularly when the danger below is considered. This state has been caused by exhaustion, depletion, or weariness. Both Ruling Lines, 2nd and 5th, while strong, are being oppressed, or confined, and advantage is being suppressed. The Subject of the Hexagram, 1st line, is at the beginning of this difficulty and represents confusion until it is determined to overcome the difficulties.

48

ABOVE: K'AN
WATER, RAIN
Danger
Abysmal

BELOW: SUN
WIND, WOOD
Gentle
Penetrating

CHING

THE NOURISHING WELL IS THE ABUNDANT
SOURCE OF WISDOM TO BENEFIT ALL.

CHING is depicted as a union of people gathered at the well for nourishment. The Chinese character symbolizes an enclosure, and in antiquity, a "dot" in the middle indicated a bucket.

CHING is a Time of Nourishment of Wisdom and Knowledge of all, characterized by Benefit to those who draw from the infinite sources of wisdom represented by the well, especially when such wisdom is employed for the benefit of others. Those who do not sincerely seek such wisdom for the benefit of all can expect misfortune or evil. Only two man-made objects are related to Hexagrams of the I CHING: Ching, this Hexagram; and Ting, #50, the Cauldron.

PROPHESIES

LUCK is neutral, and WISHES come true later with patience. LOVE works out well with patience and natural effort. MARRIAGES become harmonious with sincere concern for mutual benefit. CHILDREN of both sexes tend to be hard working and obedient, bringing happiness. If PREGNANT, expect a boy.

SICKNESS can improve with patience and proper care, and relates to organs in the lower abdominal area, particularly the kidneys. Influenza and earaches can also be expected.

MISSING PEOPLE, in the Southeast, are safe, probably hiding, and not too far away. MISSING THINGS have fallen into something else or into the water, and are most easily found when sorting. MOVING will not go particularly well now.

LOANS will be stalled until a later time. BUSINESS Ventures require patient and gradual effort for profit and success. The MARKET could go either way. Wait a short while before deciding whether to buy or sell.

CHANGING LINES

6th   6   ▬▬ ▬▬   WISDOM   CONSTRAINT

Your unselfish charity in aiding others has brought you recognition as a valuable and dependable person. Expect great good fortune.

5th   9   ▬▬▬▬   AUTHORITY   SIGNIFICANT

By allowing your talents to be used for the betterment of others, you will assume advantage or successful leadership roles.

4th   6   ▬▬ ▬▬   SOCIAL   VARIANT

Improve and educate yourself. To remain free from error wait for future opportunities to offer valuable service to others.

3rd   9   ▬▬▬▬   INDIVIDUAL   VARIANT

Your true talents are not being recognized. Change your associations to emcompass persons of superior knowledge and virtue.

2nd   9   ▬▬▬▬   ASPIRATIONS   SIGNIFICANT

Your neglect of your good qualities has brought only the influence of inferior elements. Expect no advance nor the cooperation of others.

1st   6   ▬▬ ▬▬   INSTINCT   CONSTRAINT

Your lack of concern for others has been reciprocated by their lack of concern for you. If this continues, you can expect to be forgotten and your efforts will produce no meaningful results.

DESCRIPTION

The Wind or Wood, BELOW, raises the Water, ABOVE, from the depths to the benefit of all. The water is seen within the wood, such as within a wooden bucket. The well represents a permanent source, even though the edifices of mankind come and go. So also does wisdom endure, and mankind's function is to seek it out. The single Ruling Line, 5th, also the Subject of the Hexagram, is strong and represents a superior person who is not only wise, but also has the knowledge to properly employ such wisdom.

49

ABOVE: TUI
LAKE, MARSH
Joyous
Cheerful

BELOW: LI
FIRE, SUN
Brilliance
Clarity

革

KO

REVOLUTION AND CHANGE FROM THE BELIEF
THAT CORRUPTION REQUIRES REMOVAL.

KO is depicted as revolution and change with great leadership supported by the masses.

KO is a Time of Revolution and Change brought about by the common belief that Corruption Requires Removal by such severe measures, and is characterized by Great Progress and Success when the change is made. Firm and correct measures are to be employed at this time to overcome the discord that has occurred. This is also seen as "getting rid of mottled leather."

PROPHESIES

LUCK is variable until deciding to change, and WISHES come true when constructive improvements are made. LOVE overcomes discord to succeed. MARRIAGES, initially troubled, become harmonious when courageous changes are made. CHILDREN, mostly female, are in discord with each other in youth, but find happiness as adults. If Pregnant, however, expect a boy.

SICKNESS lingers until changes in methods or doctors occur, and relates to the lungs or heart. Restrictions in vision should be expected—if you have eyeglasses, change the prescriptions.

MISSING PEOPLE, South to West, can be found by changing the method of your searching. MISSING THINGS are seen as fallen and probably buried or burned—best expect to replace them. MOVING, to change for the better, is very favorable.

LOANS will be granted after changes in reason for application. BUSINESS Ventures experience difficulties and require reorganization of personnel, facilities, and plans to restore profitability. JOBS are difficult to find and one should consider changing career objectives. The MARKET indicates a favorable time to buy.

CHANGING LINES

6th　　　　**6**　　　■■　■■　　　**WISDOM**　　　　**CONSTRAINT**

Carry revolution or change only to the degree of eliminating corruption. Knowing when to stop preserves good fortune, while going too far invites disaster.

5th　　　　**9**　　　■■■■■■　　　**AUTHORITY**　　　　**SIGNIFICANT**

The need of revolution to remove corruption is evident to all. Assuming a leadership role to accomplish this end works to the benefit of all.

4th　　　　**9**　　　■■■■■■　　　**SOCIAL**　　　　**VARIANT**

Your belief in the necessity of revolution to eliminate corruption is inspiring others. Expect to effect the desired changes and experience good fortune.

3rd　　　　**9**　　　■■■■■■　　　**INDIVIDUAL**　　　　**VARIANT**

Premature or reckless action to effect change will bring you misfortune. Consider carefully the necessity of such action if you expect any advantage or assistance.

2nd　　　　**6**　　　■■　■■　　　**ASPIRATIONS**　　　　**SIGNIFICANT**

Your patient waiting for reform should not be continued. Revolutionary change is required now to bring favorable results without error.

1st　　　　**9**　　　■■■■■■　　　**INSTINCT**　　　　**CONSTRAINT**

Circumstances are not favorable now to undertake changes. Restrain yourself and be patient, otherwise expect restraints in progress.

DESCRIPTION

The Brilliant, Fire, BELOW, fails to unite with the Joyous, Lake, ABOVE, and the influences move further apart. Growing discord is represented as the fire and water do not co-exist. The separation greatens until it is evident that the corruption and discord requires removal by revolution and change. The single Ruling Line, 5th, is the strong authority capable of leading the revolution. The Subject of the Hexagram, 4th line, is portrayed as the minister changing ordinances and codes in support of such revolution.

50

ABOVE: LI
FIRE, SUN
Brilliance
Clarity

BELOW: SUN
WIND, WOOD
Gentle
Penetrating

TING

INVIGORATING AND CULTIVATING ABLE
PERSONS IN PURSUIT OF NOBLE GOALS.

TING is depicted as the nourishing cauldron in its place amongst superior persons. Homage and supplication is made for help in pursuit of noble goals.

TING is a Time of Invigoration and Cultivation of able persons or influences in pursuit of noble goals, characterized by the attainment of Great Progress and Success. The "TING" is an ancient cauldron used both for sacrificial and feeding purposes. The Hexagram and the Chinese character both provide visual connotation with this nourishing vessel. A warning about taking only for selfish goals prevails in this Hexagram.

PROPHESIES

LUCK is very good for persons with high ideals, and WISHES come true when not selfishly motivated. LOVE is favorable to those who are not capricious. MARRIAGES endure when each regard their vows seriously. Mostly female CHILDREN are pious and obedient, bringing peace and happiness to parents. If PREGNANT, expect a girl.

SICKNESS is not severe, with complete recovery from proper care, and relates to the legs or digestive tract. Alcohol may be causing a problem. Contagious maladies with fevers and coughing may also be expected.

MISSING PEOPLE, in Southerly directions, are not difficult to find, but may be in retreat or on sabbatical. MISSING THINGS turn up on their own or are returned to you if taken by another. MOVING, associated with meaningful undertakings, goes well.

LOANS are granted for worthwhile causes. BUSINESS Ventures succeed and are profitable when high quality and fairly priced merchandise is offered to customers. JOBS, particularly those offering services to others, are favorable. The MARKET may rise a little more, but it is really a time to consider selling.

CHANGING LINES

6th 9 ▬▬▬ WISDOM CONSTRAINT

Your strength and character are equal to the tasks before you, while your consideration of others invigorates competent help. Expect great good fortune in all endeavors.

5th 6 ▬ ▬ AUTHORITY SIGNIFICANT

Your humble attitude attracts others as competent help. Hold this attitude if you expect progress or advantage.

4th 9 ▬▬▬ SOCIAL VARIANT

Shirking responsibilities in situations which exceed your capabilities drives away the competent help you need. Expect humiliation and failure.

3rd 9 ▬▬▬ INDIVIDUAL VARIANT

Your attitudes are causing your talents to go unrecognized. By cultivating improvement, you can expect this idle time to end, bringing good fortune.

2nd 9 ▬▬▬ ASPIRATIONS SIGNIFICANT

Your significant achievements bring envy, but none can find fault with your efforts. Leave the envious behind, continue your work, and expect good fortune.

1st 6 ▬ ▬ INSTINCT CONSTRAINT

You may be misunderstood when replacing the old with the new when starting endeavors. However, the product of your efforts proves you correct. Expect no blame.

DESCRIPTION

The Penetrating, Wind and Wood, BELOW, fans and fuels the Brilliant, Fire, ABOVE. The wood provides the Nourishment for the fire, while the wind increases its Brilliance, this being seen as Invigoration and Cultivation. Both Ruling Lines, 5th and 6th, are regarded as able and noble influences which are honored in this particular Hexagram. The Subject of the Hexagram, 2nd Line, represents the strong inner source of Nourishment.

51

ABOVE: CHEN
THUNDER
Movement
Arousing

BELOW: CHEN
THUNDER
Movement
Arousing

震

CHEN

SHOCKING AND PROFOUND POWER
AROUSES AWE, AS DOES THUNDER.

CHEN is depicted as the shocking power inspiring awe and reverence in the young and old alike. Those prepared respect the thunder, those unprepared fear and tremble.

CHEN is a time when Shocking and Profound Power arouses Awe and Reverence, characterized by situations being put back in order with careful observation to insure they do not again fall from order. CHEN itself is a warning, but it also moves in the rain to relieve tension—in the end all can work to advantage. An October thunderstorm is a warning of the certain approach of the darkness of winter.

PROPHESIES

LUCK is not very favorable, and WISHES come true only with proper preparation. LOVE succeeds, surprising all. MARRIAGES become happy when partners are prepared for the difficulties and pitfalls that can come along. Mostly male CHILDREN are energetic and rambunctious, but eventually develop happy, well-ordered lives. If PREGNANT, expect a boy.

SICKNESS, tends to vary, improving with rest and proper care. Mental disorders, caused by emotional shock, can be seen along with insomnia. Liver and digestive problems may occur. Be prepared when in inclement or rainy weather—wear galoshes.

MISSING PEOPLE, in the East, are in fear and danger and need to be found quickly. MISSING THINGS have been moved, or scattered on a road. They can be found now, but not later. MOVING goes well when not forced or rushed.

LOANS may be granted, but won't come easily. BUSINESS Ventures require careful planning and contingencies to overcome difficulties and produce profits. JOBS require preparedness to become favorable. The MARKET has significantly readjusted with a relatively stable period following. Expect nothing noteworthy.

CHANGING LINES

6th　　　　**6**　　━━ ━━　　**WISDOM**　　　　**CONSTRAINT**

Your preparedness against sudden shock is wisely based upon observance of others in similar situations. Remain calm and expect no trouble. Any blame is not your fault.

5th　　　　**6**　　━━ ━━　　**AUTHORITY**　　　　**SIGNIFICANT**

Sudden shocks and changes are placing you in certain peril. Adjusting to the changing circumstances allows you to avoid losses and possibly gain some advantage.

4th　　　　**9**　　━━━━　　**SOCIAL**　　　　**VARIANT**

Your lack of preparedness against the sudden change which has occurred has left you no other alternative than being drawn down by fate.

3rd　　　　**6**　　━━ ━━　　**INDIVIDUAL**　　　　**VARIANT**

Sudden shock has caused distress, but careful examination also shows new opportunity. By moving to seize this opportunity you will avoid misfortune.

2nd　　　　**6**　　━━ ━━　　**ASPIRATIONS**　　　　**SIGNIFICANT**

Sudden change has placed you in peril and resistance only greatens losses. By withdrawing until the peril passes you will find your losses restored.

1st　　　　**9**　　━━━━　　**INSTINCT**　　　　**CONSTRAINT**

Your preparedness for sudden change relieves any dread, allowing you to endure and experience good fortune in the end.

DESCRIPTION

The Arousing, Thunder, BELOW, repeated as the Arousing, Thunder, ABOVE, signifies Shocking Power. Awe is aroused by fear of the force and reverence for the movement within heaven. Such fear causes things to be put into order and merriment follows. The single Ruling Line, 1st, retains the memory of the shocking force as care and watchfulness for safety in the future. The Subject of the Hexagram, 6th line, yields with reverence to the startling movements below.

52

ABOVE: KEN
MOUNTAIN
Stillness
Silence

BELOW: KEN
MOUNTAIN
Stillness
Silence

KEN

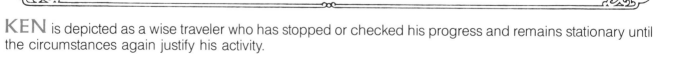

STOPPING AND REMAINING STILL IN THE APPROPRIATE TIME BRINGS NO HARM.

KEN is depicted as a wise traveler who has stopped or checked his progress and remains stationary until the circumstances again justify his activity.

KEN is a Time of Stopping or Checking activity and Remaining Still and Silent, characterized without Fault or Harm when done at the appropriate time or under the appropriate circumstances. This Hexagram warns of remaining alert to the times, detecting when a stop is required before going too far. The time of beginning anew follows so there is no need to fret.

PROPHESIES

LUCK is unfavorable, and WISHES do not come true at this time. LOVE is hindered by many obstacles. MARRIAGES are marked with strife that can best be waited out. CHILDREN, mostly male, do not show much ambition or promise early in life but awaken with goals later on. If PREGNANT, expect a boy, possibly twins, and a difficult delivery.

SICKNESS requires cessation of activities and confinement to bed if improvement is expected, and relates to the back, abdominal area, or spleen. Expect hemorrhoids, backaches, and chronic problems with arthritis or arteriosclerosis.

MISSING PEOPLE, in the Northeast, have stopped traveling, but you will not be able to find them until later. MISSING THINGS are covered by something similar and are close by, but not particularly easy to find. MOVING should not be undertaken now and stopped if in progress.

LOANS will not be granted. BUSINESS Ventures are experiencing difficulties which must be waited out instead of being forced if success is expected. JOBS are not favorable now. The MARKET suggests a time to buy, but don't expect a bargain or quick profits.

CHANGING LINES

6th   9   ▬▬▬▬   WISDOM   CONSTRAINT

Your attainment of tranquility and inner peace is providing you opportunity for good fortune in individual matters, but remain still until the time for action arrives.

5th   6   ▬▬ ▬▬   AUTHORITY   SIGNIFICANT

Your circumstances require restraint in speech, or silence. Such restraint insures that your words are heard when necessary and you will suffer no shame or regret.

4th   6   ▬▬ ▬▬   SOCIAL   VARIANT

Your circumstances demand restraint—such as stillness or silence—if you plan to remain free of fault or misfortune.

3rd   9   ▬▬▬▬   INDIVIDUAL   VARIANT

You have failed to heed warnings and find yourself in a perilous position. Remaining in such a position promises disastrous consequences. Calmly withdraw, if you can.

2nd   6   ▬▬ ▬▬   ASPIRATIONS   SIGNIFICANT

Your warnings to another to stop or remain still go unheeded. Their situation will cause you distress, but to avoid calamity stop yourself from following them.

1st   6   ▬▬ ▬▬   INSTINCT   CONSTRAINT

Stopping and patiently remaining still, silent, or inactive keeps you free from error or fault. The time for action is not close at hand.

DESCRIPTION

The Stillness, Mountain, BELOW, is doubled with the Stillness, Mountain, ABOVE. This indicates the appropriate time for stopping and remaining still. An endeavor has come to an end, and it is not yet time to begin anew. The single Ruling Line, 6th, is also the Subject of the Hexagram—remaining Still until it is time to proceed again. Just as there are appropriate times to stop, there are also times to begin anew, which follow after the time of this Hexagram.

53

ABOVE: SUN
WIND, WOOD
Gentle
Penetrating

BELOW: KEN
MOUNTAIN
Stillness
Silence

漸

CHIEN

GRADUAL PROGRESS AND DEVELOPMENT
FOR GROWTH WHEN OBEDIENT.

CHIEN is depicted as the gradual development and growth of trees, as well as progress in movement—relating here to a flock of geese.

CHIEN is a Time of Gradual Progress and Development relating to growth, characterized by Good Fortune when firmly applying principles which express proper consideration towards others. This is related to Obedience of the Natural Order. This Hexagram also portrays the happy and successful marriage, and warns against self-interest, which would work against this favorable time.

PROPHESIES

LUCK is favorable, and WISHES require patience, but they gradually come true. LOVE is successful. MARRIAGES are harmonious and long enduring. CHILDREN of both sexes tend to be quiet and obedient, but with the particular talents to favorably influence others. If PREGNANT, expect a girl.

SICKNESS, gradually improving, relates to digestive or intestinal problems. Sinus ailments or flu also require special attention.

MISSING PEOPLE, in Easterly directions, are safe and will eventually be found—consider looking to distant forests and mountains. MISSING THINGS are high, mixed with other things, and will eventually be found. MOVING is very favorable when done step by step.

LOANS are granted, but be patient with the lender. BUSINESS Ventures go well with gradual increase and expansion. JOBS improve and offer career growth. The MARKET is seen to be gradually rising—buy or hold.

CHANGING LINES

| 6th | 9 | ▬▬▬▬▬ | WISDOM | CONSTRAINT |

You can expect good fortune and attainment by modeling your efforts after others who have preceded you in similiar circumstances.

| 5th | 9 | ▬▬▬▬▬ | AUTHORITY | SIGNIFICANT |

Your patience, obedience to natural order, and concern for others during the long period of development and growth is bringing you reward. Expect good fortune.

| 4th | 6 | ▬▬ ▬▬ | SOCIAL | VARIANT |

Your continued progress and development is experiencing unstable circumstances. Flexible readjustment and gaining support from others, keeps you free from error.

| 3rd | 9 | ▬▬▬▬▬ | INDIVIDUAL | VARIANT |

Your overwhelming self-interest has separated you from others. Expect no help, failure in your objectives, and misfortune.

| 2nd | 6 | ▬▬ ▬▬ | ASPIRATIONS | SIGNIFICANT |

Your efforts and obedience to natural order have brought reward. Enjoy the good fortune and continue as you have in the past.

| 1st | 6 | ▬▬ ▬▬ | INSTINCT | CONSTRAINT |

Your progress and development brings trouble and criticism in the beginning—but with correct motives your advance will continue.

DESCRIPTION

The Stillness, Mountain, BELOW, shares influence with the Gentle, Wood, ABOVE. Most expressly seen as the gradual development and growth of a tree upon the mountain—growing in obedience with nature's order. Both ruling lines, 2nd and 5th, are in natural and corresponding positions with each other underscoring the favorableness of this Hexagram. The Subject of the Hexagram, 3rd Line, is the only unfavorable element, and it appears as overwhelming self-interest and careless disregard for others.

54

ABOVE: CHEN
THUNDER
Movement
Arousing

BELOW: TUI
LAKE, MARSH
Joyous
Cheerful

歸妹

KUEI
MEI

ABANDONING INCORRECT ATTITUDES AND
RE-ADAPTING PREVENTS MISFORTUNE.

KUEI MEI is depicted as the dissatisfaction which has resulted from one having submitted to the guile of another.

KUEI MEI is a Time when pursuit of Incorrect Goals and Objectives are characterized with Distress and Misfortune, although there is some initial happiness. Satisfaction from success is soon replaced by despair as the relationship is actually incorrect. Unlike the correct following found in SUI, #17, this situation is essentially the reverse, and incorrect following is indicated.

PROPHESIES

LUCK is poor, and WISHES come true—but they are regretted. LOVE does succeed, but does not endure. MARRIAGES, lacking harmony, are filled with distress and misfortune. CHILDREN, of both sexes, never seem to get along with others in life and are regarded as spoiled. If PREGNANT, expect a girl.

SICKNESS, severe, tends to improve, but never fully, and relates to the mouth, lungs, or possibly the heart. Liver problems appear, and a general sense of dispair gives way to dissipation—stop smoking and drinking. Use care to prevent venereal diseases.

MISSING PEOPLE, probably in the East, have met with misfortune—hurry and find them. MISSING THINGS have been moved or altered from when you last saw them, but can be found. MOVING starts out well but ends in disaster. If you have started, stop.

LOANS appear as though they will be granted, but are ultimately refused. BUSINESS Ventures show initial profits, but wrong estimates and the suppression of the correct talents provide eventual loss. JOBS appear favorable but end in chaos. The MARKET rises a little then drops—sell now.

CHANGING LINES

6th   6   ▬▬ ▬▬   WISDOM   CONSTRAINT

Superficial efforts produce empty results. You can expect no advantage or advancement from meaningless endeavors at this time.

5th   6   ▬▬ ▬▬   AUTHORITY   SIGNIFICANT

Abandoning vanity and adapting to the prevailing circumstances—even though you may not receive a position of high honor—will bring certain good fortune.

4th   9   ▬▬▬▬▬   SOCIAL   VARIANT

Permanent or substantial committments should not be made hurriedly. Take your time in deciding. Minor opportunities may be lost, but great opportunities come.

3rd   6   ▬▬ ▬▬   INDIVIDUAL   VARIANT

Capricious and flippant attitudes are denying you the relationships you seek. By abandoning these attitudes you can regain esteem, but not to the degree you originally anticipated.

2nd   9   ▬▬▬▬▬   ASPIRATIONS   SIGNIFICANT

Disappointing losses need not bring misfortune. Continuing to work towards your original goals will bring advantageous results.

1st   9   ▬▬▬▬▬   INSTINCT   CONSTRAINT

Your current position seems to provide you little or no advantage, but adapting to the circumstances and helping others brings good fortune anyway.

DESCRIPTION

The Movement, Thunder, ABOVE, subordinates to the Joyous, Lake, BELOW. Here one influence has purposely and with certain guile persuaded a force into a situation where it does not belong. Distress and misfortune follow after some initial happiness. The Ruling Line, 5th, is weak and subordinates to its correlate in Line 2. The Subject of the Hexagram, 3rd Line, is also weak and in conflict with Line 2. The incorrectness of the principle lines of this Hexagram also suggests the operation of an incorrect marriage.

55

ABOVE: CHEN
THUNDER
Movement
Arousing

BELOW: LI
FIRE, SUN
Brilliance
Clarity

豐

FENG

WITH PROSPERITY AND ABUNDANCE OF THE
GREATEST MOMENT PREPARE FOR DECLINE.

FENG is depicted as the sun, at its zenith, over prosperity. The stars indicate the possibility of eclipse or decline. The Chinese character represents "many beans," or an abundance of foodstuffs.

FENG is a Time when Prosperity and Abundance are at their Greatest, characterized with Coming Decline, in accordance with Natural Order. When things are at their greatest, they can only decline. This should cause no distress or fear but, rather, a preparation for the decline with the knowledge of this certainty.

PROPHESIES

LUCK very favorable now, but becoming less so, and WISHES are not as easily attained as you originally believed. LOVE matures, showing less intensity. MARRIAGES endure and are harmonious, but with less romance and some discord. CHILDREN, mostly female, bring happiness to themselves and their parents as they are adequately disciplined for the future. If PREGNANT, expect a boy.

SICKNESS tends to worsen. Preventitive care is necessary and relates to the liver, blood system, or heart. Headaches, fevers, or brain-related problems are also possibilities.

MISSING PEOPLE, South to East, are in increasing need of help, and should be found quickly. MISSING THINGS are mixed in with others. Locate them now or they may be destroyed or burned. MOVING starts off well, but is met with gradually increasing difficulties.

LOANS look as though they will be easily granted, but go through many difficult stages—be patient. BUSINESS Ventures, although quite profitable now, need to be prepared for a period of less success to follow. JOBS are favorable now, but carelessness could bring misfortune. The MARKET indicates a coming decline. Consider selling.

CHANGING LINES

6th   6   ▬▬ ▬▬   **WISDOM**   **CONSTRAINT**

Your failure to prepare for decline has lost you the help of associates as well as assets. Expect the current difficulties and misfortune to continue for a considerable time ahead.

5th   6   ▬▬ ▬▬   **AUTHORITY**   **SIGNIFICANT**

Your association with competent allies has brought advantage and recognition—expect good fortune as well.

4th   9   ▬▬▬▬   **SOCIAL**   **VARIANT**

Your patience, in the face of intervening obstacles, should now be coupled with strong, capable, and energetic associates to produce good fortune.

3rd   9   ▬▬▬▬   **INDIVIDUAL**   **VARIANT**

Your abilities are totally obscured by the inferior influences of others. Restrained and hindered, you can only patiently wait this period out.

2nd   6   ▬▬ ▬▬   **ASPIRATIONS**   **SIGNIFICANT**

Expect your efforts to fail when aggressively attacking the powerful, but inferior, suppressing force. Only by patiently working toward your original goals can you expect good fortune.

1st   9   ▬▬▬▬   **INSTINCT**   **CONSTRAINT**

You can associate with elements as strong as yourself during periods of prosperity, but when decline follows, failure of either influence to yield or re-adapt, invites calamity.

DESCRIPTION

The Brilliant, Sun, BELOW, with the Movement, Thunder, ABOVE, indicates the highest position of the mid-day sun, now beginning its decline into the later afternoon. This is a natural order, and with preparedness, one need have no fear of the change. The single Ruling Line, 5th, is compared to the sun at mid-day which begins yielding to the afternoon. The Subject of the Hexagram, also the 5th Line, places an individual in this greatest of positions with the message to prepare, as only lesser greatness can follow.

56

ABOVE: LI
FIRE, SUN
Brilliance
Clarity

BELOW: KEN
MOUNTAIN
Stillness
Silence

旅

LU

TRAVELING BRINGS VULNERABILITY AND
DIFFICULTY TO BE FIRMLY RESOLVED.

LU is depicted as the lodging quarters, or inn, sheltering the travelers. But it does not show the difficulties which may be found within.

LU is a Time associated with Travelling or Wandering, characterized by Small Attainments and the necessity to Firmly Resolve Difficulties to promote Good Fortune. This time speaks of exposure and vulnerability to difficulties with certain lessons for preparedness when in unknown places and guarding against overbearing behavior.

PROPHESIES

LUCK cannot be relied upon now, and WISHES only come true when they are kept small. LOVE does not succeed. MARRIAGES go poorly, but endure and attain harmony when the marital problems are eventually resolved. CHILDREN, mostly female, don't seem to "settle down," and are careless, lonely, and unhappy. If PREGNANT, expect a girl.

SICKNESS lingers, and with the passing of one ailment, along comes another, and relates to the heart or blood system. Backaches, fatigue, and problems relating to the waist can be expected. Fevers come on suddenly and may represent a contagious malady.

MISSING PEOPLE, in the South—and high—are very difficult to locate as they move about, but need your help anyway. MISSING THINGS have probably been handled by others and moved. Look where you would NOT expect them to be. MOVING can be accomplished, but be prepared for hardships.

LOANS, in small amounts, may be granted. BUSINESS Ventures are going poorly because of internal conflicts which must be firmly resolved by upper management before any expansion should be considered. JOBS are not favorable and only small successes, at best, can be expected. The MARKET, now unstable, can be expected to rise gradually in the future—but investigate carefully before buying.

CHANGING LINES

6th   9   ▬▬▬▬   **WISDOM**   **CONSTRAINT**

Your arrogant and reckless attitude has invited the disgust of others. You can expect regret, losses, and misfortune as no one will take you seriously anymore.

5th   6   ▬▬ ▬▬   **AUTHORITY**   **SIGNIFICANT**

With preparation, and consideration for others, your efforts meet with quick recognition and eventual success. Expect advancement. Good fortune will depend on you.

4th   9   ▬▬▬▬   **SOCIAL**   **VARIANT**

Your small attainments are not consistent with your ambitions and are causing you dissatisfaction. Remaining defensive and ill at ease will only prolong your misery.

3RD   9   ▬▬▬▬   **INDIVIDUAL**   **VARIANT**

Your intemperate and meddlesome behavior is driving others away from you. Such circumstances are of your own making—expect substantial loss and misfortune.

2nd   6   ▬▬ ▬▬   **ASPIRATIONS**   **SIGNIFICANT**

With modest or reserved behavior you can expect sincere and capable help. Your progress will be limited, but you will have nothing to complain about either.

1st   6   ▬▬ ▬▬   **INSTINCT**   **CONSTRAINT**

Your attention to unimportant matters has led to neglect of important matters. Expect misfortune from such neglect.

DESCRIPTION

The Sun, Brilliance, ABOVE, travels over the Mountain, Stillness, BELOW. Travelling over the mountain indicates a certain vulnerability and difficulty to be prepared for or firmly resolved, as the circumstances warrant. The single Ruling Line, 5th, is yielding to the circumstances, and is aided by the strength of the 4th and 6th Lines. The subject of the Hexagram, 4th line, is seen as the traveler at a resting place, but dissatisfied with the surroundings and lack of progress.

57

ABOVE: SUN
WIND, WOOD
Gentle
Penetrating

BELOW: SUN
WIND, WOOD
Gentle
Penetrating

巽

SUN

GENTLE, PENETRATING, MOVEMENT AND
OBEDIENTLY ADAPTING TO CIRCUMSTANCES.

SUN is depicted as a boat gently sailing across the waters with the wind filling its sails, In other words, the undertaking is obedient to the laws of Nature.

SUN is a Time of Gentle and Penetrating Movement in activities or affairs, characterized by Minor Progress and Attainment. Advantage is found by undertaking significant tasks and seeking wise advice to assist in seeing them through. A message being delivered by the "Wind" of this Hexagram is to put affairs and behavior in order.

PROPHESIES

LUCK can't be relied upon, and WISHES, when kept small, come true. LOVE, if to become successful, will depend on your adaptability. MARRIAGES experience the "ups" and "downs" of both harmony and discord. CHILDREN, many females, are obedient and considerate to parents, but frequently undertake new projects before completing the old ones. If PREGNANT, expect a girl.

SICKNESS is prolonged, wavers continually between the mild and severe, and relates to the nervous system. Venereal disease is suggested, as is lameness and leg injuries. A disabling stroke may appear unexpectedly.

MISSING PEOPLE, in the Southeast, are not too far away, probably hiding, and under the influence of another. MISSING THINGS have been moved away and hidden among other things. Seek help—they will be difficult to find. MOVING goes favorably, but don't rush or assume there will be no problems.

LOANS, when amounts are reasonable, will be granted. BUSINESS Ventures see both profit and loss. Adapting to the current market conditions will provide opportunity for future improvement. JOBS, although not ultimately satisfactory, can be advanced with the help of another. The MARKET, variable now, will be rising—consider buying.

CHANGING LINES

| 6th | 9 | ▬▬▬▬ | WISDOM | CONSTRAINT |

Your difficulties cannot be resolved by attempting to serve your own interests with insincere flattery as it only brings the disrespect of others. Expect misfortune and adversity.

| 5th | 9 | ▬▬▬▬ | AUTHORITY | SIGNIFICANT |

In spite of a poor beginning, the changes you can make now will produce good fortune. Prepare such changes in advance—then evaluate their effect. Correct and adapt as necesary.

| 4th | 6 | ▬▬ ▬▬ | SOCIAL | VARIANT |

Your education and experience are working well for you. Expect recognition of your effort and small attainment—but no great reward at this time.

| 3rd | 9 | ▬▬▬▬ | INDIVIDUAL | VARIANT |

Your inability to decide how to accomplish specific objectives produces misunderstanding, no advance, and in the end, humiliation.

| 2nd | 9 | ▬▬▬▬ | ASPIRATIONS | SIGNIFICANT |

Seek help in driving out suspicions, hidden motives, and prejudices. Once this is accomplished, you will be more favorably regarded and can expect good fortune.

| 1st | 6 | ▬▬ ▬▬ | INSTINCT | CONSTRAINT |

Your gentleness has given way to indecisiveness. Expect no advance until you firmly decide to pursue specific goals.

DESCRIPTION

The Gentle and Penetrating, Wind, both ABOVE and BELOW, symbolizes obedient movement—adaptation—in any direction. Adaptation resembles the wind in how it must adapt to the changing terrain and physical obstructions. The single Ruling Line, 5th, is honored by the other Lines, and its commands, particularly to put affairs in order, are spread to all—as if by the wind. The Subject of the Hexagram, 6th Line, is pretentuous and hypocritical, and movement, or progress, stops with this line.

58

ABOVE: TUI
LAKE, MARSH
Joyous
Cheerful

BELOW: TUI
LAKE, MARSH
Joyous
Cheerful

兌

TUI

JOY AND CHEERFULNESS ENCOURGE
PROGRESS AND ATTAINMENT.

TUI is depicted as two young daughters pleasantly proceeding in the pleasant environment of the lake and its surroundings.

TUI is a Time when Joy and Cheerfulness Encourage both individual and group efforts, characterized by Progress and Attainment. The result of Attainment, in pleasant circumstances, is Satisfaction. But even satisfaction relies on the proper attitude within oneself. The cheerfulness is passed on to others as happiness, and others naturally tend to follow this considerate leadership. Providing pleasure and satisfaction to others requires sincerity in expressions of consideration toward them.

PROPHESIES

LUCK is favorable, and WISHES come true when attitudes are correct. LOVE is happy and joyous. MARRIAGES attain satisfaction and harmony when consideration is extended between the partners. CHILDREN, mostly female, are happy—bringing happiness to the parents as well as others. If PREGNANT, expect a girl.

SICKNESS is mild, but lingering when proper care is not applied, and relates to ingestion or breathing. Asthma, stomachaches, and toothaches are indicated. There is also a suggestion of venereal disease.

MISSING PEOPLE, joyfully wandering around in the West, are probably in love, and are free from exposure to peril. They can be found without difficulty. MISSING THINGS are on the "top of the heap" and easily found. MOVING goes well, especially when not moving alone.

LOANS will be granted; use the proceeds wisely. BUSINESS Ventures show profit, and satisfied employees encourage and promote further success. However, don't become impervious to difficulties which could still arise. JOBS are favorable, with pleasant working conditions. The MARKET suggests selling—a favorable time now, but expect an unstable period in the near future.

CHANGING LINES

6th   6   ▬▬ ▬▬   WISDOM   CONSTRAINT

Using guile or flattery to attract others exposes questionable motives. You can expect no satisfying progress or attainment with this approach toward others.

5th   9   ▬▬▬▬   AUTHORITY   SIGNIFICANT

You cannot progress or expect attainment by placing your trust or confidence in inferior or self-serving elements. Study associates carefully before extending any authority.

4th   9   ▬▬▬▬   SOCIAL   VARIANT

Recognizing your distress in choosing between lowly and lofty pursuits will lead you away from the lowly decision. Expect to find joy and satisfaction.

3rd   6   ▬▬ ▬▬   INDIVIDUAL   VARIANT

Your attempts to use others solely for your own satisfaction or advantage brings disappointing results and disaster.

2nd   9   ▬▬▬▬   ASPIRATIONS   SIGNIFICANT

Finding satisfaction within your circumstances, and cheerfully communicating with others, frees you from any remorse—expect good fortune to follow.

1st   9   ▬▬▬▬   INSTINCT   CONSTRAINT

Inner satisfaction and contentment frees you of desire and envy. Expect such contentment to lead to good fortune.

DESCRIPTION

The Joyous and Cheerful Lake—doubled ABOVE and BELOW. The Pleasantness of this Hexagram encourages Progress and Attainment. Both Ruling Lines, the 2nd and 5th, indicate firmness within, and as each are close to an outwardly yielding influence (the 3rd and 6th Lines respectively), they do not contain the conflict normally associated with uncorresponding positions. The Subject of the Hexagram, 6th Line, even though it has the ability to attract others, contains questionable or ulterior motives.

59

ABOVE: SUN
WIND, WOOD
Gentle
Penetrating

BELOW: K'AN
WATER, DARK
Danger
Abysmal

HUAN

SCATTERING EXPOSES THE INFERIOR AND ALLOWS REASSEMBLY OF THE SUPERIOR.

HUAN is depicted as the progress of a boat on a journey, The obstructions have been eliminated and the boat is carried forward by the gentle, but penetrating, wind.

HUAN is a Time when Scattering Exposes and Eliminates Inferior elements hindering progress, and Reassembling the Favorable or Superior elements for Attainment. It is characterized by Progress and Success in undertakings when such Dispersion is correctly accomplished. This Hexagram speaks favorably of this operation, and pent-up emotions, anxieties, and fears can likewise be dispersed at this time, relieving the blockage of personal progress.

PROPHESIES

LUCK is favorable, and WISHES come true as the damaging or distressing elements are eliminated. LOVE succeeds with persistent efforts to overcome obstacles. MARRIAGES become harmonious when issues causing controversy are eliminated. CHILDREN, mostly male, are stubborn, but can be favorably disciplined and educated. If PREGNANT, you may be suprised by a girl.

SICKNESS lingers and will worsen unless proper care is applied early. Illness relates to emotional distress as well as liver or urinary problems. Uterine problems are also indicated.

MISSING PEOPLE, in the North, are cold and isolated—needing attention and care. MISSING THINGS are difficult to find and have probably been dispersed—perhaps having been sold off by another. MOVING goes well once initial problems are resolved.

LOANS will be granted, but not on the first attempt. BUSINESS Ventures, with persistent determination to overcome obstacles, become successful. JOBS become favorable once obstacles are overcome. The MARKET shows a dropping trend and suggests an excellent time to trade off unfavorable issues for favorable ones.

CHANGING LINES

6th   9   ▬▬▬▬▬   **WISDOM**   **CONSTRAINT**

Remove yourself from troublesome situations or worries at this time, and expect freedom from anxiety without criticism from your associates.

5th   9   ▬▬▬▬▬   **AUTHORITY**   **SIGNIFICANT**

Your dispersion of accumulated wealth for the common benefit and progress brings satisfactory results as well as personal satisfaction.

4th   6   ▬▬ ▬▬   **SOCIAL**   **VARIANT**

Only a very few have the courage to dissolve their current associations in order to bring the most favorable back together, but those who do can expect great good fortune.

3rd   6   ▬▬ ▬▬   **INDIVIDUAL**   **VARIANT**

Your progress will depend upon your dispersion of self-interest to achieve success at this time. Such a sacrifice will, however, bring no regret.

2nd   9   ▬▬▬▬▬   **ASPIRATIONS**   **SIGNIFICANT**

Replacing anxiety, mistrust, or fear with more temperate attitudes, especially towards mankind, frees you from remorse.

1st   6   ▬▬ ▬▬   **INSTINCT**   **CONSTRAINT**

Don't rely on your individual efforts to expose and eliminate obstacles restricting progress. By securing competent help and support, you can expect success and good fortune.

DESCRIPTION

The Danger, Water, BELOW, is frozen with the Penetrating, Wind, ABOVE, warming and thawing, and the blockage caused by the ice is being relieved. As the blockage is freed, the inferior elements are eliminated, and the superior forces (rivers and lakes) are reassembled. The single Ruling Line, 5th, is strong and represents the power which can correctly disperse and then reassemble to restore order. The 5th Line is also the Subject of the Hexagram and relates this favorable attribute to common benefit. A special courage, making possible the accomplishment of such a transition, is related in the 4th Line as a startling revelation.

60

ABOVE: K'AN
WATER, DARK
Danger
Abysmal

BELOW: TUI
LAKE, MARSH
Joyous
Cheerful

節

CHIEH

LIMITATION AND REGULATION PROVIDES PROGRESS WHEN NOT EXCESSIVELY APPLIED.

CHIEH is depicted as a superior person, conscious of limitations—represented by the courtyard. The Chinese character actually symbolizes the limiting joints of a bamboo stalk.

CHIEH is a Time of Limitation and Regulation as affairs are restored to order, characterized by Progress and Attainment when restrictions are sufficient to restore the order, but not excessive beyond the restoration of order. Although difficulty and peril are present, cheerfulness can be expected to provide favorable conclusions.

PROPHESIES

LUCK is favorable when pleasant attitudes are maintained, and WISHES come true, but with difficulty—be patient. LOVE is successful with patience and understanding. MARRIAGES become harmonious with the consistence efforts of both partners to accentuate favorable aspects of the relationship. Mostly male CHILDREN tend to be obedient and peaceful, resulting from correct discipline applied by the parents. If PREGNANT, expect a boy.

SICKNESS is prolonged, and relates to the mouth, breathing system, kidneys or urinary tract. Recuperation is possible with clinical restraints. Digestive upsets resulting from diets can be expected. Alcohol worsens any situation.

MISSING PEOPLE, North to West, may be to embarrassed to return, and are possibly bitter over a soured love affair. MISSING THINGS are covered, close by, and can be found. Search patiently. MOVING brings nothing but difficulty. If possible, postpone it until later.

LOANS are granted, but have limitations or conditions you hadn't expected. BUSINESS Ventures become profitable by patiently and systematically completing projects or resolving difficulties. JOBS are hard to obtain, but persistent efforts eventually bring reward. The MARKET may rise a little more, but expect a quiet and stable time to follow. Best investments are probably utilities.

CHANGING LINES

| 6th | 6 | ▬▬ ▬▬ | WISDOM | CONSTRAINT |

In spite of correct motives, severe limitations and restrictions provide failure and misfortune. This degree of regulation cannot long endure and eventually disappears completely.

| 5th | 9 | ▬▬▬▬ | AUTHORITY | SIGNIFICANT |

Cheerful moderation and personal restraint set an example for others. Expect respect, cooperation, progress, and good fortune.

| 4th | 6 | ▬▬ ▬▬ | SOCIAL | VARIANT |

Limiting and moderating your lifestyle to conform to a more natural order conserves energies and allows peaceful progress and success.

| 3rd | 6 | ▬▬ ▬▬ | INDIVIDUAL | VARIANT |

Your unlimited and selfish pursuits will bring distress—expect to blame no one but yourself for the consequences.

| 2nd | 9 | ▬▬▬▬ | ASPIRATIONS | SIGNIFICANT |

Your failure to proceed at this time causes misfortune now and losses of opportunity later.

| 1st | 9 | ▬▬▬▬ | INSTINCT | CONSTRAINT |

Confidently knowing when to stop, and when to proceed, provides attainment without error.

DESCRIPTION

The Cheerful, Lake, BELOW, requires regulation as the Danger, Water, ABOVE, continues flowing and filling. Such regulation controls water levels as the river unites with the Lake. The single Ruling Line, 5th, represents the strength required to correctly achieve union. Here cheerfulness, in the presence of danger, is also suggested as an attribute. The Subject of the Hexagram, 1st Line, is at the base of the cheerfulness and, with certain knowledge of limitations, correct progress is attained.

61

ABOVE: SUN
WIND, WOOD
Gentle
Penetrating

BELOW: TUI
LAKE, MARSH
Joyous
Cheerful

中孚

CHUNG
FU

SINCERITY FROM WITHIN THE HEART
ADVANCES RELATIONSHIPS WITH OTHERS.

CHUNG FU is depicted as progress in journeys through cooperation. The cranes, in the flora around the edge of the lake, dramatize inner sincerity when relating with others.

CHUNG FU is a Time when Inner Sincerity and Truth advance relationships with all others, characterized by Good Fortune and Advantage in Movement or Undertaking significant tasks. The advantageousness of this Hexagram comes from the help and support of others which have been influenced by the inner sincerity. The authors remind the reader not to confuse CHUNG FU with "KUNG FU", which is primarily a study of martial arts.

PROPHESIES

LUCK is favorable, and WISHES come true when sincere concern is expressed towards others. LOVE is successful. MARRIAGES are harmonious and peaceful when partners are concerned for each other. CHILDREN of both sexes are contented—bringing happiness to parents. If PREGNANT, expect a girl.

SICKNESS can become very grave and relates to the heart, liver, or kidneys. Anxieties need to be abandoned. Heart attacks and peritonitis may suddenly appear.

MISSING PEOPLE, in the West, have found satisfaction in new relationships and are not interested in returning. MISSING THINGS may have fallen into the hands of another, but are returned or reappear after a long period of time. MOVING is favorable—but be sure of your need to move.

LOANS will be granted. BUSINESS Ventures show increased sales and profit when sincere regard is applied to the quality of products or services. JOBS are particularly favorable now. The MARKET shows a gradual rise in the near future, but don't let blind faith alter your good judgement.

CHANGING LINES

6th   9   ▬▬▬▬▬   **WISDOM**   **CONSTRAINT**

Even sincerity can be carried to an arrogant extreme. Believing you have become more superior than others brings certain downfall.

5th   9   ▬▬▬▬▬   **AUTHORITY**   **SIGNIFICANT**

Your sincere regard for others attracts their help and support—expect easy progress.

4th   6   ▬▬ ▬▬   **SOCIAL**   **VARIANT**

No fault is found when you abandon selfish or self-serving relationships and pursue the virtuous and noble.

3rd   6   ▬▬ ▬▬   **INDIVIDUAL**   **VARIANT**

Although sincere, your dependency upon relationships with another causes either grief or happiness, depending on the moods of the other. Satisfaction can only be determined by yourself.

2nd   9   ▬▬▬▬▬   **ASPIRATIONS**   **SIGNIFICANT**

Your sincere concern for others brings personal satisfaction as very close and special relationships are shared with others.

1st   9   ▬▬▬▬▬   **INSTINCT**   **CONSTRAINT**

By remaining honest and sincere towards others, you can expect good fortune. Schemes or designs, however, will provoke disaster.

DESCRIPTION

The Gentle, Wind, ABOVE, moves over the Pleasant, Lake, BELOW. Gentleness and pleasantness reflect the operation of sincerity within. The lake is touched by the wind, as are other persons favorably touched by inner sincerity. The single Ruling Line, 5th, is the perfectly sincere leader, and all others form close union with this perfection. The Subject of the Hexagram, 4th Line, is moving away from inferior influences by following the example of perfection in the 5th Line.

62

ABOVE: CHEN
THUNDER
Movement
Arousing

BELOW: KEN
MOUNTAIN
Stillness
Silence

小過

HSIAO
KUO

GENTLE BEHAVIOR PREDOMINATES AND SMALL ENDEAVORS WORK ADVANTAGEOUSLY.

HSIAO KUO is depicted as the bird ascending into certain peril without conscious regard of the danger.

HSIAO KUO is a Time when Small Issues in behavior, undertakings, and material wealth predominate. It is characterized with Great Good Fortune when it is recognized that descending or holding, rather than ascending, is required to produce satisfactory changes or transitions. It is of the opposite effect of TA KUO, #28, (the Preponderance of the Great).

PROPHESIES

LUCK is favorable in small issues, and WISHES come true when not ambitious. LOVE succeeds and, with gentleness, endures. MARRIAGES are not harmonious unless egos are set aside. CHILDREN, mostly male, are troubled and may not have satisfying lives. If PREGNANT, however, expect a girl.

SICKNESS can become very severe unless all activity ceases, and relates to the liver, kidney, or other vital organs in the lower abdominal area. Injuries to limbs—hands, arms, legs, or feet—are also indicated.

MISSING PEOPLE, in an Easterly direction, may be destitute—without even bus fare—and difficult to locate. MISSING THINGS have probably been swept away or stolen—don't expect to find them unless they have no value. MOVING does not go well as there are too many obstacles.

LOANS will be granted in small amounts only. BUSINESS Ventures are troubled, and closing down unprofitable operations or projects will lead back to recovery. JOBS, temporary, are available, but permanent positions won't be offered until later. The MARKET will be rising, then declining—suggesting the need for great care when buying or selling.

CHANGING LINES

6th   6   ▬▬ ▬▬   **WISDOM**   **CONSTRAINT**

Your advance, without having resolved the smaller matters requiring your attention, is bringing misfortune and injury upon you through your own fault.

5th   6   ▬▬ ▬▬   **AUTHORITY**   **SIGNIFICANT**

Recognize your weakness or inabilities. The competent help you require will not volunteer and must be laboriously sought out.

4th   9   ▬▬▬▬   **SOCIAL**   **VARIANT**

Neither advance nor withdraw, but hold your position, as any decisive change places you in jeopardy. Avoiding change at this time, you can expect freedom from error or harm.

3rd   9   ▬▬▬▬   **INDIVIDUAL**   **VARIANT**

Careless disregard for small matters requiring your attention are leading to great misfortune and possibly physical injury. Evaluate such matters and protect yourself.

2nd   6   ▬▬ ▬▬   **ASPIRATIONS**   **SIGNIFICANT**

No fault or harm will come to you now if you accept the restraints which have been imposed upon you.

1st   6   ▬▬ ▬▬   **INSTINCT**   **CONSTRAINT**

In spite of warnings for the need of economy you have allowed extravagance to continue. Expect misfortune.

DESCRIPTION

The Arousing, Thunder, ABOVE, is contained within the Silent, Mountain, BELOW. Thus moving thunder is restrained from great movement as would normally be the case on the plains, and the sense of success associated with gentleness of behavior, smaller undertakings, and economy is indicated. The two Ruling Lines, 2nd and 5th, both indicate a yielding during transition, also represented by this Hexagram. The Subject of the Hexagram, 4th line, shows the advantage of holding firm but avoiding the misfortune from attempts of ascent which are beyond means to accomplish.

63

ABOVE: K'AN
WATER, DARK
Danger
Abysmal

BELOW: LI
FIRE, SUN
Brilliance
Clarity

CHI
CHI

ENDEAVORS ARE ACCOMPLISHED. AFTER COMPLETION ONLY LESSER ORDER FOLLOWS.

CHI CHI is depicted as the satisfactory completion of a journey. All events have come to order.

CHI CHI is a Time when Endeavors and efforts have brought Successful Completion, establishing perfect order, and is characterized by Progress and Success in small matters, along with Good Fortune. The time of perfect completion can only be followed by lesser degrees of order. No distress should follow as this is in accord with the natural order.

PROPHESIES

LUCK, good until now, begins to diminish, and WISHES are realized less frequently. LOVE, contented now, begins to show discontent. MARRIAGES will begin to experience unexpected problems which upset the harmony of this time. CHILDREN, of both sexes, get along while young, but become more argumentative they grow older. If PREGNANT, expect a boy.

SICKNESS, is marked with relapse, but recuperation is possible. Illness relates to the heart, blood system, or kidneys. Diminished eyesight or hearing are also indicated.

MISSING PEOPLE, probably in the North, are easily found, but choose to remain away. If brought home they only leave again. MISSING THINGS are on top of something, maybe floating, and can be found easily, but will probably be lost again. MOVING, probably completed now, should not be started again at this time.

LOANS should be secured quickly, otherwise you will have more difficulty. BUSINESS Ventures are going well, but complacency may set in, bringing even severe difficulties. JOBS should be obtained now—offers may be withdrawn. The MARKET is favorable now, but declines are indicated—consider selling.

CHANGING LINES

6th　　　　**6**　　　━━　━━　　　**WISDOM**　　　　**CONSTRAINT**

Your attitude assuming that this favorable time will last forever places you in deep peril. Only by proceeding with caution and sincere effort can you move away from peril.

5th　　　　**9**　　　━━━━━　　　**AUTHORITY**　　　　**SIGNIFICANT**

To maintain your successful position, maintain sincere and dedicated effort—otherwise your contributions will fail to be recognized and you will fall from the favor of others.

4th　　　　**6**　　　━━　━━　　　**SOCIAL**　　　　**VARIANT**

Your doubts are well founded—you are exposed to hidden dangers. Continue to take precautions and correct any faults.

3rd　　　　**9**　　　━━━━━　　　**INDIVIDUAL**　　　　**VARIANT**

Undertaking tasks of which you are not fully capable will cause loss, hardship, and prolonged delays—but you will eventually succeed. Secure the most competent help available.

2nd　　　　**6**　　　━━　━━　　　**ASPIRATIONS**　　　　**SIGNIFICANT**

You may need to make a temporary sacrifice to adjust to current circumstances. Accept this situation and any losses will be restored.

1st　　　　**9**　　　━━━━━　　　**INSTINCT**　　　　**CONSTRAINT**

You can expect to avoid danger or misfortune by not proceeding at this time—or by making very careful preparations before proceeding.

DESCRIPTION

The Brilliant, Fire, BELOW, has been extinguished by the Danger, Water, ABOVE. The completion is symbolized by the quenching of the fire, and the lines of this Hexagram are in perfect and natural order. From such perfect order there only follows lesser degrees of order. The single Ruling Line, 2nd, has yielded to insure that perfect order is attained. The Subject of the Hexagram, 3rd line, also suggests completion, but only after much effort and time.

64

ABOVE: LI
FIRE, SUN
Brilliance
Clarity

BELOW: K'AN
WATER, DARK
Danger
Abysmal

未濟

**WEI
CHI**

ENDEAVORS ARE YET UNDONE. WITH SINCERE
EFFORTS FOR COMPLETION ORDER FOLLOWS.

WEI CHI is depicted as a courageous journey underway with much to do—and a long distance to travel—before completion.

WEI CHI is a Time when Endeavors or Projects are undone and there is much yet to do, it is characterized with Progress and Success when resolute and diligent efforts are applied to the tasks at hand. An exciting time, but not a time when the faint-hearted or indecisive can expect to successfully prevail. It is particularly interesting to note that the I CHING does not complete its commentary with an ending, but rather a transition to another beginning.

PROPHESIES

LUCK, now poor, is improving, and WISHES come true with diligent effort and hard work. LOVE is moving away from a period of discord. MARRIAGES are beginning to show signs of improvement—but still need a lot of effort by both partners. CHILDREN, of both sexes, are serious and will become hard working and prosperous adults. If PREGNANT, expect a boy.

SICKNESS gradually improves—expect recuperation—and relates to the urinary tract, kidneys, or sex organs. Heart attack or strokes may unexpectedly appear. Hearing or visual impairments are indicated. Fevers can be expected, as well as measles in children.

MISSING PEOPLE, in the South, are in difficulty—you can expect them to contact you or return on their own. MISSING THINGS are high and difficult to see—requiring patience to find. If wood or paper, they may have been burned. MOVING succeeds, but expect difficulties when starting.

LOANS will be granted later. BUSINESS Ventures return to profitable status with diligent effort to correct or overcome problems. JOBS are becoming available, but don't accept the first offer. The MARKET may be recovering from a staggering loss, but improvements now suggest a favorable time to buy.

CHANGING LINES

6th   9   WISDOM   CONSTRAINT

The actual arrival of success is unimportant when one has the satisfaction of clear and perfect conduct. But without such conduct, the success fails to appear at all.

5th   6   AUTHORITY   SIGNIFICANT

Your efforts to advance are becoming successful due to your planning and preparation. Expect capable help to volunteer now and good fortune to follow.

4th   9   SOCIAL   VARIANT

Your careful and tireless preparation can now be used when acting or advancing. Expect success and good fortune as remorse or regret disappear.

3rd   6   INDIVIDUAL   VARIANT

Changes are imminent but you are unprepared to take any action. If you attempt to advance, you can expect misfortune. Any preparation you make now provides advantage for future advancement.

2nd   9   ASPIRATIONS   SIGNIFICANT

The time has not yet come to take action. Continuing to prepare for the proper opportunity will provide success and good fortune when the opportunity appears.

1st   6   INSTINCT   CONSTRAINT

Your unprepared advance forces you into a humiliating retreat. Reassess your abilities and learn from this experience.

DESCRIPTION

The Brilliance, Sun, ABOVE, is ascending over the Danger, Water, BELOW. The dawn (beginning) has passed, but the complete disorder of this Hexagram suggests much to do before completion. The single Ruling Line, 5th, has yielded between two stronger positions and represents a successful transition, or return, to order. The Subject of the Hexagram, 4th line, is strong and represents diligent and enduring effort to restore order. The lines of this Hexagram are all out of natural position, implying that only greater degrees of order follow.

STEP 4: ELEMENTARY ANALYSIS
OF THE TRIGRAMS

STEP 4 provides the Player the fundamentals for elementary analysis of the Trigrams. The Player's ability to correctly analyze a Trigram will improve with experience and application, and with the accumulation of such knowledge, it is expected that the Player will want to seek more insight into the representations of these three meaningful lines.

This Step is organized to provide understanding of the prevalence of influences, the attributes of influences, as well as some purely entertaining aspects of Oriental culture—closely, but not correctly, associated with the I CHING.

With experience, the Player will determine the depth of analysis sought for any question and will choose where to terminate within this Step. Also, with such experience, the Player will derive "short-cuts" which provide meaningful interpretations of the prophesies. The publisher also offers **I CHING, The Advanced Techniques,** and asks the Player to note that other publications are also commercially available which provide various methods of analysis.

THE PRINCIPLES OF MUTUAL CREATION AND DESTRUCTION. The I CHING routinely resolves the prevailing influence between any associative influence with the use of a "Principle of Mutual Creation and Destruction." This concept was introduced in Step 2, but is expanded here for the Player as it is the elementary method used to determine significant trends in the I CHING prophesies.

CREATION has the character of giving birth. Viewed from the standpoint of the newborn this is advantageous because it has received something it didn't have before—life. From the standpoint of the creators this is not quite as advantageous since they have taken something from themselves and passed it on to another — even though it can be expected to be based upon love. This is a natural passing, and although it detracts from the originators, it provides for the future and continuity of the natural order.

DESTRUCTION has the character of taking for itself. Viewed from the standpoint of the prevailing adversary it is advantageous since it has acquired something from the other. From the standpoint of the oppressed it is unfavorable since involuntary sacrifice is made.

EQUALITY occurs when the associative influences are the same, and it signifies a supportive situation which is best related with peer groups, or as brothers and sisters.

These precepts, when representing a prevailing situation, are important. Compare the opposing concepts—has advantage been found because life has been given for the future, or has advantage been found by the destruction of a supposed opposition. There is some relief in the philosophy of the I CHING, however, since forceful destructions are normally intended to be applied against inferior or immoral influences.

These precepts also have reciprocal influences which either act favorably or unfavorably in opposition.

— Life, from Creation, is revered, and love is passed back to the origin, which is probably the parents.

— Destruction, or destructive ability, tends to pass back fear or hatred.

To address comparative conditions a Subject and Object need to be introduced. In the I CHING, the Subject, or "Self" as most strictly interpreted, is the Subject of the consultation, and it is the Subject's position within the Universal Order which is being determined.

The Object, strictly interpreted as "Other," is representative of the influences most directly interfacing with the Subject, and the prevailing influence may be either the Subject or Object, being resolved by the Principle of Mutual Creation and Destruction.

Even "YES-NO" questions are resolved by the I CHING with these precepts.

— Creation, when received from another source, is strongly positive—YES.

— Creation, when given to another, is mildly negative—NO.

— Destruction, when applied to another, is mildly positive—YES.

— Destruction, when received from another, is strongly negative—NO.

The third precept of equal influence is considered favorable from the standpoint of being supportive, even though it does not act as either a creative or destructive force. In antiquity these five operations; 1-Being Created; 2-Destroying; 3-Neither, or Equality; 4-Creating; and 5-Being Destroyed; were seen as the emulation of all life cycles and, consequently, the operation of physical phenomena were applied to these operations in the form of five "Live Elements": Earth, Water, Wood, Fire, and Metal.

EARTH—the foundation—was associated with the ability to Create internal things, and assigned the character of EARTH Creating METAL (as metallic ore).
EARTH was also associated with the the ability to Destroy fluid things, and assigned the character of EARTH Destroying WATER (by absorbtion and receptivity).

WATER was associated with the ability to Create living things—trees, flowers, plants, even mankind—and assigned the character of WATER Creating WOOD (as nourishment).
WATER was also associated with the ability to Destroy burning things, and assigned the character of WATER Destroying FIRE (as extinguishing).

WOOD was associated with the ability to Create burning things, and assigned the character of WOOD Creating FIRE (as fuel).
WOOD was also associated with the ability to Destroy its own foundation, and assigned the character of WOOD Destroying EARTH (as it grows and extracts sustenance from the Earth).

FIRE was associated with the ability to Create substantive things, and assigned the character of FIRE Creating EARTH (as the ash from burned or consumed items).
FIRE was also associated with the ability to Destroy hardened things, and assigned the character of FIRE Destroying METAL (as observed when the FIRE melts the METAL).

METAL was associated with the ability to Create things by condensation from its hard and cool nature, and assigned the character of METAL Creating WATER (as condensation).
METAL was also associated with the ability to Destroy living things, and assigned the character of METAL Destroying WOOD (most commonly seen as cutting wood with an ax or saw).

Even in antiquity it was evident to the original authors of the I CHING that there were more than five elements occurring in nature, but the Player should note that these five "Live Elements" are associated with specific abilities to create or destroy within a cyclic representation of each other. The diagram on page 213 relates this cyclic association somewhat more graphically. Note also the inclusion of the "Five Viscera," which are the organs believed to be governed by the five Live Elements.

The "Five Virtues"—Benevolence, Purity, Propriety, Wisdom, and Truth—are bestowed upon all persons at birth by the operation of the T'AI CHI, and their development is dependent upon the behavior of the individual throughout life. Therefore they are not associated to the Live Elements when relating to Creation and Destruction. The same is true of the "Five Poisons" which are represented by the viper, scorpion, centipede, toad, and spider.

Other "elements," such as Air, were not associated with the Creative-Destructive pattern as were the Live Elements. But Air, on the other hand, is the stage on which the dramatization and interplay of the Live Elements takes place, and the Wind (Trigram SUN) is associated with movement from place to place, while CHEN is associated with movement in an arousing sense. Note that both of these Trigrams are governed by the Element WOOD.

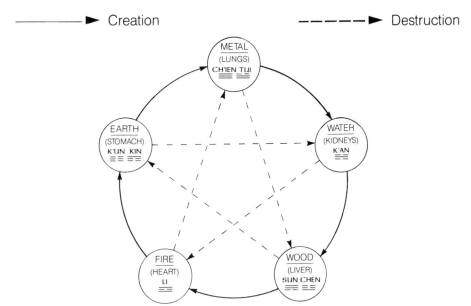

——————▶ Creation   – – – – –▶ Destruction

The simplified Table of Step 2 is repeated here for easy reference.

WATER Creates WOOD   WATER Destroys FIRE
EARTH Creates METAL   EARTH Destroys WATER
WOOD Creates FIRE   WOOD Destroys EARTH
FIRE Creates EARTH   FIRE Destroys METAL
METAL Creates WATER   METAL Destroys WOOD

Step 2, in this publication, routinely coincides the play of the "House" with a resultant Personification of the Line. In all cases the Personification of the Line was determined by the Principle of Mutual Creation and Destruction. The same comparison can be made when using the Subject and Object Trigrams of Hexagrams.

When the SUBJECT and OBJECT are the same,
    the personification is: Brothers, Sisters, and Peers.
When the SUBJECT Creates the OBJECT,
    the personification is: Sons, Daughters, Descendants.
When the SUBJECT Destroys the OBJECT,
    the personification is: Wife, Husband, Money, Business.
When the OBJECT Creates the SUBJECT,
    the personification is: Fathers, Mothers, Ancestors.
When the OBJECT Destroys the SUBJECT,
    the personification is: Officials, Bosses, Troublemakers.

This familiar personification of the Trigrams is, however, more commonly based upon all six Trigrams associated with a prophesy: two from the Present/Recent Past (Pen Kua); two from the Motive or Internal Hexagram (Hu Kua), see Step 2; and two from the Future Hexagram (Shih Kua). These relate to advanced techniques which are defined in **I CHING, The Advanced Techniques.**

Regardless, the interaction of the Subject Trigram ("S"), interrelates with the Object ("O"), and the prevailing influences are determined. The actual scheme can become much more complex, but the Player should be able to easily relate with the fundamental principles. The Subject Trigram (the Trigram with an "S" in its lines) compares with the Object Trigram (the Trigram with an "O" in its lines), which is always the opposite of the Subject. Our original Sample, T'AI, #11 (see also page 73), shows the Subject on the 3rd Line (Lower Trigram of CH'IEN, governed by METAL) and the Object on the 6th Line (Upper Trigram of K'UN, governed by EARTH).

The Composite of Hexagram T'AI, #11, Copied from Step 2.

PEACE, HARMONY. THE BAD DEPARTS, THE GREAT ARRIVES. SUCCESS, GOOD FORTUNE.

ABOVE: K'UN	Earth, Land	Natural, Receptive	Mother
BELOW: CH'IEN	Heaven, Sky	Creative, Firmness	Father

Line		Mark	Time	Element
6	▬▬ ▬▬	O N	5pm - 7pm	METAL
			Sons, Daughters, Descendants	
5	▬▬ ▬▬	R	9pm - 11pm	WATER
			Wife, Husband, Money, Business	
4	▬▬ ▬▬	N	1am - 3am	EARTH
			Brothers, Sisters, Peers	
3	▬▬▬▬▬	S N	7am - 9am	EARTH
			Brothers, Sisters, Peers	
2	▬▬▬▬▬	R	3am - 5am	WOOD
			Officials, Bosses, Troublemakers	
1	▬▬▬▬▬	N	11pm - 1am	WATER
			Wife, Husband, Money, Business	

House: KU'N, 4th Position; EARTH   [54]
The Primary Hexagram of the 1st Month, (FEBRUARY).

As EARTH Creates METAL, a positive conclusion is applied to both the Subject, wherein it was created by the operation of the Object, and the Object itself, for even though it is held to be diminished, it has been bestowed with love and respect. Other operations also decide the degrees of favorableness of Hexagrams, but T'AI, Peace and Harmony, is certainly a vivid example of this effect.

Other issues within the philosophical scope of the I CHING are also resolved with the Principle of Mutual Creation and Destruction and are identified with advanced topics, although a simplistic and entertaining example is related with the Yearly and Animal Symbols on page 223.

RELATIONSHIPS OF TRIGRAMS WITHIN HEXAGRAMS. As related on Page 214, the Trigrams play a particular and active role in determining the meaning of a prophesy.

The I CHING characterizes the Upper Trigram within a Hexagram as being associated with high and noble ideals, and the Line representations carry this thought further. Referring to the uppermost right-hand diagram on page 23, the Player will find that the upper Trigram contains the lines associated with Wisdom, Authority, and Society.

An easy way to view the I CHING is as a set of two triangles. The Upper triangle is pinnacled with Wisdom at the top. Association with Wisdom is a supreme precept of I CHING—it relates to the Wisdom of knowing when to stop or go, as well as the Wisdom of knowing when our relationships—with ourselves and with others—are correct or incorrect. This is represented as the concept that the application of wisdom is of greater importance than the mere acquisition of wisdom. One of the lines addresses this, indicating that it may be easy to know what to do, but difficult to do that which is correct.

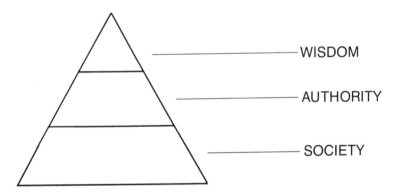

Compared to Wisdom, the lessons of Authority are simple—the exercise of good analytical judgment, remaining pure in conduct and principle, and expressing concern for others always seems to produce favorable results.

The Line labeled "Society" is the interface between Authority and the persons within the Society. The Lower Trigram will represent one of many which interface directly to the administrator represented by Society. Conflict generally exists between the higher ideals of the Upper Trigram and the individualistic ideals of the Lower Trigram which follows on the 3rd Line. But Society has the effect of prevailing over the individual.

The I CHING characterizes the Lower Trigram within a Hexagram with individualistic, materialistic, and generally less noble endeavors. The pinnacle of the Lower Triangle is shown as Individual or Self Interest.

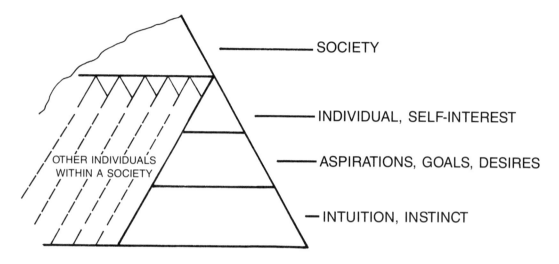

SOCIETY

INDIVIDUAL, SELF-INTEREST

ASPIRATIONS, GOALS, DESIRES

INTUITION, INSTINCT

OTHER INDIVIDUALS
WITHIN A SOCIETY

Note that the individual is represented as only one, but within a society of many.

Aspirations, Goals, and Desires are regarded favorably when noble. They represent the desire to succeed or reach higher degrees of attainment.

Intuition and Instinct generally form the base of human behavior, even including primal needs. For this reason the I CHING considers this bottom line as the beginning.

Each of the Eight Trigrams have particular relationships with each other, as well as each having its own attributes, which are also considered when evaluating the Hexagram. T'AI, #11, shown on page 214, portrays a successful union between the Mother, K'UN, and Father, CH'IEN, and particular favorableness is implied as the Heaven, CH'IEN, has yielded its high place and raised the Natural, Earth, K'UN, to the elevated position.

Similar dramatizations of the interaction between the two Trigrams can be found in all of the Hexagrams, and the Description associated with each Hexagram in Step 3 begins its commentary with the description of this interaction.

RELATIONSHIPS OF TRIGRAMS WITH OTHER TRIGRAMS. The Eight Trigrams are seen as relating to one another in two distinctly different ways. The First—believed to have been originated by Fu Hsi—is called the Early Heaven Order, and is based upon polarity. This order is used in conjunction with Astrology and is described within the Advanced Techniques.

The Second is believed to have been originated by King Wen and is called the Later Heaven Order. This order is cyclic and best relates to the Hexagrams which were also clarified by King Wen. This book has used this order throughout, and the cycle is shown as the "Hu Tien," which we have expanded as shown on page 217.

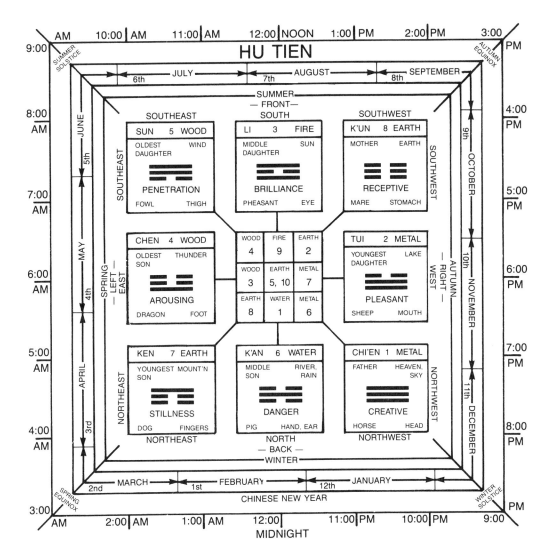

THE CHINESE LUNAR CALENDAR DOES NOT EXACTLY CORRESPOND TO WESTERN CALENDARS.

The Hu Tien relates each trigram as it exists in the cycle of time and influence. The Primary Attributes are displayed for each Trigram, and the Magic Square of 15 is shown in the center of the Hu Tien.

The Magic Square of 15 is used with Advanced Techniques, but note that any three numbers added in line (with the exception of the "10") total 15. Both 5 and 10 appear in the center to represent opposite influences and this square is used, in part, in determining the 10 Celestial Stems.

THE ATTRIBUTES OF THE TRIGRAMS. The Table representing the Attributes of the 8 Trigrams, pages 220-221, defines each Trigram with its most predominant and frequently used Attributes. Differences exist between different publications, and duplication of Attributes will occasionally occur. We have avoided printing the duplications in this text, but an example of how these duplications can be derived is shown in the paragraphs which address K'AN and TUI below.

The Trigrams, and their Attributes, were introduced on page 28 of Step 2, and the Primary Attributes have been expanded or elaborated upon throughout this text. The table which begins on page 220 associates each of the Trigrams with their Primary Attributes at the top, followed by their most encompassing characteristics.

Types of Persons, Professions, Places, Parts of the Body, Illnesses, Foods, Plants, and Animals follow and can be used as guidelines from which similar characteristics can be derived. For example: CH'IEN, #1, is indicative of Presidents or Kings—the governing persons of state—thus Prime Ministers or Emperors could be equally appropriate.

K'AN, #6, relates to liquids, particularly flowing liquids. TUI, #2, relates to liquids in a static sense. The ancient character derivation for water, ≈≈≈ is easily visualized as flowing water and the form of the Trigram K'AN, ☵ typifies the flowing water of a river. By closing off the direction for water to flow (remember, water always flows downward), ☱ another Trigram, TUI, is formed.

(Note that the bottom line of TUI is closed, while the bottom line of K'AN is open.) Hence, TUI typifies the Lake, Marsh, or low place such as a Valley—but not as low as the Abyss represented by K'AN.

Because of similarities between the formation of Trigrams, duplications occur between their Attributes. Although this text lists venereal disease as an Illness associated with K'AN, it is also an Illness associated with TUI. Both K'AN and TUI tend to be careless or reckless and when combined, such as in Hexagram K'UN, #47, warnings of excessive sexual activity, or alcohol use, are provided by the I CHING. Another similarity which K'AN and TUI share is K'AN—the Fisherman, and TUI—the Seafarer.

Every conceivable Attribute would be too lengthy to list and too burdensome to use, and an element of judgment is required on the part of the Player.

A general Attribute of CH'IEN, #1, is roundness, while K'UN, #8, is associated with squareness. In the introductory material we have presented the concept of opposites, and as the opposites are combined they represent an entirety. Ancient Chinese coins are believed to be a manifestation of this concept—being round and representative of Yang on the outside, and with an internal square hole to represent Yin. This can also be stated as "Heaven and Earth are combined to form the Universe."

Positions within homes or houses are similarly derived. With the understanding of K'AN being associated with running water, it should not be difficult to associate K'AN with the Bathroom.

Colors require more introspection and study of the I CHING to fully understand their particular assignments. The Trees and Grass of SUN, #5, can be easily equated to Green. Yellow and Black are both colors associated with Earth, hence both K'UN, #8, (Earth), and KEN, #7, (Mountain), share these colors.

The remaining Attributes at the bottom of the listings of the individual Trigrams in the Table are taken from the positioning within the HU TIEN, page 217. The weather equates to cycles experienced in the Northern Hemisphere. When this material is being used in the Southern Hemisphere, these cyclic representations should be reversed.

In Step 3, introductory explanations were given regarding how the Attributes of Trigrams affect Prophesies.

Hexagram PO, #23, (page 126), shows the Mountain falling down upon the Earth (Trigram KEN, #7, Above and K'UN, #8, Below.) From the particular Attributes this may be seen as an Apartment House falling into a Field—or into a certain state of disrepair.

PO, #23, may well be the least favorable Hexagram. But when the roles of the two Trigrams are reversed (K'UN, #8, Above and KEN, #7, Below) a supreme concession is indicated and the Attributes associated with K'UN are exhalted above those of KEN. The resulting Hexagram, CH'IEN, #15, is probably the most favorable.

Greater emphasis is placed upon these Attributes when using Advanced Techniques and methods using numbers, frequencies, positions, and the like, are presented in depth within the Plum Blossom I—which in itself is a fascinating amplification of the I CHING.

Don't be surprised, however, if you consult the I CHING regarding weather, and upon receiving a response of Hexagram CH'IEN, #15, you find that the Cloudiness of a Low Pressure Area clears to a more Temperate and Mild Climate within a day or two. (Study the two Trigrams, KEN, #7, and K'UN, #8, remembering that KEN is the Subject and K'UN is the Object.)

1 CH'IEN

FATHER	HEAVEN, SKY
	CREATIVE POWER
	FIRMNESS
	HORSE—HEAD
GREATER YANG	ELEMENT: METAL

IDENTITY WITH THE UNIVERSAL ORDER.

Power; Wisdom; High Status; Wealth;
Courage; Leadership; Contentment.

ELDERLY MEN; Husbands; Presidents;
    Kings; Commanders; Sages.
GOVERNING Officials; Managers; Sales;
    Mechanics; Lawyers.
PARLIAMENT; Offices; Fortresses;
    Shrines; Racetracks.
HEAD; Skull; BRAIN; Pineal Gland;
    Mind; BONES.
STROKES; Tumors; Headaches; Senility;
    Broken Bones; Insanity; Dizziness.
FRESH FRUITS; Natural Teas; Rye; Oats; Grains.
CHRYSANTHEMUMS; Fruit Trees; Herbs.
HORSE; Tiger; Lion; Dragon.

Roundness; Autos; Planes; Gems;
    Clocks; Insignia; Emblems.

The Study. RED; White.

NORTHWEST—RIGHT/REAR   7:30pm-10:30pm
Early December to Mid-January, Winter.
Clear, Crisp and Cold.

2 TUI

YOUNGEST DAUGHTER	LAKE, MARSH
	JOYOUS
	PLEASANT
	SHEEP—MOUTH
GREATER YANG	ELEMENT: METAL

SENSUALITY AND JOYFULNESS.

Laughter; Sexual Desires; Setbacks;
Sorcery; Speaking; Lecturing; Amiable.

GIRLS, Daughters, Immature or Incompetent
    People; Waitress; Concubine.
ENTERTAINERS; Public Relations; Dentists;
    Bankers; Seafarers; Barmaids.
THEATRES; Brothels; Banks; Valleys;
    Gardens.
MOUTH; Throat; LUNGS; Breathing
    System; Chest; Breast; TEETH;
ASTHMA; Breathing Disorders; Impeded
    Speech; Toothaches; Coughing.
MUTTON; Wine; Coffee; Fish; Honey; Tea; Rice.
GARDENIAS; Magnolias; Lake plants.
SHEEP; Deer; Birds; Monkeys.

Stringed Instruments; Articles of
    Sensual Pleasure.

The Bedroom. WHITE; Gold.

WEST—RIGHT   4:30- 7:30pm
Mid-October to Late November, Autumn.
Rain; Mist; Fog and Smog.

5 SUN

OLDEST DAUGHTER	WIND, WOOD
	GENTLENESS
	PENETRATION
	ROOSTER—THIGH
LESSER YANG	ELEMENT: WOOD

INTROSPECTION FOR IMPROVEMENT.

Care; Neatness; Statesmanship;
Empathy; Credit; Concentration.

MIDDLE-AGED WOMEN; Business People;
    Teachers; Mediators; Travelers.
CONTRACTORS; Builders; Shippers;
    Manufacturers; Travel Agents.
FACTORIES; Schools; Terminals; Ports;
    Construction Sites; Forests.
THIGHS; Legs; NERVOUS SYSTEM.
LAMENESS; Epilepsy; Hysteria; Influenza.
PASTA; Onions; Garlic; Cauliflower; Chicken.
LILIES; Poppies; Grass; Trees.
FOWL; Snake; Unicorn; Crane.
Rope; Wire; String; Lumber; Cabinets;
    Chests; Binding or Holding Devices;
    Hypnosis; Psychiatry; Desk.

The Hallway. GREEN; Blue.

SOUTHEAST—LEFT/FRONT   7:30am-10:30am
Early June to Mid July; Spring-Summer.
Windiness, and Tornadoes.

6 K'AN

MIDDLE SON	WATER, RAIN
	DANGER
	ABYSMAL
	PIG—EAR, HAND
LESSER YANG	ELEMENT: WATER

SPIRITUAL CLEANSING, BAPTISM.

Difficulties; Peril; Hardship; Crimes;
Cunning; Worries; Confined Activity.

YOUNG MEN; Rebelious People; Trouble-makers;
    Sick, Evil or Dead People.
PRINTERS; Chemists; Druggists;
    Writers, Fishermen; Bartenders.
DAMS; Funeral Parlors; Liquor Stores;
    Canneries; Waterfalls; Wells; Rivers.
EARS; Hands; KIDNEYS; Urinary Tract; Sex Organs.
DEAFNESS; Venereal Disease.
DAIRY PRODUCTS; Hard and soft Drinks; Pork; Salt.
LOTUSES; Reeds; Swamp Plants; Algae.
PIG; Rat; Fox; Bat.
Paints; Varnishes; Inks; Oil; Petrol;
    Medicine; Liquids of all Types.
    Canyons and Cliffs.

The Bathroom. BLACK, RED.

NORTH—REAR   10:30pm-1:30pm
Mid-January to Late February. Winter.
Heavy Rains and Floods; Dark; Cold.

3 LI

MIDDLE DAUGHTER	FIRE, SUN
▬▬▬▬▬▬	BRILLIANCE
▬▬▬ ▬▬▬	CLINGING
▬▬▬▬▬▬	PHEASANT—EYE
LESSER YIN	ELEMENT: FIRE

INSPIRATIONS TO SELF AND OTHERS.

Intelligence; Clarity; Sound Judgement; Intuition; Correspondence;

YOUNG WOMEN; Beauties; Intelligent and Beneficial People.
ARTISTS; Models; Judges; Diplomats; Optometrists; Beauticians; Barber.
GALLARIES; Law Courts; Lighthouses; Beacons; Lit Streets; Volcanoes.
EYES; HEART; Blood System.
BLINDNESS; Heart Attacks; Blood Disorders; Clotting; Fevers; Burns.
DRIED FRUITS; Shellfish; Peanuts. Shr..np; Crab; Lobster.
TOMATOES; Watermelons; Maple; Pepper.
PHEASANT; Shellfish; Tortoise; Oyster.
Books; Paintings; Lights; Stocks; Bonds; Pets; Arrows and Armor; Calligraphy; Bookstores; Nest; Net.

The Patio. RED; Purple.

SOUTH—FRONT   10:30am-1:30pm
Mid-July to Late August; Summer.
Clear, Warm and Dry.

4 CHEN

OLDEST SON	THUNDER
▬▬▬ ▬▬▬	MOVEMENT
▬▬▬ ▬▬▬	AROUSING
▬▬▬▬▬▬	DRAGON—FOOT
LESSER YIN	ELEMENT: WOOD

EXTERNAL AND INTERNAL GROWTH.

Surprise; Determination; Shock;
Birth; Newness; Renewal;

MIDDLE-AGED MEN; Princes; Innovators; Inventors; Sports and Famous Persons.
ENGINEERS; Technicians in Electrical and Electronic Industries; Hunters.
AUDITORIUMS; Power or Radio-TV Stations; Stadiums; Surfside.
FEET; LIVER; Gall Bladder.
GOUT; Corns; Bunyons; Hepatitis; Liver Disease.
GREEN VEGATABLES; Citrus Fruits. Peaches; Plums; Prunes.
EVERGREENS; Bamboo; Game Foods; Sprouting Plants.
DRAGON; Eagle; Swallow; Cricket.
Guns; Fireworks; Telephones; Gongs; Pianos; Noisemakers; Trumpets; Motivation and Enathusiasm.

The Living Room. BLUE; Green.

EAST—LEFT   4:30am-7:30am
Mid-April to Late May; Spring.
Thunderstorms; Clearing and Milder.

7 KEN

YOUNGEST SON	MOUNTAIN
▬▬▬▬▬▬	STILLNESS
▬▬▬ ▬▬▬	SILENCE
▬▬▬ ▬▬▬	DOG—FINGERS
GREATER YIN	ELEMENT: EARTH

INTROSPECTION AND INNER AWARENESS.

Inactive; Quiet; Honest; Stubborn;
Frugal; Cautious; Independent.

BOYS; Priests; Faithful and Sincere People; Thinkers; Meditators; Guard.
CLERGYMEN; Monks; Graduate Students; Philosophers.
CHURCHES; Monastaries; Apartment Houses; Dormatories; Libraries.
FINGERS; Back; SPINE; Rectum; NOSE; Pancreas.
FATIGUE; Backache; Hemorroids. Constipation.
PRESERVED FOODS; Nuts; Mushrooms; Red Meat
MANGOES; Avocadoes; Bananas.
DOG; Bull; Leopard; Mouse.

Cased and Packaged Goods; Bolts of Non-Moving and Stored Items; Warehouses; Beds; Tables.

The Bedroom. BROWN; Yellow; Black.

NORTHEAST—LEFT/REAR   10:30am-1:30pm
Early March to Mid-April; WINTER-SPRING.
Cloudiness tending to Clear; Mild.

8 K'UN

MOTHER	EARTH, LAND
▬▬▬ ▬▬▬	NATURAL STRENGTH
▬▬▬ ▬▬▬	RECEPTIVENESS
▬▬▬ ▬▬▬	MARE—STOMACH
GREATER YIN	ELEMENT: EARTH

PHILANTHROPY, RENDERING OF SERVICES.

Strong; Responsive; Respectful;
Devoted; Docile; Obedient.

ELDERLY WOMEN; Wives; Queens; Leaders of Large Social Groups.
HUMANITARIANS; Doctors; Nurses; Union Leaders; Farmers; Gardeners.
HOSPITALS; Fields; Homes; Ghettos; Farms; Large Social Gatherings.
ABDOMEN; Stomach; SPLEEN; Lower Torso; SKIN.
ULCERS; Digestive Disorders. Diarrhea; Chronicness.
POTATOES; Yams; Beets; Ginger.
BULB FLOWERS; Taro; Cotton.
MARE; Ox; Cow; Ant; Cat.

Squareness; Clothing; Pillows; Mattresses; Cushions; Sheets.

The Kitchen. Black; YELLOW; Brown.

SOUTHWEST—RIGHT/FRONT   1:30pm-4:30pm
Early September to Mid-October. SUMMER-AUTUMN. Cloudy; Low-Pressure Systems.

To the novice Player, Trigrams may seem elusive, but with a little study and application it will be seen that they are, indeed, the basis of the I CHING Prophesies.

In Appendix A, Examples of Prophesies, more use is made of the Attributes of the Trigrams, and the Player is invited to compare his or her own assessment with the Samples.

In the practical sense this completes Step 4. The first time through this process may have seemed confusing and laborious, but you will find that the knowledge gained will progressively speed your analyses and lend greater accuracy to your interpretation of the Prophesies. You will also find more fulfilling aspects of your own life or lifestyle when you begin applying the Wisdom of the I CHING.

The remainder of this Step addresses a highly entertaining aspect of Oriental culture, although not strictly related to the I CHING.

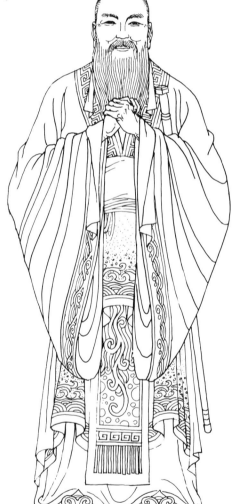

CONFUCIUS, CIRCA 500 B.C.

"If I had 50 more years to live, I'd devote them all to the study of I CHING."

CHINESE YEARLY AND ANIMAL SYMBOLS. The Chinese yearly Cycle of Sixty, or Cathay, is a composite representation of the 12 Terrestrial, or Horary, Branches and the 10 Celestial Stems, as they equate to the 5 Live Elements. The Table which follows on page 224 displays the 76th, 77th, 78th Cycles of Sixty within the current age. The 12 Branches and 10 Stems, briefly explained on page 226, are detailed fully in **I CHING, The Advanced Techniques.**

The Elements associated with a particular year can be used to establish prevalence between any two given years, as described earlier in this Step under the explanations for Mutual Creation and Destruction. As an example: one born in 1940 would be associated with a parental position when compared to one born in 1943, as METAL (1940) gives birth to WATER (1943), and each is associated further with the traits of the animals—1940 the Dragon, 1943 the Ram.

When comparing dates with the Table it must be taken into consideration that the Chinese New Year begins on approximately the 5th of February—thus January normally represents the preceeding Yearly Symbol. For example, if the date (such as a birthdate), January 10, 1947, were being considered, that date would fall under the yearly symbol of 1946—Ping Hsu, FIRE, the Year of the Dog.

Determining the Chinese New Year (mid-January to mid-February) actually requires a Chinese calendar to be specific, since the lunar cycles of the Chinese calendar and the inter-calendary months vary the actual New Year's Day over a 30 day range. The actual date in 1986 was February 9th. A perpetual calendaring scheme is supplied with **I CHING, The Advanced Techniques,** but is not included within this Primer.

The Animals represented do not actually relate to the I CHING and are believed to have been passed on to the Chinese from East Indian cultures. They are now commonly associated with the Chinese, and persons will frequently refer to the time of their birth as occurring during "The year of the Dog," or whatever their associated symbol happens to be.

The Animals, and their characteristics, associated with the Yearly Cycles are summarized on page 225 and are for entertainment. Remember that prophesies are not based upon these representations.

YEARS			YEARLY NAME	ELEMENT		ANIMAL	
1864	1924	1984	Chia Tzu	WOOD,	Mu	RAT,	Shu
1865	1925	1985	I Chou	WOOD,	Mu	OX,	Niu
1866	1926	1986	Ping Yin	FIRE,	Ho	TIGER,	Hu
1867	1927	1987	Ting Mao	FIRE,	Ho	HARE,	T'u
1868	1928	1988	Wu Ch'en	EARTH,	T'u	DRAGON,	Lung
1869	1929	1989	Chi Ssu	EARTH,	T'u	SNAKE,	She
1870	1930	1990	Keng Wu	METAL,	Chin	HORSE,	Ma
1871	1931	1991	Hsin Wei	METAL,	Chin	RAM,	Yang
1872	1932	1992	Jen Shen	WATER,	Shui	MONKEY,	Hou
1873	1933	1993	Kuei Yu	WATER,	Shui	ROOSTER,	Chi
1874	1934	1994	Chia Hsu	WOOD,	Mu	DOG,	Ch'uan
1875	1935	1995	I Hai	WOOD,	Mu	BOAR,	Chu
1876	1936	1996	Ping Tzu	FIRE,	Ho	RAT,	Shu
1877	1937	1997	Ting Chou	FIRE,	Ho	OX,	Niu
1878	1938	1998	Wu Yin	EARTH,	T'u	TIGER,	Hu
1879	1939	1999	Chi Mao	EARTH,	T'u	HARE,	T'u
1880	1940	2000	Keng Ch'en	METAL,	Chin	DRAGON,	Lung
1881	1941	2001	Hsin Ssu	METAL,	Chin	SNAKE,	She
1882	1942	2002	Jen Wu	WATER,	Shui	HORSE,	Ma
1883	1943	2003	Kuei Wei	WATER,	Shui	RAM,	Yang
1884	1944	2004	Chia Shen	WOOD,	Mu	MONKEY,	Hou
1885	1945	2005	I Yu	WOOD,	Mu	ROOSTER,	Chi
1886	1946	2006	Ping Hsu	FIRE,	Ho	DOG,	Ch'uan
1887	1947	2007	Ting Hai	FIRE,	Ho	BOAR,	Chu
1888	1948	2008	Wu Tzu	EARTH,	T'u	RAT,	Shu
1889	1949	2009	Chi Chou	EARTH,	T'u	OX,	Niu
1890	1950	2010	Keng Yin	METAL,	Chin	TIGER,	Hu
1891	1951	2011	Hsin Mao	METAL,	Chin	HARE,	T'u
1892	1952	2012	Jen Ch'en	WATER,	Shui	DRAGON,	Lung
1893	1953	2013	Kuei Ssu	WATER,	Shui	SNAKE,	She
1894	1954	2014	Chia Wu	WOOD,	Mu	HORSE,	Ma
1895	1955	2015	I Wei	WOOD,	Mu	RAM,	Yang
1896	1956	2016	Ping Shen	FIRE,	Ho	MONKEY,	Hou
1897	1957	2017	Ting Yu	FIRE,	Ho	ROOSTER,	Chi
1898	1958	2018	Wu Hsu	EARTH,	T'u	DOG,	Ch'uan
1899	1959	2019	Chi Hai	EARTH,	T'u	BOAR,	Chu
1900	1960	2020	Keng Tzu	METAL,	Chin	RAT,	Shu
1901	1961	2021	Hsin Chou	METAL,	Chin	OX,	Niu
1902	1962	2022	Jen Yin	WATER,	Shui	TIGER,	Hu
1903	1963	2023	Kuei Mao	WATER,	Shui	HARE,	T'u
1904	1964	2024	Chia Ch'en	WOOD,	Mu	DRAGON,	Lung
1905	1965	2025	I Ssu	WOOD,	Mu	SNAKE,	She
1906	1966	2026	Ping Wu	FIRE,	Ho	HORSE,	Ma
1907	1967	2027	Ting Wei	FIRE,	Ho	RAM,	Yang
1908	1968	2028	Wu Shen	EARTH,	T'u	MONKEY,	Hou
1909	1969	2029	Chi Yu	EARTH,	T'u	ROOSTER,	Chi
1910	1970	2030	Keng Hsu	METAL,	Chin	DOG,	Ch'uan
1911	1971	2031	Hsin Hai	METAL,	Chin	BOAR,	Chu
1912	1972	2032	Jen Tzu	WATER,	Shui	RAT,	Shu
1913	1973	2033	Kuei Chou	WATER,	Shui	OX,	Niu
1914	1974	2034	Chia Yin	WOOD,	Mu	TIGER,	Hu
1915	1975	2035	I Mao	WOOD,	Mu	HARE,	T'u
1916	1976	2036	Ping Ch'en	FIRE,	Ho	DRAGON,	Lung
1917	1977	2037	Ting Ssu	FIRE,	Ho	SNAKE,	She
1918	1978	2038	Wu Wu	EARTH,	T'u	HORSE,	Ma
1919	1979	2039	Chi Wei	EARTH,	T'u	RAM,	Yang
1920	1980	2040	Keng Shen	METAL,	Chin	MONKEY,	Hou
1921	1981	2041	Hsin Yu	METAL,	Chin	ROOSTER,	Chi
1922	1982	2042	Jen Hsu	WATER,	Shui	DOG,	Ch'uan
1923	1983	2043	Kuei Hai	WATER,	Shui	BOAR,	Chu

CHARACTERISTICS RELATING TO THE ANIMAL, OR YEARLY, SYMBOL.

RAT (MOUSE) people are athletic and persausive. They are impulsive and romantic lovers. They should embrace Dragon and Monkey people, and avoid Horse people.

OX people are assertive, quick-tempered, and stubborn. They tend to be vain in love, with many lovers. They should embrace Snake and Rooster people, and avoid Ram people.

TIGER people are of noble character, gregarious, but not interested in details. They are faithful and passionate lovers. They should embrace Dog and Horse people, and avoid Monkey people.

HARE (RABBIT) people are peaceful and charming. They are shy in love but seek virtue. They should embrace Boar and Ram people, and avoid Rooster people.

DRAGON people are energetic, high-strung, and talk a lot. They fall in love quickly, but not too deeply. They should embrace Monkey and Rat people, and avoid Dog people.

SNAKE people are wise and self-sufficient. They are sexually appealing, but vain in love. They should embrace Ox and Rooster people, and avoid Boar people.

HORSE people are happy, but also deep thinkers. They are always passionate lovers, but are generally stubborn. They should embrace Tiger and Dog people, and avoid Rat people.

RAM (SHEEP) people are scholarly and sensitive. They are cautious, but love very deeply. They should embrace Hare and Boar people, and avoid Ox people.

MONKEY people are talented and have great memories. Because of their aloofness they need to be careful in love. They should embrace Dragon and Rat people, and avoid Tiger people.

ROOSTER people are cheerful, intelligent, and active. They tend to be fickle, loving often—but lightly. They should embrace Snake and Ox people, and avoid Hare people.

DOG people are capable, very friendly, and logical thinkers. They tend to be lazy or inconsiderate in love affairs. They should embrace Horse and Tiger people, and avoid Dragon people.

BOAR (PIG) people are emotionally steady and physically strong. In love affairs they are indecisive, but both need and give love. They should embrace Hare and Ram people, and avoid Snake people.

THE TWELVE TERRESTRIAL BRANCHES. The 12 Terrestrial Branches, also referred to as the 12 Horary Branches to relate them with their identity to Horoscopes, divide time segments into 12 equal divisions. The Player will note that in Step 2 the authors took the liberty of referring to these branches as "Hourly" Branches, since they divide the Day into 12 two-hour segments.

The 12 Terrestrial, or Horary Branches, also divide years, and groups of years within a Cycle of Sixty (explained previously on page 223). The Hu Tien, page 217, displays each of the 12 Branches as they relate to the Hours. An interesting and entertaining parallel, however, can be drawn from the 12 Branches and the 12 Zodiac signs of Occidental astrology. The Chinese Animal Symbol is fully related to current years in the Table on page 224.

HOURLY BRANCH	(NAME)	ANIMALS	(NAME)
11pm– 1am	T'zu	Rat	Shu
1am– 3am	Ch'ou	Ox	Niu
3am– 5am	Yin	Tiger	Hu
5am– 7am	Mao	Hare	T'u
7am– 9am	Ch'en	Dragon	Lung
9am–11am	Ssu	Snake	She
11am– 1pm	Wu	Horse	Ma
1pm– 3pm	Wei	Ram	Yang
3pm– 5pm	Shen	Monkey	Hou
5pm– 7pm	Yu	Rooster	Chi
7pm– 9pm	Hsu	Dog	Ch'uan
9pm–11pm	Hai	Boar	Chu

THE TEN CELESTIAL STEMS. The 10 Celestial Stems can be seen evolving from the Magic Square of 15 (page 217), as in the center both a 5 and 10 are represented to indicate opposite polarities. The 10 Celestial Stems combine with the 5 Live Elements in the following order:

CELESTIAL STEM	(NAME)	CHARACTERISTIC	ELEMENT	(NAME)
1	Chia	Trees	WOOD	Mu
2	Yi	Wood used as Timber	WOOD	Mu
3	Ping	Lightning	FIRE	Huo
4	Ting	Burning Material	FIRE	Huo
5	Wu	Land, Hills, etc.	EARTH	T'u
6	Chi	Pottery, Earthware	EARTH	T'u
7	Keng	Metallic Ore	METAL	Chin
8	Hsin	Metallic Items	METAL	Chin
9	Jen	Salt, Sea Water	WATER	Shui
10	Kuei	Fresh Water	WATER	Shui

The 10 Celestial Stems and the 12 Terrrestrial Branches form the foundation for the astrological aspects of the I CHING, which are addressed as an Advanced Topic.

In closing this Step, and the book itself, an interesting parallel to Western astrology is presented. The "Twenty-Four Solar Terms," from antiquity, are coincided with the months of the year. Both Oriental and Occidental (Zodiacal) astrological affiliations divide at the same dates and portray the same characteristics. The actual days vary slightly from year to year, as the Lunar Cycle also varies calendar dates. The Chinese terms are equated with early agricultural considerations, but these dates—even to-day —continue to have particular importance. Ch'ing Ming, "Clear and Bright," is still the day reserved for worship—respectful consideration—of one's ancestors.

DATE		NAME	CHARACTER	ZODIAC
22	December	Tung Chih	Winter Solstice	Capricorn
6	January	Hsiao Han	Little Cold	"
21	January	Ta Han	Great Cold	Aquarius
5	February	Li Ch'un	Spring Begins	"
19	February	Yu Shui	Rain Water	Pisces
5	March	Ching Shih	Excited Insects	"
20	March	Ch'un Fen	Vernal Equinox	Aries
5	April	Ch'ing Ming	Clear and Bright	"
20	April	Ku Yu	Grain Rains	Taurus
5	May	Li Hsia	Summer Begins	"
20	May	Hsiao Man	Early Harvests	Gemini
6	June	Mang Chung	Cultivation of Crops	"
21	June	Hsia Chih	Summer Solstice	Cancer
7	July	Hsiao Shu	Little Heat	"
23	July	Ta Shu	Great Heat	Leo
7	August	Li Ch'iu	Autumn Begins	"
23	August	Ch'u Shu	Summer Heat Departing	Virgo
8	September	Pai Lu	White Dew	"
23	September	Ch'iu Fen	Autumnal Equinox	Libra
8	October	Han Lu	Cold Dew	"
23	October	Shuang Chiang	Frost Descends	Scorpio
7	November	Li Tung	Winter Begins	"
22	November	Hsiao Hsueh	Little Snow	Sagittarius
7	December	Ta Hsueh	Great Snow	"

PERSONAL NOTES

APPENDIX A — EXAMPLE PROPHESIES

The following examples represent the types of questions most commonly asked of the I CHING. Because of the character of the questions the Hexagrams have been evaluated differently. In the following Examples "CHAN", and the Chinese character below (literally interpreted as "Prophesy"), preceed the authors' interpretation of the response from the I CHING Oracle. The final sentence, in bold face type, is the conclusive answer to the question.

WILL JAMES AND I MARRY WITHIN A YEAR?

The Coin Toss method of consulting the I CHING Oracle was selected from Step 1 and line values of 6,8,8,7,6, and 7 were obtained for Lines 1 through 6 respectively (page 17). The following two Hexagrams were formed and identified from Step 2.

PRESENT/RECENT PAST				FUTURE		
══ X ══	R		(F,M,A) Controlling	═══════	R	(B,O,T)
	S				S	
═══════				═══════		
══ ══				══ ══		
══ X ══	R	O	(F,M,A)	══ ══	O	(F,M,A)
#35 CHIN				**#25 WU WANG**		

The influence is moving from a pure YIN to a YANG-YIN in the future with the YANG influence slightly favored. (page 23, by following the Polarity Sequence backward from #35 to #25.)

The Present/Recent Past indicates CHIN, #35, "Progress and Recognition from Enlightened and Virtuous Efforts," and CHIN is identified as a Hexagram of the 1st Month, Feb. (page 55).

The Future indicates WU WANG, #25, "The Unexpected Appears even with Honest and Sincere Efforts," and WU WANG is identified as a Hexagram of the 8th Month, Sept. (page 50).

The Ruling, Subject, and Object Lines are noted as well as the Personifications of the two Changing Lines.

The Controlling Line is selected (Two Lines Changing, page 71). Notice that the Ruling Line 5 continues, but that the Ruling Line 1 does not. The Personification of the Ruling Line 5, also the Controlling Line, changes from "Father, Mother, Ancestor" to "Boss, Official, Troublemaker."

"Rapid and Easy Advancement" is indicated by CHIN (page 151) and the Prophesies regarding Wishes, Love, and Marriage, read "Wishes come true . . . Love easily succeeds . . . Marriages are harmonious with rewarding benefits." The Controlling Line, 5th Line Changing, reads "With well-ordered and virtuous effort you have no need of concern for gain or loss. Expect further progress and advantage."

"Natural Order with Progress, be wary of Unexpected Complications" is indicated by WU WANG (page 131).

CHAN

The Authors' Interpretation of the Response. A very favorable situation is indicated. The change from total YIN to YANG-YIN; the change in family relationships away from the parental—which also rule; the prophesy; and the controlling line all reflect a very favorable matrimonial response. Continue sincere efforts, but let things happen naturally. Avoid taking advantage of this favorable situation for personal interest. Be on guard for a troublesome source in the future, possibly an employer (boss) or official. **"Yes, you and James can expect to be married within the year, and probably in seven months."** (The difference between the 1st and 8th month). **"You and James can also expect a favorable beginning of your marriage."**

SHOULD I TAKE THE JOB
AT SMITH AND SMITH COMPANY NOW?

The Yarrow Stick method of consulting the Oracle was selected from Step 1. The values of 3 (Lower Trigram LI), 1 (Upper Trigram CH'IEN), and 1 (Changing Line) were obtained (pages 19-20). The following Hexagrams were formed and defined from Step 2.

PRESENT/RECENT PAST		FUTURE	
▬▬▬▬ O		▬▬▬▬	
▬▬▬▬ R (W,H,M,B)		▬▬▬▬ R (B,S,P)	
▬▬▬▬		▬▬▬▬ S	
▬▬▬▬ S (B,O,T)		▬▬▬▬	
▬▬▬▬ R		▬▬ ▬▬ S	
▬▬▬▬ ⊙ (F,M,A) Controlling		▬▬ ▬▬ (F,M,A)	
#13 T'UNG JEN		**#33 TUN**	

The influence is moving from YANG to YIN in the future. The Changing Line is moving from YANG to YIN. The Present/Recent Past indicates T'UNG JEN, #13, "Peaceful Union among Colleagues. Progress, Success." T'UNG JEN is identified as a Hexagram of the 6th Month, July (page 44).

The Future Hexagram indicates TUN, #33, "Strength Yields and Withdraws as Appropriate to the Circumstances," and T'UNG JEN is also identified as a Hexagram of the 6th Month, July (page 54).

The Ruling, Subject, and Object Lines are noted, as well as the Personification of the single Changing Line. The Subject (Self) is moving from YANG to YIN in the future and is moving downward, as does the YIN influence. The Lower Trigram, LI—Brilliance, is changing to KEN—Stillness, while the Upper Trigram, CH'IEN—Creative, is experiencing no change. The personification of Ruling Line 5 is changing from "Wife, Husband, Money, Business" to "Brothers, Sisters, Peers."

In this instance a less than positive response is being formed. The Internal or Motivating Hexagram of T'UNG JEN, #13, is #44—KOU "Inferior Elements Appear as Temptation" (page 33).

The Controlling Line is the single Changing Line (page 71) and the Personification remains constant as "Fathers, Mothers, Ancestors."

"Progress and Success" are indicated when collaborating with colleagues of "Similar Interests" by T'UNG JEN (page 106) and the Prophesy regarding Jobs suggests availability with much competition. The controlling Line reads "With honesty and openness between all, you and your colleagues now advance without error."

Yielding, Withdrawing," and possibly "Isolation"—due to the rise of lesser influences—is indicated by TUN (page 146).

CHAN

The Authors' Interpretation of the Response. A declining situation is projected—the employment offer may seem attractive, but has little basis for growth or advancement in the future. All factors which were used for evaluation indicated a decline from YANG to YIN resulting in Stillness, and possibly stagnation, even though levels of responsibility and authority remain essentially the same. **"No, especially if you are changing jobs or moving away from colleagues with whom you work well now. The Smith and Smith offer provides you no particular advantage or growth."** Your own personal situation would have to be closely related to this response. The response does NOT indicate any particular adversity or crisis—only a decline to stillness. If you are unemployed now, disgruntled with current employment, or are looking for employment with a retiring character, you may choose to accept the Smith and Smith offer in any event.

CAN I FIND MY DOG? IS HE SAFE?

The Coin Toss method of consulting the I CHING Oracle was selected from Step 1 and line values of 8,6,8,8,9, and 8 were obtained for Lines 1 through 6 respectively (page 17). The following two Hexagrams were formed and identified from Step 2.

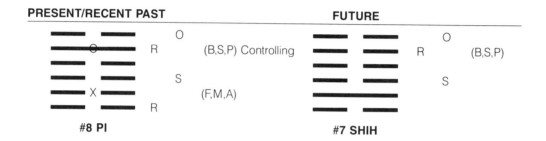

PRESENT/RECENT PAST		FUTURE	
O		O	
R	(B,S,P) Controlling	R	(B,S,P)
S		S	
	(F,M,A)		
R			
#8 PI		**#7 SHIH**	

This evaluation uses several "short-cuts" to get to the response without analyzing inappropriate material.

The Present/Recent Past indicates PI, #8, "The Group is United and Held Together with Sincere and Loyal Relationships"; the 3rd Month, April; and that the Hexagram is of the 8th Position, indicating Return, even though health was not specifically addressed (page 41).

The Future indicates SHIH, #7, "Army, Strength Stored in a Mass of People. Organization and Leadership"; also the 3rd Month, April; and also the 8th Position, indicating Return (page 41).

The Controlling Line is selected (Two Lines Changing, page 71).

Notice that the Trigram for Danger, K'AN, is present in both Hexagrams but not the major factor in either. In fact it is declining as it relates to future influence, while Naturalness and Receptivity (K'UN) are rising.

In addition to both Hexagrams representing "Return" by their 8th Positions, they also both indicate the 3rd Month, April, from which a sense of immediacy can be gathered.

"Success in Loyally Joining" is indicated by PI (page 97) and the Prophesies of Missing People and Missing Things read "in the North, are safe and can be found easily . . . when you get help." If one were to visualize standing, facing South, on the HU TIEN (page 217), the missing Object is found behind the searching Subject. The construction of the Hexagram PI, #8, also suggests a higher elevation and the Hu Tien further suggests cold and darkness. Attributes of the Upper Trigram, K'AN, suggest water, canyons, and cliffs as well (page 220). The 5th Controlling Line (Changing) reads "Wise leadership provides choices without fear and requires no submission. Continuing in this manner, you can expect good fortune.

"Organization and Leadership Producing Success" is indicated by SHIH, #7 (page 95).

CHAN

The Authors' Interpretation of the Response. The necessity of seeking and organizing help is indicated, as is "Return"— but return on own volition is NOT indicated. The desire to return does exist, but there is some factor preventing return, such as; the dog is in the care of some other concerned party who does not know how to contact the searchers; the dog may be disoriented and unable to find its way back; or the dog may have been left in an unfamiliar place (driving off during a camping trip) and is without adequate means to return. **"Yes, you can find your dog—probably North and at a higher elevation. The dog is safe, and possibly 'penned-in' for the night. Get friends or family to help in an organized search starting from where he was last seen and begin looking North. You will be able to find the dog now, but if you wait too long you may lose the opportunity to find him forever."**

* * * * * * * * * * * * * * * * * * *

The Worksheet Example for Coins, constructed on pages 18 and 24, and completed on page 73, was evaluated in the same manner as these preceeding examples. The authors invite Players to evaluate the Worksheet regarding Yarrow Sticks, page 21, on their own.

Accuracy and speed in evaluating prophesies increase with practice, but any response must be evaluated on the basis of the Player's individual circumstances.

* * * * * * * * * * * * * * * * * * *

The Program, **I CHING IN 4 EASY STEPS,** has the ability to produce Prophesies by either the Coin Toss, Yarrow Stick, Random Number Generation, or an Advanced By-Pass method.

Although this *Primer* organizes the elements of the I CHING in progressive steps, it still requires referencing of different pages. Some Players will use many books to evaluate a single response. The Program, however, contains the essential components of the I CHING text, as translated and interpreted herein, as a Data Base on a computer diskette. Consequently the Program can generate, and print, responses from the I CHING Oracle very quickly and in substantial volume.

Even with the Program the Player is urged to sincerely consider the question and seriously evaluate the response to gain full value from this ancient, but contemporary, philosophical system.

APPENDIX B — VOCABULARY

"WORDS are anchors that restrict thought." The words themselves are unimportant. Producing the correct thought is the goal of this vocabulary.

Fundamentals which have been explained within the text of this publication, even though they may be represented by a single word or phrase, are not necessarily duplicated within this vocabulary.

ASPIRATIONS. The character associated with the 2nd Line of a Hexagram—the desires, goals, ambitions, and "Aspirations" which contribute to the patterns of individual lives.

ARMY. In antiquity the "Army" was represented as a "Social" whole. All members contributed, particularly in defense. The young and strong men were the warriors; the nobility was required to contribute foodstuffs and materiel; the women maintained armaments; and the infirm, old, or very young maintained supplies and fodder. Even though fuedal, this system insured that the "Army" was united in purpose.

ATTAINMENT. Accomplishment of particular goals and objectives, not intended to be as all-encompassing as "Success."

AUTHORITY. The character associated with the 5th Line of a Hexagram—the position of precipitating and continuing action, enforcing obedience, or issuing commands. In the I CHING authority is exercised for the common good.

BLAME. The consequential attitude of others, or one's own, toward adverse behavior or acts—generally manifested as criticism.

CHAOS. A state of disorder or confusion which the I CHING associates with adversity or misfortune.

COMMUNITY. The collection of "Individuals" which exist within a "Society." The "Community" shares and works toward common goals, Its smallest unit is viewed as the "Family" while the largest unit is viewed as the "Society."

CONSTRAINT. Either the 1st or 6th Line of a Hexagram which constrains or bounds the Theme of the Hexagram. The 1st Line (Bottom or Beginning) eases into the Theme of the Hexagram while generally retaining some of the influence of the preceeding Hexagram in the Orderly Sequence. The 6th Line (Top or Ending) completes any influence indicated by the Theme and begins addressing the Theme of the following Hexagram.

CORRECT. Proper behavior or attitudes which, in themselves, tend to promote "Good Fortune" or "Success."

CORRESPONDENCE. The associative condition between two Lines within a Hexagram where one is YANG and one is YIN. "Correspondence," also referred to as "Matched," relates to the 1st and 4th Line, the 2nd and 5th, and the 3rd and 6th. This occurs as the two Trigrams of the Hexagrams are compared. The condition of "Correspondence" is regarded as more favorable as both influences are present, while two YANG influences may be too overbearing and two YIN influences may not be assertive enough.

CRITICISM. The voiced opinion of others, or one's own, which may be based upon either valid evaluation or misunderstanding. It originates from generally assumed adverse acts, or where improvement can be expected.

DIFFICULTY. Obstacles in one's path through life which require resolution. Such resolution usually adds to the character of the individual. Although many lines address "Difficulty," there are 4 Hexagrams which address "Difficulty" specifically:
CHUN, #3—The "Difficulty" associated with New Beginnings.
K'AN, #29—"Difficulty" requiring great perseverance to resolve.
CHIEN, #39—"Difficulty" associated with personal restraint or injury.
K'UN, #47—"Difficulty" associated with exhaustion, depletion, or weariness.

DISASTER. The superlative of "Misfortune" which can be associated with physical destruction as well.

DRAGON. An Eastern Dragon symbolizes the dynamic and arousing force within. Unlike the Western medieval monster, it is the genius of strength and goodness. It is the spirit of change and life itself. It awaits the time and rouses slowly, appearing in the storm clouds. Its claws are seen as forks of lightning, and its green scales the glistening of rain and wind swept pine trees. Its voice is heard in thunder, and the Trigram CHEN, Arousing and Thunder, carries the attribute of the "Dragon."

ERROR. Intemperance or incorrectness in behavior or beliefs. A situation requiring correction. Also MISTAKE and FAULT.

EVIL. "Misfortune" or "Disaster" associated with the character of nefariousness or treachery.

FAILURE. A significant and counterproductive lack of accomplishment relative to the question asked of the Oracle. Existing in degrees, it can only be evaluated by the individual.

FAMILY. The smallest unit of "Community," where joy, goals, assets, griefs, liabilities, etc., are commonly shared to promote "Attainment" for both the individuals within the "Family," as well as the "Family" itself. Occidental "Family" relationships are not regarded with as much importance as are their Oriental counterparts, and in a cultural sense, the I CHING tends to move away from emphasis on individualism except when the "Sage" is considered.

FAULT. See ERROR.

FORCE. An aggressive or assertive action to implement action or conclusion. "Force" is never applied beyond which is necessary to achieve the desired result.

GOOD FORTUNE. Favorable position relative to the question of the Oracle. Probably enduring and possibly financial.

GREAT GOOD FORTUNE. The superlative of "Good Fortune."

GREAT UNDERTAKINGS. The superlative of "Undertakings."

HARM. Personal, and possibly physical, damage from operation within incorrect or less than virtuous circumstances.

HELP. The support or assistance of colleagues within a "Community" to an individual, and specifically the "Subject" of a "Prophesy."

INDIVIDUAL. The character associated with the 3rd Line of a Hexagram—the "Individual" or "Self" interests of this Line normally tend to be in conflict with the interests of "Society" (Line 4). The I CHING gives less regard to "Individual" interests than to those of "Community."

INSTINCT. The character associated with the 1st Line of a Hexagram—the primal behavior or response at the beginning of awareness, conditioned by either an inborn tendency or an acquired aptitude.

INTUITION. Similiar to "Instinct," and also associated with the 1st Line of a Hexagram, but more closely related to a knowledge without conscious reasoning or logical evaluation. The response from the I CHING Oracle is regarded as intuitive since there is the unconscious knowledge of positions within the Cosmic Order or TAO.

MAN-MADE. The I CHING views and makes evaluations upon natural phenomena, but two Hexagrams unexpectly relate to "Man-Made" objects:
CHING, #48—The Well, "Nourishment" and sources of wisdom to benefit all.
TING, #50—The Cauldron, "Nourishment" for the "Attainment" of noble goals.
Notice both also relate to "Nourishment," a natural requirement.

MARRIAGE. Even in antiquity mutual consideration and respect were important precepts of "Marriage."

Several lines within the I CHING relate to "Marriage," as do specific Prophesies, and 4 Hexagrams in particular address "Marriage."
HSIEN, #31—Mutual attraction and wooing to "Marriage."
HENG, #32—Enduring and sincere relationships existing within the "Marriage."
CHIEN, #53—Gradual development following the act of "Marriage."
KUEI MEI, #54—An unsuccessful "Marriage" due to incorrect motives.
Note also that a "Marriage" is not solely limited to the wedded relationship between a man and woman.

MASTER. A "Player" regarded as supremely competent in a particular endeavor, or endeavors, such as the I CHING. Peers and colleagues confer the title "Master" as a sign of deep respect and confidence—assigning the title of "Master" to oneself tends only to expose oneself as a charlatan.

MATCHED. See CORRESPONDENCE.

MISFORTUNE. Unfavorable position relative to the question of the Oracle. Probably enduring and possibly financial.

MISTAKE. See ERROR.

MODESTY. Oriental cultures, even today, regard "Modesty" as a high virtue which is associated with inner confidence and peace requiring no ostentatious display. Occidental cultures tend to associate "Modesty" with embarrassment or meagerness. In addition to language barriers, this cultural difference often furthers misunderstanding between the ethnic divisions.

NATURAL. An attribute associated with a Line of a Hexagram. This "Naturalness" associates with the favorableness of either a Strong (Solid—YANG) or Yielding (Broken—YIN) influence when related with the character of the Line. The "Natural" states of the Lines are:
6, Wisdom—Yielding, Broken, YIN.
5, Authority—Strong, Solid, YANG.
4, Society—Yielding, Broken, YIN.
3, Inidividual—Strong, Solid, YANG.
2, Aspirations—Yielding, Broken, YIN.
1, Instinct—Strong, Solid, YANG.
Page 23, and Step 2 in general, describes these relationships more thoroughly.

NOURISHMENT. When addressed by the I CHING "Nourishment" is not merely a physical fulfillment, but more a time of resting, recuperation, or the gathering of strength, including the gathering of strength from spiritual considerations or sources. There are four Hexagrams which specifically address "Nourishment":
HSU, #5—The "Nourishment" derived from resting and patiently waiting.
I, #27—"Nourishment" for growing, food and spiritual cultivation.
CHING, #48—"Nourishment" for common benefit, drink, and wisdom.
TING, #50—"Nourishment" of high ideals for pursuit of noble goals.

OBJECT. Indirect influence either upon or by the "Prophesy." Each Hexagram has an "Object" Line which is within an "Object" Trigram. Both this Line and the Trigram contain the indirect influences.

ORACLE. The composite and collective wisdom of the I CHING which, having been acquired through the centuries, is passed on to the sincere "Player."

OTHER. The personification of the "Object" of the Hexagram.

PLAYER. A participant, in any varying degree, of a particular endeavor, such as I CHING, T'AI CHI CHUAN (an exercise and physical training system), etc. In the Orient "Player" is not necessarily associated with "Games" and, indeed, can be an extremely serious participant.

PROPHESY. The response of the I CHING Oracle which is interpreted and evaluated by the individual according to the circumstances relating to the "Subject."

REGRET. The sorrow or remorse, usually visited upon oneself, which arises from an intemperate act or attitude.

REWARD. Advantage received from one's own efforts. A promotion, raise, or esteemed recognition which is individually fulfilling.

SAGE. A wise person who has chosen to remain aloof from the daily turmoil to create incomparable values for the future. The cover of this publication depicts the "Sage" presenting the T'AI CHI with its YANG and YIN elements.

SELF. The personification of the "Subject" of the Hexagram.

SIGNFICANT. Either the 2nd or 5th Line of a Hexagram which is "Significant" in defining the Theme of the Hexagram.

SOCIETY. The character associated with the 4th Line of a Hexagram—the position of expressing the "Authority" to the "Community" and vice versa. In antiquity, as well as today, a Minister occupied this normally precarious position.

SUBJECT. Direct influence either upon or by the "Prophesy." Each Hexagram has a "Subject" Line which is within a "Subject" Trigram. Both this Line and the Trigram contain the predominant influences.

SUCCESS. A significant and productive degree of accomplishment relative to the question asked of the Oracle. Existing in degrees, it can only be evaluated by the individual.

UNDERTAKINGS. Activities requiring personal character, stamina, capital, etc. It is more commonly associated with "Great Undertakings," which referred to the crossing of the Yellow River in ancient times— then a particularly dangerous feat. Also notice the appearance of the river in the Illustrations of Step 3, where "Undertakings" or "Great Undertakings" are indicated.

VARIANT. Either the 3rd or 4th Line of a Hexagram which varies the Theme of the Hexagram with either favorable or unfavorable interactions between "Society" and the "Individual."

VICTORY. Success associated with the defeat of an adversary or an adversarial situation. "Victory" is never allowed to continued on to perdition of the vanquished.

VIRTUE. Excellence in morality, goodness, and "Correctness," as they relate to behavior and attitudes. The passing of knowledge to attain "Virtue" is the true committment of the I CHING.

WISDOM. The character associated with the 6th Line of a Hexagram—the knowledge, experience, and perception which leads one through the proper courses in life. Wisdom is manifested in correct behavior.

WISE ADVICE. Advice or counsel sought and applied from another, or others, who are assumed to have particular knowledge and experience relating to the question of the Oracle. "Wise Advice" is derived from the ancient phrase "See a Great Man." The source of this counsel is also implied from a spiritual source such as God, when relating to Occidental religions, and the Tao of Eastern religions.

YOU. Assumed to be the Superior Person striving for high ideals and goals, which include the reaching of one's inner consciousness. Ancient texts actually refer to "Superior Man" in this capacity, but the term is not generally used in this text. "You" is also assumed to be the "Subject" of the consultation. When the "Subject" is taken as another, then He, She, It, etc., can be used as appropriate.

YOUR. Indicates possession of characteristics or attributes by "You."

APPENDIX C — INDEX
AND CROSS REFERENCE OF SUBJECTS

KGI Publishing maintains a Mail Order system for items associated with the I CHING series of products as, in some areas, they may be difficult to obtain through regular sources of supply. The following items are available through this Mail order system Pricing is subject to change without prior notice.

I CHING, The Illustrated Primer. Additional copies of this
      Book (Each)..$ 19.95
      Add Shipping and Handling Charge.. 1.50
      California Residents Add 7% Sales Tax................................. 1.40

I CHING IN 4 EASY STEPS. The Software Program replicating the published material contained herein. This Package includes one copy of this book; a single double-density, double-sided 5-1/4 inch diskett capable of executing the I CHING program on IBM-PC, and compatible type personal computers; a set of 3 each, specially struck I CHING coins styled from the T'ang Dynasty, 621-975 AD; and installation and instruction booklet. The Program does not include graphics and can be operated with conventional display screens or monitors The Coins and diskette are illustrated on page 243.
      Each Program Package.. $ 69.95
      Add Shipping and Handling Charge.. 1.50
      California Residents Add 7% Sales Tax................................. 4.90

      Software and Coins without Book .... $ 59.95
      Add Shipping and Handling Charge 1.50
      California Residents Add 7% Sales Tax................................. 4.20

I CHING, The Advanced Techniques. This Book provides the Horoscopes and Astrology which are based upon the I CHING. Other advanced techniques such as Plum Blossom I, Geomancy (Positioning), Lo and Ho Mapping, are included in this test. The illustrations which appear as fine-line art in I CHING, The Illustrated Primer are included in the Horoscope section as full color artwork from Mr. Yang's renderings.
      Each Book .... $ 49.95
      Add Shipping and Handling Charge.. 1.50
      California Residents Add 7% Sales Tax................................. 3.50
**Publishers date is 15 May 1987, Distribution will be made prior to 15 June, 1987.
Advance orders will be filled with autographed First Editions, First Printings

———— RELEASE PENDING ————

I CHING, The Advanced Techniques. This Program Package replicates the published material described on the previous page on IBM-PC, amd compatible, type personal computers. The program Package includes the Book, I CHING,The Advanced Techiques; A double -sided, double density disket capable of executing the Horoscope and Advanced Techniques; A set of 3 specially struck I CHING coins from the T'ang Dynasty, 621-975 AD; and an installation and execution instruction booklet.

Each Program Package.. $ 119.95
Add Shipping and Handling Charge.. 2.00
California Residents Add 7% Sales Tax 8.40
** Publishers date is 15 May 1987, Distribution will be made prior to 15 June, 1987.
Advance orders will be filled with autographed First Editions, First Printings

———— RELEASE PENDING ————

THE YEARLY I CHING.   A spiral-bound book with a single double-sided double density 5-1/4 inch diskette. The book also contains the installation and execution instructions. This package is produced Yearly and serves as a Daily Calendaring and Memorandum function with relationships to the I CHING. Either the I CHING IN 4 EASY STEPS or the I CHING, The Advanced Techniques Program Package is required to support this package. The book is prepared yearly beginning 1 January and continuing until the next years's Chinese Bew Year (approximately February 5th). Include the year requested when ordering
    1987   (4685)   The Year of the Hare, Ting Mao
    1988   (4686)   The Yeat of the Dragon, Wu Ch'en; etc.
Each Program Package.. $ 59.95
Add Shipping and Handling Charge 1.50
California Residents Add 7% Sales Tax 4.20
** Publishers date is 15 November of each year. Distribution will be made prior to 10 December of each preceeding Year.
Book only..
                                                                                        $ 14.95

I CHING Coins.A set of 3 coins replicated from the T'ang Dynasty, 621-975 AD. Packaged in a convenient plastic case.
Each Coin Set (of 3)... $ 4.95
Add Shipping and Handling Charge... .75
California Residents Add 7% Sales Tax... .35

NOTE: IBM is a Registered Trademark of IBM Corporation.

To Order, use the following format and include the full ammount in the form of a check or money order (only), do not send cash.

Please note that the minimum order we can process is $10.00 and that all prices are expressed in terms of U.S.A. monetary units, Roreign exchange adjustments will be required for orders using monetary units other than that of the United States, and taxes, etc, may also have to be applied.

When ordering software it is advised to include the make and model, allowing the publisher to insure that the intended equipment is in fact *compatible*. Inquires as to the availability of software for other types of personal computers are also invited.

Telephone or C.O.D. orders will not be accepted and the Retail Outlet must be included to process your order.

AN EXAMPLE ORDER FORM

1 each I CHING, The Advanced Techniques, Book .... $ 51.45
1 each Yearly I CHING 1990 .... $ 61.45
2 each I CHING Coin Sets.. $ 11.40
     Total amount enclosed... $ 124.30

I have a Compaq-256 Personal Computer. The Retail Outlet through which I became familiar with KGI Publications' I CHING material is:
     KGI Bookstore, San Jose, California.

Send the ordered items to:

     Name

     Address

     City, State, Zipe Code

Mail you order (with check or money order) to:

     KGI Publications
     7280 Blue Hill Dr. #4
     San Jose, CA 95129

Except as noted above, allow 4 weeks for delivery. (Please note that money orders normally produce speedier deliveries due to the reduction in approval times.)

For the publishers current catalog of all I CHING products send $1.00 and 2 self-addressed stamped envelopes to KGI Publications at the above address.

SET OF THREE COINS,
REPLICATED FROM THE T'ANG DYNASTY,
621-975 A.D., See Page 13.

The Diskette Label depicts one of the several character representations of "I CHING" which Artist/Illustrator Ken C. Yang has prepared for this material. Serious students of Oriental calligraphy will be able to identify the different styles with the different periods of history.

THE SOFTWARE DISKETTE AND ENVELOPE.

The "Ba Kua" on the Diskette Envelope is in the "Good Fortune" arrangement with the T'ai Chi in the center.

The "Ba Kua", or "8 Sets of Lines", is also depicted on the front cover of this publication. Various arrangements of the 8 Trigrams about the T'ai Chi are used to represent different relationships. The above arrangement, "Good Fortune," is commonly placed at the doors of homes to ward off bad luck.

The Authors' preferred I CHING worksheet, which may be photocopied by the reader of this publication for personal use—but which may not be sold or reprinted in any other publication without express written authorization from the publisher—is printed below.

Players are urged to save their personal responses from the I CHING Oracle to allow evaluation of trends of dated prophesies.

I CHING WORKSHEET

QUESTION	DATE

YANG
TAIL = 3

YIN
HEAD = 2

6th

5th

4th

3rd

2nd

1st

RECENT PAST, PRESENT

NO.	NAME
TITLE	

ABOVE

BELOW

FUTURE

NO.	NAME
TITLE	

ABOVE

BELOW

—X— 3 HEADS = 6 CHANGING

——— 2 HEADS, 1 TAIL = 7

— — 1 HEAD, 2 TAILS = 8

—O— 3 TAILS = 9 CHANGING

INTERNAL, MOTIVATING

PROPHESY REMARKS

KGI PUBLICATIONS